SAVING PERSUASION

The Board of Syndics of Harvard University Press
has awarded this book the thirty-fifth annual
Thomas J. Wilson Prize, honoring the late director
of the Press. The prize is awarded to the book
chosen by the Syndics as the best first book
accepted by the Press during the calendar year.

Bryan Garsten

Saving Persuasion

A Defense of Rhetoric and Judgment

HARVARD UNIVERSITY PRESS

Cambridge, Massachusetts, and London, England   2006

Library of Congress Cataloging-in-Publication Data

Garsten, Bryan.
  Saving persuasion : a defense of rhetoric and judgment / Bryan Garsten.
    p. cm.
  Includes bibliographical references and index.
  ISBN 0-674-02168-1 alk. paper
    1. Persuasion (Rhetoric)—Political aspects. 2. Communication in politics. 3. Political
psychology. 4. Democracy. 5. Judgment. I. Title.

JA85.G38 2006
320.01'4—dc22   2005052757

To my parents

"It looks to me, Socrates, as if you two are hurrying to get away to Athens,"
said Polemarchus.

"That's not a bad guess," I said.

"Well," he said, "do you see how many of us there are?"

"Of course."

"Well, then," he said, "either prove stronger than these men or stay here."

"Isn't there another possibility?" I said. "That we persuade you to let us go?"

"Could you really persuade," he said, "if we don't listen?"

"There's no way," said Glaucon.

"Well, then, think it over, bearing in mind we won't listen."

    —Plato, *Republic*

Contents

Acknowledgments

I feel very lucky to have been surrounded by wise advisers and good friends while I wrote this book. I really do not know how to thank them adequately, so instead I will just acknowledge my debts. Chief among them is what I owe to Harvey Mansfield, to his quiet wisdom and his generous and gentlemanly spirit. A rare combination of philosophic thoughtfulness and spirited argument, he teaches with an unobtrusive grace, gently indicating where I might go while leaving me free to make my own discoveries and mistakes. Many of the ideas in this book were first inspired and later sharpened in long conversations with Russ Muirhead, whose incisive advice helped to shape every chapter and whose generous enthusiasm for the project repeatedly helped to rekindle my own interest in it. Michael Sandel offered the perfect mix of encouragement and critical interrogation, raising penetrating questions at just the right moments and consistently prodding me to follow my arguments through to their conclusions. Richard Tuck introduced me to whole new areas of study, drew me into the historical and philosophical issues at the heart of the project, and challenged me to rethink the conventional wisdom on every one of those issues. My writing partner, Tamara Metz, read many drafts of each chapter with the right mix of sympathy and detachment, and her intelligent questions helped to shape each one. Jill Frank and Sharon Krause both read much of the manuscript and offered excellent advice. In addition, I have learned quite a bit from conversations and exchanges about various parts of the project with Danielle Allen, Arthur Applbaum, Seyla Benhabib, Ben Berger, Ronald Beiner, Noah Dauber, Ioannis Evrigenis, Robert Fannion, David Fott, Anna Garsten, Jeffrey Green, Jill Horwitz, Andrew Kuper, Melissa Lane, Bruno Macaes, Karuna Mantena, Jason Maloy, George Marcus, Nicole Mellow, David Meskill, Mary Nichols, Chad Noyes, John Parrish, Matthew Price, Andrew Sabl, Andrea Sangiovanni, Malcolm Schofield, Kathryn Sensen, Susan Shell, Gary Shiffman, Steven Smith, Travis Smith, Annie Stilz, Norma Thompson, Elliott Visconti, and Robert Wokler.

As I revised the manuscript for publication, my new colleagues and students at Williams College and Yale University provided warm intellectual friendship. I also benefited a great deal from the comments of three outside reviewers for Harvard University Press and from the encouragement and advice of Michael Aronson. Thanks are also due to Tonnya Norwood and Rebecca Hartshorn for editorial and logistical assistance.

The chapters on Aristotle and Cicero were presented at annual meetings of the American Political Science Association in 2001–2002; those on Cicero, Hobbes, Rousseau, and Kant were presented at the New England Political Science Association in 2001–2004. The Hobbes chapter was presented and discussed as part of the International Hobbes Association panel at the American Philosophical Association meetings in San Francisco in 2002. I also presented different parts and versions of the project to audiences at the Political Theory Colloquium and the Center for Ethics and the Professions at Harvard, at the Humanities and Social Sciences Workshop at Williams College, and at the Political Theory Workshop and the Whitney Humanities Center at Yale. After each of these presentations I learned something from the questions raised and the comments given.

For financial support during graduate school at Harvard I am grateful to the Graduate School of Arts and Sciences, the University Center for Ethics and the Professions, the Earhart Foundation, and the Harvard Program on Constitutional Government. The Center for European Studies at Harvard offered a wonderful place to work for two years, and the Whitney Humanities Center at Yale generously provided financial assistance for the final preparation of this book through the Frederick W. Hilles Publication Fund.

The last and greatest debts are to my family. My mother, father, and sister, Lauren, provided a sort of "family compound" to which I retreated often and from which I always emerged happier. To my wife, Anna, whose ever-expanding patience and love still fill me with wonder, I owe more than I could say. And to our son, David, born as the book was being put to bed, I owe the feeling of rebirth.

SAVING PERSUASION

Introduction: Persuasion

In democracies, quiet people rarely enter politics. Democratic political life is dominated for the most part by people who like to talk. Of course, there are exceptions, a few politicians who defy this expectation and build a reputation for quiet efficiency or inconspicuous integrity. But the quintessential democratic politician is a smooth talker, winning and inspirational in front of crowds and irresistibly persuasive behind closed doors. Democratic politicians are often good storytellers, adept with compliments and able to charm even some of their critics. On the strength of these talents, they enjoy the popularity of a successful general without having mastered the art of war. They have mastered a different art, a certain way of speaking to their fellow citizens. While they may seem to talk for many reasons—to amuse, to inspire, often just to pass the time—they usually have an additional purpose. They talk to bring people to their side. In democracies we are ruled more often by speech than by force, and a democratic politician is one who knows how to use speech as a means of influence and a technique of rule. If quiet people rarely enter democratic politics, that is because they know that no matter what virtues of mind or character they might bring to the job, their shyness is itself a liability. The practiced, persuasive talk that marks a true democratic politician is not a superfluous talent but one central to his or her success.

To find the source of political power in a society, it is always helpful to notice what ambitious people want. In democracies they want to be heard. When Alexis de Tocqueville visited America, he noticed that legislators clamored above all for their chance to speak; he saw that they chafed at rules of procedure requiring their silence and jumped at opportunities to voice their views.[1] Today there are still few powers in a legislature greater than the power to set the agenda—to determine who can talk, what can be

1

discussed, and for how long. It may be true that in Washington "money talks," but campaign strategists and lobbyists often value money for its ability to buy speaking time and a large audience. In general, if people want to wield political power in a democracy, they must look for opportunities to talk to their fellow citizens, to impress them, and to persuade them. Persuasive talk is the currency of the democratic realm.

What are we to make of this feature of democratic politics? In ancient Athens the rhetorician Gorgias defended the prominence of persuasive speech by asserting that it brought freedom to the people and rule to those who could persuade them.[2] But how could it do both at once, unless freedom meant being subjected to the rule of persuasive speakers? In the seventeenth century Thomas Hobbes offered such a danger as reason to be suspicious of democratic government, which he thought tended to devolve into an "aristocracy of orators."[3] Along with Hobbes we may ask, why should the best speakers be allowed the upper hand in a society of equals? Is persuasion anything other than a form of manipulation?[4]

This anxiety must be balanced, however, against an opposing consideration. If persuasion is a technique of rule, it is a technique so indirect as to often undermine its own power. The word "persuade" arises etymologically from the same root as the words "suave" and "sweet," which reminds us that democratic persuasion requires insinuating oneself into the good graces of one's audience. Persuasive talk aims to sway people by learning their tastes and offering them what they crave. For this reason democratic politicians have always risked becoming servants rather than rulers, catering to their audience's sweet tooth.[5] Politicians have always been accused of pandering, and, while few plead guilty to the charge, many will admit at least to having felt the temptation.

Thus the practice of persuasion seems prone to two forms of corruption. In trying to persuade, democratic politicians may end up manipulating their audiences, or they may end up pandering to them. These twin dangers reveal something about the nature of persuasion as an activity. When we persuade, we want to change our listeners' minds by linking our position to their existing opinions and emotions. In our desire to change their minds lies the danger of manipulating, and in the effort to attend to their existing opinions lies the risk of pandering. The two vices thus arise from the dual character of persuasion itself, which consists partly in ruling and partly in following. In this way persuasion shares more generally in the character of democratic citizenship, which requires citizens to both rule and be ruled.[6] Persuasion is one of the characteristic activities of democratic politics.

The study of persuasion, or the art of rhetoric, was for this reason thought to be a fundamental part of a democratic citizen's education throughout much of Western history. In ancient Athens and Rome, in medieval schools and Renaissance cities, in early modern Europe and nineteenth-century America, both scholars and statesmen taught their students that a well-functioning republican polity required citizens who could articulate arguments on either side of a controversy, link those arguments to the particular opinions and prejudices of their fellow citizens, and thereby facilitate the arguing and deliberating that constituted a healthy political life. Politics naturally gives rise to controversy, and rhetoricians taught citizens how to engage in controversy through speech rather than force. While there have been critics of rhetoric since Socrates, for much of Western history their attacks failed to unseat the study of rhetoric from its central place in education.

Since the sixteenth and seventeenth centuries, however, this view about the importance of rhetoric has come under renewed and distinctive attack, and the full fruition of that attack can be seen in our contemporary suspicions of rhetoric. Today schools and universities rarely teach the art of persuasion, and when they do, they more often give the topic to literature scholars than to professors of politics. Political theorists tend to focus on reasonable dialogues of justification rather than passionate exchanges of rhetoric. While actual politicians have not abandoned persuasion (how could they?), they prefer not to acknowledge their art. They understand that when they hear an argument described as "rhetorical," it is being either decried as manipulative or dismissed as superficial. In both theory and practice today, the reigning view of rhetorical speech is that it is a disruptive force in politics and a threat to democratic deliberation.

This book aims to challenge that conventional wisdom. Its guiding motivation is the thought that a politics of persuasion—in which people try to change one another's minds by appealing not only to reason but also to passions and sometimes even to prejudices—is a mode of politics that is worth defending. Persuasion is worthwhile because it requires us to pay attention to our fellow citizens and to display a certain respect for their points of view and their judgments. The effort to persuade requires us to engage with others wherever they stand and to begin our argument there, as opposed to simply asserting that they would adopt our opinion if they were more reasonable. This way of proceeding can be contrasted to the sort of argumentation described in many recent theories of deliberation, which can seem insensitive to the particularities of people's lives and leave them feeling alienated from the results of public discussions.

Because a number of factors conspire against it, we cannot take the practice of persuasion in politics for granted. Relatively few people are interested in listening to arguments, much less in having their minds changed. Politics, when it does not descend into violence, is more often a realm of interests than of arguments, more often a marketplace than a forum.[7] When political controversy does proceed through public discourse, it often decays quickly into the sort of exchange that allows room for neither persuasion nor deliberation, the sort of exchange in which ideologues voice increasingly radicalized versions of their positions to audiences who already agree with them. In today's increasingly polarized political landscape, public debate often devolves into groups of like-minded individuals talking to one another, leaving other citizens increasingly alienated.[8] In addition, various features of modern politics—such as the prominence of bureaucracies with their rule-governed decision-procedures, the dominance of mass media with its emphasis on visual images, the weakening of parties relative to special-interest groups, and the slow but inexorable drift toward more plebiscitary forms of democratic decision-making—conspire to close off spaces in which persuasion might occur. The very possibility of persuasion needs to be protected.

This book aims to make the case for a politics of persuasion by examining the intellectual roots of the modern suspicion of persuasive rhetoric and then challenging them, pointing the way toward an understanding of deliberation in which rhetoric plays a central role. The book aims to show how deeply the early modern attack on classical rhetoric influenced the social contract tradition in political thought and how it continues to influence contemporary theories of public reasoning indebted to that tradition. The modern suspicion of rhetoric arose, I suggest, from a crisis of confidence about citizens' capacity to exercise practical judgment in public deliberations. This crisis was fueled by observation of the especially dogmatic religious character of public debate in early modern England, where a prophetic rhetoric of conscience put on display the most dangerous tendencies of rhetorical speech.

While democratic citizens will always have reason to be on the lookout for demagogues and to adopt institutions designed to avoid the effects of demagogy, we go too far when we aim to eliminate rhetoric from deliberation altogether. Even if we hope to draw citizens into deliberating reasonably with one another, we cannot help but begin by appealing to them as we find them—opinionated, self-interested, sentimental, partial to their friends and family, and often unreasonable. The moment in which politicians face citizens' everyday opinions, the rhetorical moment, cannot be avoided in democratic politics. In the final chapter of the book I suggest that attention to this moment yields an understanding of deliberation that challenges recent theories of deliberative democracy.[9] The rhetorical approach to deliberation differs from these recent theories in that it appeals to no concept of public reason, accepts that publicity and transparency are not always best, and suggests that partiality, passion, and even prejudice have a legitimate and often productive role to play in democratic deliberations.

Persuasion and Judgment

Before we go further, it may be helpful to explain more precisely the way in which this book uses certain key words: *rhetoric, persuasion,* and *judgment.* The term *rhetoric* has acquired a variety of meanings. Some scholars use it to refer to the characteristics of a particular community's discourse, such as that of economists, while others use it to refer to particular tropes and styles of poetry or literature; for others still, the term encompasses all of human communication. For the purposes of this project, I will follow a long tradition of understanding rhetoric as speech designed to persuade. If this definition seems to leave out a whole host of familiar rhetorical practices, including certain techniques of manipulation and deception that regularly earn the name "rhetoric" in ordinary conversation, that is because I do not aim to defend those practices here—or at least, I aim to defend them only insofar as they can be viewed as necessary to the politics of persuasion.

When we try to persuade, we use the arguments, images, and emotions most likely to appeal to the particular audience in front of us. Rhetoricians who teach the art of persuasion have always instructed their students to treat different audiences differently, to study their distinctive and peculiar passions and their particular commitments, sentiments, and beliefs.

Persuasion can thus be distinguished from the mode of discourse that has been identified as central to much liberal political theory, that of justification.[10] Justification treats different audiences similarly, in deference to the ideal of equality. When we justify a course of action, we argue that it is just, legitimate, or reasonable. We ask for our listeners' consent insofar as they take on the role of impartial or reasonable judges and adopt the shared public perspective that John Rawls and others have called the standpoint of "public reason," but we do not ask for more than that. We stop short of what persuasion might require. We show why any reasonable person should accept our view but not necessarily why these particular people listening here and now should do so. Instead, we ask our listeners to join us on a different plane, a place where "questions of political justice can be discussed on the same basis by all citizens, whatever their social position, or more particular aims and interests, or their religious, philosophical, or moral views."[11] We treat every citizen as being equally capable of giving and receiving public reasons. Of course, we acknowledge that many, perhaps most, of us are not fully reasonable in our actual opinions and judgments. But we do presume that our listeners could be reasonable, that they could step into the role of someone exercising public reason as a standard. In this way we respect their equality, for it is when citizens step into that role that they become most equal and most alike. And it is because they can become alike in this way that we assume they can agree on basic standards of justification. In presuming this sort of equality, theories of justificatory liberalism tend to assume the possibility of universal agreement even if they do not call upon us to always reach consensus.[12] Though these theories can permit a great deal of "reasonable disagreement," they can do so only because they presume that we can agree, for the most part, about what sort of disagreement is reasonable. In contrast to the classical-humanist tradition of rhetoric, which assumed that people disagreed and asked how they could engage in controversy through speech rather than force, the modern liberal tradition of justification assumes that people can find some shared point of agreement and asks how they can engage in deliberation within the boundaries set by that underlying agreement.

Persuasion does not rest upon a commitment to any underlying agreement. Rhetorical appeals need not and, in fact, must not take the intention to think reasonably for granted. They frequently start from premises or attitudes shared only by members of the present audience. Often they rely on premises that are not even made explicit; these premises are supplied by the audience itself. In trying to bring an audience from the conventional wisdom to thoughts or intentions they might not otherwise have adopted, rhetoric intends to wield influence over them. In this sense rhetoric is a form of rule. Rhetorical speech is therefore political even when its explicit subject matter seems to lie far from the realm of policies and justice. The political aspect of persuasive speech suggests why its conditions and techniques should fall within the realm of political theory. It also suggests why liberal thought, in its broadest sense, is suspicious of rhetoric. Liberalism's aversion to persuasion is a symptom of its more general aversion to rule.[13]

The way in which persuasion aims to rule, however, is distinctive. While the word "rhetoric" as used today often refers to one of the vices of democratic speech, the term changes its valence when defined as an effort to persuade. *Persuasion* in the strict sense identifies a way of influencing that is neither manipulation nor pandering. The speaker who manipulates his audience so as to bring them to a belief or action without their consent, as Kant thought orators moved men "like machines," has not persuaded but coerced.[14] In contrast, the speaker who merely finds out where his audience itches and then scratches there, as Plato thought pandering Athenian orators did, has not managed to change his listeners' minds at all.[15] To truly persuade people is to induce them to change their own beliefs and desires in light of what has been said. Though we speak of "being persuaded" in the passive voice, we recognize the difference between being persuaded and being indoctrinated or brainwashed; the difference lies in the active independence that is preserved when we are persuaded. Though overbrazen orators and their enemies have long compared persuasion to a drug or a magical capacity that does the work of coercion without the need for physical force, such metaphors exaggerate an orator's power and pervert the meaning of persuasion.[16] An orator does not coerce; he merely puts words into the air. In the brief moments of conscious or unconscious reflection that occur while we listen to a sales pitch or a campaign speech, an active process of evaluation and assimilation occurs in our minds. We cannot make use of the energy of food simply by coming into contact with it; our bodies must actively digest it. An analogous process of digestion must occur before our mind internalizes the suggestions of any speaker. Unlike actual digestion, however, mental digestion is a process over which we can exercise some control. We reject arguments that seem far-fetched or suspicious. Being persuaded is not the same as learning, but it is related. When someone sits back and decides, "All right, you have persuaded me," he is not merely describing something that has happened to him. In spite of the grammar, he is describing something he has done. That, at least, is the presumption in the very idea that there is such a thing as persuasion that lies between manipulation and pandering. It is the presumption of democratic politics.

This concept of persuasion points, in turn, to the human capacity for practical judgment. By *judgment* I mean the mental activity of responding to particular situations in a way that draws upon our sensations, beliefs, and emotions without being dictated by them in any way reducible to a simple rule. This kind of judgment may involve integrating new information into existing patterns of thought, readjusting those patterns to make room for a new perspective, or both. There are several sorts of judgment—logical, aesthetic, moral, political, and perhaps others—but the concept I have in mind is linked most closely to what Aristotle called practical wisdom, or *phronesis,* and what Aquinas discussed as prudence, and it is also linked to our idea of common sense.[17] When speaking of prudence and common sense, we may notice that while judgment is a general human capacity, some people are better at using it than others. People with good judgment are adept at evaluating and responding to difficult and ambiguous situations. They have a certain instinctive sensitivity and appreciation for nuance that allows them somehow to focus on appropriate similarities and differences, noticing how a particular situation is similar to previous ones in their experience and how it is different. We can imitate such people by trying to follow their example, but we cannot come up with a set of rules that will, if followed, assure us of being able to replicate their good judgment. Still, we each have judgment to some degree, and often it improves with use.

Practical judgment understood in this way is closely linked to the activity of deliberation. We only deliberate about how to respond in situations where there is no clear or definite answer, where we can control our response to some extent, and where certain responses seem to be better than others. As Aristotle noted, people do not deliberate about things they cannot control, such as the orbits of the stars or the coming of the rains; nor do we deliberate about matters that are wholly in the hands of others, such as what policy citizens of a neighboring state should adopt.[18] We deliberate about what we can do ourselves. People who have good judgment are skilled at this sort of deliberation. Their skill consists not only in having the requisite intellectual quickness and cleverness but also in having the right dispositions or habits of affective responses. They will not often be overwhelmed by their passions or by fear, hunger, or lust; nor will they fall prey to the distorting influences of insecurity or vanity. They will feel such emotions but they will feel them, more often than not, in ways that contribute to their ability to judge well rather than in ways that distort that capacity. Partly from nature and partly by education, they will have gained certain dispositions that allow them a measure of self-possession; from that relatively steady perspective they will be able to imagine accurately and empathetically what it would be like to take various courses of action. They will also be able to examine the various options available to them with some measure of detachment. Thus they will view the objects of their judgment with a mixture of sympathy and detachment, and they will be able to do so because they have certain traits of character, a keen perceptivity and relatively steady habits of emotional response. When people have all these traits, they find that they can draw upon their various perceptions, feelings, and opinions to respond in a relatively deliberate way to whatever particular situation confronts them.[19]

When speakers or writers try to persuade us of something, they are confronting us with a particular situation in speech. If they are neither indoctrinating us nor simply repeating what we already think, they are appealing to our capacity to respond to what they are saying by drawing upon and reorganizing our existing patterns of thought and emotion—they are appealing to our capacity for judgment. Since judgment is so closely linked with deliberation, so too is the practice of persuasion. While we might be tempted to say that the persuasive speaker trying to engage us in deliberative judgment appeals ultimately to our capacity for reason, this is not always so. It is possible to appeal to judgment through speech that is not wholly reasonable—indeed it is often necessary to do so. This follows from the character of judgment. Since judgment emerges from and draws upon a whole complex of emotions, dispositions, and tacit knowledge, a persuasive speaker often engages judgment by appealing to passions and images as well as reasons.

While judgment is spoken of less frequently than reason and emotion in discussions of political psychology, it should be a familiar idea nonetheless. Judgment is at least as natural and intuitive a concept as "reason" or "desire" and is probably closer to experience than either of those abstract terms. To speak of desire without an object seems appropriate only for the most basic impulses of hunger and lust; to speak of reason in the abstract rather than of particular reasons or arguments seems equally vague. Yet political theorists recognize both reason and desire as important human capacities without objection. Judgment may be difficult to analyze, but neither its existence nor its importance can plausibly be questioned.

Because of the link between persuasive rhetoric and judgment, an argument for saving the possibility of persuasion in democratic politics is an argument for protecting the practice of judgment. It seems to me that this is a crucial project. Today we are more than ever governed by rules that eliminate space for even the smallest exercises of judgment. These rules are created by both private and public authorities, by legislators, bureaucrats, and corporate managers, all interested in minimizing the uncertainty associated with judgment. A worker at a department store cannot look around and decide whether going to the restroom at a particular moment will interfere with customer satisfaction but must instead follow a scrupulously detailed procedure for taking breaks; a factory worker cannot evaluate the risk of arranging machinery in a way that long experience in the trade might suggest but must instead comply with OSHA code developed far from the factory floor. Today's culture of rules and codes not only eliminates the risk of imprudence but also the responsibility that breeds prudence.[20]

Of course, persuasive rhetoric does not address these problems. The point is rather that the modern suspicion of rhetoric arises from the same impulse to minimize the risks of judgment that is on display in our culture more generally. In fact, I will argue that we cannot understand the modern suspicion of rhetoric without noticing certain peculiarly modern anxieties about the uncertainties and dangers involved in judgment.

Dogmatism and Demagogy

The body of this project is divided into two parts. The first shows how the thought of Hobbes, Rousseau, and Kant undermined the classical-humanist tradition of rhetoric. The second examines that tradition as it was displayed in its most subtle and sophisticated expositors, Aristotle and Cicero, and as it might be mined for insights relevant to a modern theory of rhetorical deliberation.

In Part One, three broad lines of argument will be advanced. The first is that the early modern attack on rhetoric proceeded by asking citizens to alienate their capacity for private judgment to a sovereign public authority. The origin of the attack thus lies in Hobbes's recommendation that citizens should distance themselves from their everyday political opinions and judgments by creating a sovereign to judge controversial matters for them. This aspect of Hobbes's political theory should be seen, I argue, as a response to the threat posed by preaching orators, who Hobbes thought used rhetoric to divide citizens into factions and to encourage citizens to take their own private judgments or consciences as more authoritative than their rulers', thus sowing the seeds of discord and civil war. Hobbes suggested that if those citizens had already agreed to allow the sovereign to make judgments for them and to take his laws as their "public conscience," they would not be swayed by the rhetoric of the preaching orators. He therefore asked citizens to alienate to the sovereign precisely the faculty of judgment to which persuasion appealed. Deeply suspicious of the role that this faculty played in politics, Hobbes sought to minimize its influence. His suspicion arose not only from a philosophical skepticism about the grounds of judgment but also, I suggest, from having seen the dogmatism of private judgment as it displayed itself in the Puritan rhetoric of conscience. He constructed his new understanding of sovereignty, based on the alienation of judgment, as a way to immunize citizens against the rhetoric of revolutionary preachers. In the two chapters that follow I argue that both Rousseau and Kant, in spite of their more republican sympathies and in spite of their significant departures from Hobbes, nevertheless adopted his attack on persuasive rhetoric by accepting the basic structure of his theory. They asked citizens to distance themselves from their private judgments and to judge from a sovereign, unitary, public standpoint instead.

The second argument running through Part One concerns the manner in which citizens can be persuaded to leave behind their private judgments. They must be persuaded to make a second-order judgment to replace their first-order judgments with a sovereign public point of view. They must be drawn to consensus on a basis that will not be upset by future arguments, a basis more fundamental than the agreement of any particular political opinions. Citizens must be persuaded not to be persuaded in the future. This effort requires a rhetoric of its own, with a different character than the rhetoric it aims to eliminate. In the need for a rhetoric against rhetoric we can see what might be called the "rhetorical moment" in each of these antirhetorical theories. In that moment the rhetoric against rhetoric aims to create a source of shared identity deeper than opinion. Hobbes begins with the passions, Rousseau with pity and patriotism, and Kant with a public conception of reason. In turning to these bases of unanimity, the rhetoric against rhetoric aims to create sources of unity that, once accepted, cannot be dislodged by persuasive arguments. Thus the rhetoric deployed in the rhetorical moment of these theories, often unacknowledged and yet uncompromising in its demands on all citizens, can be more invasive and more dogmatic than the forms of persuasion it aims to replace.

The rhetoric against rhetoric can arise in at least three distinct incarnations, each of which emerges in a different way from the efforts to minimize the politics of persuasion. In Hobbes we find a rhetoric of representation, which aimed to hide citizens' subjection to sovereignty by convincing them that they had authorized the actions of their rulers. In Rousseau we find a rhetoric of prophetic nationalism, which sought to instill in citizens a prerational, quasi-religious sense of sympathetic identification with their fellow citizens. And in Kant we find a rhetoric of public reason, which demanded deference to philosophers and scholars by claiming that they could best approximate the enlightenment that the citizens themselves had not yet achieved. We will see that each of these three types of rhetoric against rhetoric arose from a fundamental mistrust of ordinary opinion and judgment. Each aimed to minimize the space for persuasion in politics, and each sought, in a different way, to obscure the work of ruling accomplished in the rhetorical moment. Today all three types of rhetoric against rhetoric can still be found in politics and political theory, suggesting how deeply the attack on persuasion and the mistrust of judgment that motivated it still influence us.

The third broad theme running through Part One concerns what might be called the aestheticization of rhetoric. Rhetoric that aims to work beneath the level of argument, wielding its influence on unarticulated passions and identities and emerging from a mistrust of practical judgment rather than from an appeal to it, begins to concern itself directly with the senses. The rhetoric against rhetoric at work in each of the three thinkers investigated in Part One is linked somehow to a particular sense: vision in Hobbes, hearing (music) in Rousseau, and taste in Kant. The time period during which the classical art of rhetoric declined under the influence of these theories was the period during which modern aesthetics was born, and this seems not to have been a coincidence.[21] Rhetoric and judgment, displaced from the realm of morals and politics, were reconstituted in a discipline of their own, and the study of rhetoric gradually became a literary enterprise rather than a political one. The shift was eventually consolidated in schools and colleges. At Harvard University, for example, the first Boylston professor of rhetoric was John Quincy Adams, who lectured on public oratory and who was famously eloquent himself in speaking against the slave trade. Since then, however, that professorship has been occupied by literary critics and poets, most recently the poets Seamus Heaney and Jorie Graham.[22] One curious consequence of this evolution is that today the argument for paying more attention to rhetoric in politics has often been cast as an argument for treating politics as a realm of aesthetics. But the category of the aesthetic was born partly out of the impulse to distance rhetoric and judgment from moral and political thought, and the result of treating politics aesthetically is usually to import into the moral and political realm a deep skepticism about the grounds on which we make judgments.[23] The aestheticization of rhetoric tends to call into question the rationale for appealing to judgment and therefore tends to undermine the practice of persuasion. To treat politics as a subfield of aesthetics is, I suggest in Part One, to further Hobbes's attack on rhetoric rather than to resist it.

A better way of resisting that attack can be found in ancient accounts of the politics of persuasion. In Part Two, I suggest that we focus especially on those accounts that attended to both the promise and the danger of rhetorical controversy. Rather than studying the ancient sophists, who seem to have praised rhetoric unqualifiedly, I have chosen to study Aristotle and Cicero, who both reflected on the limited power of speech and on the harm that orators and demagogues could do and who therefore devoted attention to domesticating persuasion as well as accommodating it. The defenses of rhetoric that we find in Aristotle and Cicero are interesting precisely because they acknowledge and try to respond to the dangers of demagogy. Aristotle responded by attempting to reform rhetoricians' own understanding of what it takes to successfully master the art of rhetoric. He tried to draw them toward a kind of deliberative rhetoric that would supplement rather than threaten the rule of law, and he did so not by imposing moral constraints from outside the activity of persuasion but by reconceptualizing that activity from the inside, thus showing how persuasion could only be mastered as an art if it appealed to the capacity for judgment that citizens developed within the context of their city. Cicero, less intellectual and more political than Aristotle, responded to the danger of demagogy somewhat differently. Forced into political exile by his opponents and bitter about his exclusion from the public forums in which he had gained fame and influence through his speaking, he was led to reflect on the moral and political conditions under which a sustainable politics of persuasion could survive. In Cicero's thoughts on the link between rhetoric and republican politics we find demonstrated the vested interests that he, and orators in general, had in protecting those conditions.

From the studies of Aristotle and Cicero I draw out ideas that seem fundamental to any theory of political persuasion in which controversy is facilitated rather than suppressed and in which the danger of demagogy does not consistently overwhelm the possibility of deliberative judgment. From Aristotle I derive concepts of *situated judgment* and *deliberative partiality,* which together suggest the surprising idea that rhetorical appeals to people's partial and passionate points of view can often be a good means of drawing out their capacity for judgment and so drawing them into deliberation.

From Cicero I derive the importance of certain forms of firm moral conviction to the politics of persuasion and also the importance of preserving institutional spaces for controversy. In the final chapter of the book I show how these concepts bear on recent approaches to deliberative democracy, point the way toward an understanding of deliberation that is open to the contributions of rhetorical persuasion, and suggest that one benefit of modern representative or constitutional democracy, properly understood, is the way that it aims to facilitate a healthy politics of persuasion.

The Long Shadows of the Past

Any project that aims to challenge modern ideas by recalling older ones risks falling into nostalgia. Defenders of rhetoric often invoke a utopian past in which wise and eloquent politicians provided effective leadership through the majesty of their words alone. A glance at the journalism about recent presidential campaigns in the United States reveals this sort of nostalgia at work in a host of complaints about the candidates' lack of eloquence and in wistful comparisons with figures from the past, such as John F. Kennedy. But the same magazine that lodged such a complaint during one recent campaign had also run an article after Kennedy's inaugural address that looked nostalgically back to Adlai Stevenson. In Stevenson's day, in turn, commentators despaired about the state of oratory compared to the great models of the nineteenth century. In the nineteenth century many rhetoricians looked back longingly to the Renaissance, which was itself characterized by and named for its backward-looking imitation of the ancients. And even Cicero himself, the great exemplar and spokesman for the classical tradition of rhetoric, lamented the decline of oratory in his time.[24] For one reason or another, nostalgia is one of the most persistent vices of writings about rhetoric. It is a vice that this book aims to avoid.

For political theorists the danger of nostalgia often arises in the temptation to glorify the virtues of a "contestatory" or "agonistic" mode of politics that modern liberal society is said to have eclipsed. To avoid nostalgia on this point, we must attend carefully to the reasons that the early moderns gave for seeking to tamp down the politics of persuasion and minimize the role of private judgment. The truth that lies behind their suspicions is that judgment is an uncertain, ambiguous, and fallible activity, easy to manipulate and prone to collapse into either dogmatic self-assertion or deferential submission. A politics of persuasion carries within it the potential to quickly slide into destructive forms of controversy.

This warning against a nostalgic view of rhetoric also has a long history of its own. A common trope found in Diderot, Hume, and Gibbon is that the fall of the Roman republic and its political culture of rhetorical controversy brought about the rise of a relatively peaceful and stable regime under Augustus and his successors.[25] Against those who lamented the decline of rhetoric these authors pointed out that oratory and eloquence arose only in tumultuous times when gifted speakers could draw angry or frightened people into partisan mobs. Romans, it was suggested, should have been happy to sacrifice eloquence if doing so brought relief from the tumult. Though the origin of the case against nostalgia goes back at least to the Greeks, one of the clearest statements of it came near the end of Tacitus's *Dialogue on Oratory*. After listening to the other speakers in the dialogue lament the decline of oratory since the fall of the republic, the character Maternus argues that orators were opportunists who took advantage of aristocratic feuds and other forms of political confusion to claim authority: "All this [confusion] tore the commonwealth in pieces, but it provided a sphere for the oratory of those days and heaped on it what one saw were vast rewards."[26] Maternus claims that orators "made public meetings also the opportunity of launching characteristically spiteful tirades against the leading men of the state."[27] He argues that the decline of oratory can be traced in large part to the rise of centralized authority and rule-bound courts, the very developments that finally brought peace to Rome. When speaking of the greatness of eloquence in the past, he says, we often forget the political disorder that gave rise to such speeches:

> The art which is the subject of our discourse is not a quiet and peaceable art, or one that finds satisfaction in moral worth and good behavior: no, really great and famous oratory is a foster-child of license, which foolish men called liberty, an associate of sedition, a goad for the unbridled populace. It owes no allegiance to any. Devoid of discipline, it is insulting, off-hand, and overbearing. It is a plant that does not grow under a well-regulated constitution . . . Likewise at Rome, so long as the constitution was unsettled, so long as the country kept wearing itself out with factions and dissensions and disagreements, so long as there was no peace in the forum, no harmony in the senate, no restraint in the courts of law, no respect for authority, no sense of propriety on the part of the officers of state, the growth of eloquence was doubtless sturdier, just as untilled soil produces certain vegetation in greater luxuriance. But the benefit derived from the eloquence of the Gracchi did not make up for what the country suffered from

their laws, and too dearly did Cicero pay by the death he died for his renown in oratory.[28]

Maternus ends his contribution to the dialogue by rebuffing his nostalgic colleagues for failing to appreciate the peace and tranquility of their day. Unlike them, he has turned his efforts to poetry, where rhetorical inclinations can find some outlet in times of peace.

Thus runs the argument against nostalgia for rhetorical politics. While it provides a useful warning to those who are overeager to revive rhetoric, it probably needs little further elaboration today. Most people already associate rhetoric with the dangers of demagogy and divisive, opportunistic politics. The modern political thought in which we are steeped takes Maternus's argument seriously. One might go so far as to say that Hobbes and his intellectual descendants turned Maternus's observation about the correlation between rhetoric and tumult into a guiding and cardinal rule of politics: minimize the opportunity for rhetoric. From Hobbes's proposal that we take the sovereign's judgments as our own, to the contemporary Kantian-liberal insistence that we decide reasonably and universally, one central goal of modern political theory has been to purge politics of the contentiousness that fuels and is fueled by oratory and the tumult that Maternus says "tore the commonwealth in pieces." The contemporary connotations of the word "rhetoric" testify that we are likely to take Maternus's point seriously even without prompting.

Perhaps we take it more seriously than Tacitus himself intended. When Maternus explains further why rhetoric is not necessary in imperial Roman politics, he presents a utopian picture of his country:

> If a community could be found in which nobody ever did anything wrong, orators would be just as superfluous among saints as are doctors among those that need no physician . . . What is the use of long arguments in the senate, when good citizens agree so quickly? What is the use of one harangue after another on public platforms, when it is not the ignorant multitude that decides a political issue, but a monarch who is the incarnation of wisdom? What is the use of taking a prosecution on one's own shoulders when misdeeds are so few and so trivial, or of making oneself unpopular by a defence of inordinate length, when the defendant can count on a gracious judge meeting him halfway?[29]

No one familiar with Tacitus's dark view of the principate—his depictions of Tiberius, or of the shouting matches in the senate—could read this passage without some appreciation of its irony.[30] It is hard not to wonder, in fact, if that irony does not extend to Maternus's dismissal of republican liberty as "license" in the previous passage. The utopian description of imperial politics cannot be read without calling attention to discrepancies between its words and reality and therefore calling for improvement of the reality. Maternus's description allows Tacitus to outline what benefits imperial rule would have to bring to justify the eclipse of republican liberty. Thus while Maternus's speech may seem at first to rebuff those nostalgic for the republic, on deeper consideration it offers a nostalgia of its own, or at least an ironic demonstration of how imperial rule—politics without rhetoric—falls short. By failing to attend to Tacitus's own ironic rhetoric, we may be led to overstate the case against rhetoric. Tacitus's approach acknowledges the danger of nostalgia but nevertheless quietly presses opponents of rhetoric to prove that they do not rely on as utopian a picture of imperial politics as Maternus does. In our tendency today to study rhetoric as literature or poetry, we find ourselves following Maternus's advice to those who are interested in oratory but who must live in an empire rather than a republic. Does our literary approach to rhetoric signal an abandonment of republican politics?

Of course, responding to concerns about nostalgia by turning to a classical author for insight may not be persuasive. Leaving Tacitus aside, then, we can confront the charge of nostalgia more directly. The reason to consider classical and humanist sources when reflecting on persuasion today is not that their societies offer models for our own, but that their reflections on rhetoric were not distorted by the lens supplied by post-Reformation politics. That early modern lens threatens to distort our view of the subject. While religious rhetoric may be more visible recently both within the United States and on the world stage, the political challenges that it poses are not the same as those faced by early moderns such as Hobbes, who were responding to wars of religion in a different context. In responding to our challenges, we should be on guard against blindly falling into patterns of thought we have inherited from that period.[31]

As I will suggest in more detail in the final chapter, today we confront not only religious fanaticism but also a distinctively modern form of zealotry born as a response to liberalism. The frustration of being left out of the rewards and discourse of Western liberalism, a sense of alienation that is only intensified by the liberal preference for toleration over engagement, has produced responses to modernity that are as dogmatic and dangerous as the religious fanaticism that liberalism was meant to contain. And to make mat-

ters more confusing, these sentiments of alienation often present themselves as manifestations of religious fervor. This leaves us in a delicate position, caught between two forms of dogmatic rhetoric that seem to require
opposite solutions. Religious zealotry seems to call for the modern liberal
strategy that arises from Hobbes's attack on rhetoric. The alienation and fanaticism that arise in response to liberalism, however, seem to call for an alternative strategy which engages more directly with religious opinion. The
first strategy seems too hostile to the politics of persuasion, and the second
too vulnerable to demagogy. In this situation there is reason to study the
writings of authors who sought to contain demagogy without eliminating
the politics of persuasion altogether.

That is the perspective that certain classical theories of rhetoric can offer.
Neither Aristotle nor Cicero, we will see, offered naively optimistic accounts
of rhetorical politics. Both worried about demagoguery. But rather than attempting to rule rhetoric out of political debate, they tried to show under
what conditions it might become a means of facilitating a more deliberative
sort of controversy. Because they did not face the challenge posed by the
politicization of creedal, monotheistic religious claims, these ancient authors do not provide adequate solutions for us today. But they can help us
free ourselves from the post-Reformation perspective on political theory
that has gripped us for too long. There is a danger not only in falling into
nostalgia for the ancient past but also in failing to escape the long shadow of
a more recent past. The truth is that our dilemmas are our own and that we
must do our thinking for ourselves. The historical work that comprises most
of this book aims to help set the stage for and inform that project.

On Method

While this is a book about political rhetoric, it is not a study of great oratory.
I spend no time extolling the great orators of the past and offer only an
oblique hint about how we might decide what makes a speech great. Other
authors and editors have compiled collections of impressive oratory and
decried the absence of artful public speaking in our time.[32] In the recent
popularity of these books we see that the absence of skillful rhetoric has not
gone unnoticed by thoughtful democratic citizens. But a wistful longing to
be inspired by another Winston Churchill or Martin Luther King Jr. does
not suffice, because it does not address the deep reasons for the decline of
rhetoric. The cynicism that arose from politicians' lies about Vietnam and

Watergate cannot fully explain this decline. Nor are the growing importance of the mass media and the refined practice of opinion polling wholly responsible for rhetoric's demise—though these latter developments do reveal and reinforce its lowly status.[33] Nor is the suspicion of rhetoric we find today simply the natural suspicion of smooth talkers. That healthy skepticism is bolstered and transformed by the influential strain of modern political theory to which I draw attention in this book.

I have chosen to write about well-known, canonical figures in the history of political thought rather than the more obscure authors who wrote lengthier treatments of rhetoric itself. Histories of rhetoric such as Thomas Conley's helpful textbook, *Rhetoric in the European Tradition,* already offer surveys of the rhetorical tradition and thoughtful reflections on it.[34] But they offer little more than brief remarks about how the rhetorical tradition is relevant to the mainstream history of political thought, and they often speak more to students of belles lettres than to those interested in politics. In particular, existing works on the rhetorical tradition tend not to do justice to the central political problems that rhetoric causes—the problems of manipulation and pandering, which come together in the danger of demagogy. Thus they tend to simply dismiss as unfair the attacks on rhetoric found in authors such as Plato, Hobbes, Thomas Sprat of the Royal Society, Locke, and Kant, complaining that such thinkers have foisted an undeservedly bad reputation upon the noble tradition of rhetoric. In this work I am, as already indicated, more sympathetic to these attacks. I inquire into what political concerns lay behind them, and I argue that any attempt to incorporate insights from the rhetorical tradition must take these reservations into account. For these reasons I have not followed other defenders of rhetoric in extolling the ancient sophists. Instead I turn to Aristotle and Cicero, who took Plato's warnings about demagogy seriously and whose defenses of rhetoric were therefore more modest than those advanced by the sophists and their recent champions.[35]

In a similar way, the argument found here also distinguishes itself from the strand of recent political theory that exalts contestatory or agonistic politics and portrays constitutions and institutions primarily as a threat to it.[36] While my argument for saving persuasion makes a similar case for preserving a realm of truly political action against the impulse to quell disputes that can be found in some liberal theory, I am less sanguine about the dangers that accompany such political action. Therefore, while the first part of this work criticizes the attacks on the rhetorical tradition found in early modern thought, the second part joins Aristotle and Cicero not in glorifying rhetoric so much as in trying to find ways to tame it. The final chapter makes the case that representative institutions of constitutional democracy, properly understood, aim to foster and facilitate a politics of persuasion rather than to eliminate it. The challenge is to defend a place for rhetorical controversy by showing that it can be kept in its place. This requires delineating the boundaries of rhetoric's competence. Persuasion is a central part of democratic politics but not the whole of it.

The approach to rhetoric in this book also differs from postmodern views that label all public statements as "rhetoric" in an effort to reveal the way in which they are used to hide or rationalize exercises of power. With the word "rhetoric" I aim to describe a particular activity of persuasion, with its own internal standards and with a distinct and delimited function within a political regime. I do not use the notion of rhetoric to unmask the interests that lie behind principles claiming to be objective nor do I suggest the impossibility of judging between such principles. To the contrary, I argue that a theory of rhetorical deliberation must rest on a substantial faith in the possibility of making judgments.

Finally, any project on rhetoric must face the objection that speech is superficial, that a true understanding of democratic politics requires us to look not at what people say but at what they do. Why study what politicians say when they so often misdirect, mislead, and equivocate? Would it not be better to seek the reality behind their rhetoric? This is the insight that drives modern behavioral political science, which focuses on interests. Interests are preferences revealed in action rather than articulated in argument. Sophisticated students of political science do not claim that people are inherently self-interested but more modestly assert that people's behavior can best be modeled by leaving behind the motives they profess and instead attributing certain interests to them. It must be admitted that while this approach can lead to a crude reductionism, it is nevertheless often a sensible way to approach political behavior, especially if one's goal is to describe broad patterns of action. Nor does this approach rule out attention to rhetoric; recent political science has placed a great deal of attention on the way that certain forms of "framing" influence individuals' perceptions of their interests and their calculations about how to pursue them.[37] However, a different and deeper attention to rhetorical argument becomes necessary if our goal shifts from that of describing or predicting broad patterns of action to that of explaining how political actors should understand themselves

and what they are doing. Political actors make arguments about their actions. While a model based upon interests may offer a more reliable description of their behavior, this does not itself imply that political actors should
understand themselves or their peers according to that model. That conclusion would follow only if we add the premise that reliability is the most important guideline for political action. As we shall see, this premise has its
roots in Machiavelli's advice that princes who want to secure their own rule
should base their actions on the "effectual truth" rather than on what
people profess and also in Hobbes's view that religious wars could be more
reliably avoided if the purpose of political rule was broadly understood to
concern worldly interests rather than divine reward. The alleged superfi-
ciality of rhetoric is therefore not so much an observation as it is a theoretical
claim about the purpose of political knowledge, and as such it is properly
studied in the realm of political theory.

In each of the following chapters I try to do two things at once. I raise a
puzzle that arises within each thinker's work and also a more general question about persuasion in democratic politics. The internal puzzle is usually
one related to issues raised by previous and prominent interpreters. In engaging with and challenging these interpreters, I aim to contribute to current debates about how to understand the canonical authors. My approach
is to attend to the historical situation of each author insofar as it helps to il-
luminate his treatment of the general and enduring political questions that
are raised in his thoughts. The treatment of the interpretive puzzles is in
each case directly related to the larger argument about persuasion made in
the book as a whole.

   The purpose of these chapters is to make visible what has been hidden—
a decision at the founding of modern political thought—and to subject that
decision to the scrutiny it deserves today. The campaign against the sort of
deliberative rhetoric that aimed to draw upon citizens' judgments arose at
first as a response to the fact that religious arguments had grown too dogmatic to be susceptible to deliberative refinement. Whether this campaign is
one whose legacy we should unquestioningly accept depends a great deal
on the extent to which we think political judgments today retain the character of exclusionary theological claims. My instinct is that in spite of the
new visibility of religious rhetoric—and perhaps because of it—a more direct engagement with political opinion is both possible and necessary. Considering how such an engagement with opinion might be facilitated was the

project of the rhetorical tradition. To call for the continuation of that project is not to offer a nostalgic search for ancient solutions to modern problems. Rather, it is to cast off the harness of one early modern argument, a harness that prevents us from exploring the question of how citizens' capacity for judgment can best be engaged in a politics of persuasion.

Part of what we might gain from renewed attention to this question is the ability to articulate precisely what is lost in a politics without persuasion: a feel for how to render moral and political principles psychologically attractive, a prudent sensitivity to the particular passions and interests of different audiences, and a decent respect for the knowledge of probabilities enshrined in common sense and ordinary experience. But I also hope to show the limits of the ideal of persuasion. Sensitivity to existing opinions can easily become capitulation to unjust prejudices, and attempts to inspire political engagement often create turmoil. The goal of this study is to find a place for political rhetoric while firmly putting it in its place. Persuasion cannot be saved without also being tamed. In Chapter One we will see that no one has made the case for why it needs taming more persuasively than Thomas Hobbes.

PART I

Against Rhetoric

CHAPTER 1

The Rhetoric against
Rhetoric: Hobbes

Man's tongue is a trumpet to war and sedition.

—Hobbes, *De Cive* 5.5

Thus *stupidity* and *eloquence* unite to subvert the commonwealth; in the manner in which once upon a time (as the story goes) the daughters of *Pelias*, king of Thessaly conspired with *Medea* against their father. Wishing to restore a decrepit old man to his youth, they cut him in pieces by the advice of *Medea* and placed him on the fire to cook, in the vain hope that he would be rejuvenated. In the same manner the mob in their stupidity, like the daughters of *Pelias*, desiring to renew their old commonwealth and led by the *eloquence* of ambitious men as by the sorcery of *Medea*, more often split it into *factions* and waste it with fire than reform it.

—Hobbes, *De Cive* 12.13

Like Plato, Hobbes both attacked the art of rhetoric and made masterful use of it. Though some readers have sought to evade this tension, Hobbes did not make it easy for them. Throughout his political writings he criticized orators and rhetoricians even as he deployed their favorite techniques. In *Leviathan*, where the tension is most obvious, he associated metaphors with the art of rhetoric and insisted that they should be "utterly excluded" from "demonstration, Councell, and all rigourous search of Truth."[1] He characterized his book as a work of both demonstration and council, proudly claiming that "no other Philosopher hitherto, hath put into order, and sufficiently, or probably proved all the Theoremes of Morall doctrine" and expressing the hope that sovereigns might take advice from it.[2] Yet not only did Hobbes fill the book with metaphors; he titled it with one. He introduced the work by setting forth in elaborate detail a master metaphor, the commonwealth as "artificial man." He elaborated this metaphor with a series of submetaphors, through which particular organs of the state were likened to organs or faculties of the artificial man; magistrates were the joints, punishment the nerves, laws the will, and so on. And he had each edition of *Leviathan* illustrated with a frontispiece depicting a metaphorical vision of the commonwealth.[3] In *De Cive*, where his arguments against eloquence and metaphors were even clearer and where he took pains to adopt a scientific or geometrical method of analysis, he nevertheless dramatized his points with vivid metaphors and similes, such as those quoted in the epigraphs to this chapter: the tongue was a trumpet of war, and eloquence was like the sorcery of Medea.[4] Other rhetorical images, techniques, and metaphors in Hobbes's various writings could be adduced, but the general puzzle is clear: How can we best understand the fact that he both attacked the art of rhetoric and used it so effectively?[5]

It is tempting to reduce the difficulties in Hobbes's thought by emphasizing one side of this tension at the expense of the other. An earlier generation of scholars put the accent on Hobbes's antirhetorical science, highlighting its novelty and treating the rhetoric as a superficial matter of form, a vestige of the tradition he had left behind.[6] More recent scholarship, notably Quentin Skinner's *Reason and Rhetoric in the Philosophy of Hobbes*, has shifted in the other direction, stressing Hobbes's use of rhetoric and inferring his debt to the humanist tradition.[7] In this chapter I take a different approach by focusing on Hobbes's rhetoric and yet insisting on his novelty. While Hobbes certainly made use of the rhetorical techniques he had learned as part of his humanist education in rhetoric, he turned those techniques against the heart of the tradition from which they came.

The classical and Renaissance tradition of rhetoric, with Cicero as its center of gravity, had viewed eloquence as a means of articulating the best arguments on each side of a controversy. In Hobbes's hands, rhetoric became a means of avoiding controversy rather than engaging in it.[8] Viewing political opinions as irremediably dogmatic, insistent, and subjective, Hobbes entertained a deep mistrust of citizens' capacity to exercise the sort of practical judgment that would have been required to make political controversy susceptible to compromise or deliberation. In all three major versions of his political thought (*Elements*, *De Cive*, and *Leviathan*) he displayed his distrust of judgment and public deliberations by emphasizing the speed with which verbal disagreements tended to devolve into war. It was this mistrust, I will suggest, that fundamentally distinguished his rhetoric from that of the humanist Ciceronian tradition.[9]

There is more at stake in the question of how best to understand Hobbes's use of rhetoric than his historical relation to Renaissance humanism. The character of Hobbes's rhetoric was closely tied to the structure of his political theory, and it reveals his intention to base politics on a shared and overwhelming interest in avoiding controversy about the most fundamental political issues. Hobbes did not use metaphors and other rhetorical tropes as a way to articulate an argument for deliberating citizens. Rather, he used such devices as a way to close off deliberation so that his advice would not be merely another opinion but the founding and final one.[10] He sought to persuade citizens to alienate their judgments to the sovereign, to agree to abide by its determinations on controversial matters rather than judging for themselves. Hobbes's peculiar conceptions of consent and representation, which rest upon this alienation of judgment, cannot fully be understood without noticing how deeply suspicious he was of the traditional practice of rhetoric. If Hobbes thought that citizens had to be persuaded to disregard their private judgments and reasons, that was in large part because he saw no other way of bringing them to disregard the reasons being supplied to them by seditious orators and preachers. Hobbes's suspicion of rhetoric as it was practiced in his time is what led him to propose that citizens allow their private judgments to be displaced by what he called, in chapter 37 of *Leviathan*, "publique reason."[11] Hobbes seems to have been the first political philosopher to use the English phrase "public reason" to describe a distinct class of arguments that citizens should accept as legitimate in public affairs even if they do not do so in private. Of course, there are a host of distinctions to be made between Hobbes's use of the phrase and that found in contemporary Kantian-Rawlsian theories of public reason. Still, insofar as these recent theories inherit not only the phrase but also the basic contractual structure of Hobbes's approach, they have roots in his effort to quell the seditious practice of political debate that he associated with the classical-humanist tradition of controversial rhetoric.

Rhetoric and Controversy

In a sense we can solve the puzzle about rhetoric in Hobbes simply by restating it. If the question is how Hobbes could have both attacked rhetoric and used it, the answer is that he used rhetoric to attack rhetoric. While he used traditional forms or techniques of rhetoric, he put those forms to a novel use and offered rhetoric a new function. The new function of rhetoric was to end its old function.

The old function of rhetoric was to facilitate controversy. Rhetoricians taught their students how to argue on any side of any question. A successful orator displayed his skill as Cicero reported Carneades had during his trip to Rome, arguing first on one side, then on the other. The practice of arguing both sides of a question *(in ultramque partem)* was defended because of the uncertainty inherent in words of moral and political evaluation, such as *good* and *just*.[12] Rhetoric was a manner of engaging in public deliberation, and one only deliberated about what was controversial or uncertain.

The new function of Hobbesian rhetoric was to minimize uncertainty and controversy. The new rhetoric moved men to act according to the dictates of science. It motivated and managed, but it did not invent arguments of its own. It was a servant of science. Rather than exposing citizens to the arguments for various sides of an issue and thus facilitating controversy, the new rhetoric promoted certainty or consensus by aligning the will with the conclusions of science, conclusions that were, by definition, uncontroversial or incontrovertible. The first task of the new rhetoric was thus to eliminate the realm of controversy in which the old rhetoric had found its place. The new rhetoric sought to end the practice of rhetoric as it had traditionally been understood.

Hobbes did not announce a "new rhetoric," but he suggested its possibility in the way that he attacked the tradition of rhetoric while using its techniques. Elements of his new approach to rhetoric can be traced to earlier thinkers, notably Machiavelli and Luther, and also to lesser-known figures such as Petrus Ramus and Omer Talon.[13] It was Hobbes, however, who collected and organized these elements into a comprehensive view of morals and politics, and it was his new political science that sought to end rhetoric as a practice of controversy.

In emphasizing the distinction between Hobbes's own rhetoric and that which he attacked, I aim to challenge the characterization of *Leviathan* found in Quentin Skinner's important book on the subject. Citing Hobbes's use of rhetorical techniques, Skinner describes *Leviathan* as a part of the humanist tradition of rhetoric: "The *Leviathan* constitutes a belated but magnificent contribution to the Renaissance art of eloquence . . . [It] is a work in which the humanist ideal of a union between reason and rhetoric is not merely defended but systematically realised."[14] To explain why Hobbes would have returned to the Renaissance humanist tradition after having proudly introduced a new science of politics, Skinner turns to his intellectual biography. He proposes that Hobbes twice executed a drastic about-face in his opinion about rhetoric. First, after discovering Euclid's *Elements,* Hobbes "proceeded to pull up his own humanist roots" and turned from eloquence to geometrical science.[15] This part of the story is familiar, and there is little debate about Hobbes's change of direction. Aristotle had offered geometry as precisely the sort of subject that did not require eloquence, and English Renaissance humanists such as Thomas Wilson repeated the point; Wilson noted on the first page of his *Arte of Rhetorique* (1560) that "*Geometrie* rather asketh a good square, then a cleane flowing tongue to set out the art."[16] When Hobbes praised and imitated the method of geometers in *Elements* and *De Cive,* he was openly attacking the rhetorical approach to politics. Skinner's real innovation is to say that a second turnabout occurred, reversing the first, at about the time that *Leviathan* was written. According to Skinner, Hobbes underwent "a remarkable change of mind . . . Hobbes now endorse[d] in large measure the humanist analysis of the relations between reason and rhetoric which he had earlier sought to challenge and supercede."[17]

This second reversal proposed by Skinner is the one that deserves scrutiny. For while it is true that Hobbes believed eloquence would make his argument more attractive, that fact alone is not enough to make *Leviathan* a "contribution to" or an "endorsement of" the Renaissance humanist rhetorical tradition. That tradition is best characterized not only by the use of rhetorical techniques, but also, and more fundamentally, by the function that those techniques were meant to perform. The mere presence of rhetorical tropes and tricks in *Leviathan* does not by itself suggest that Hobbes reconsidered the opposition to rhetoric that he articulated in *Elements* and *De Cive.* The main beliefs animating his hostility to rhetoric did not change between the *Elements* and *Leviathan.* Hobbes always believed (even before the English Civil War) that controversy was above all other things to be avoided. In *Elements, De Cive,* and *Leviathan* he consistently portrayed rhetoric as an art of controversy for the proud and vain, for those who desired applause and were willing to sacrifice both political stability and truth for the sake of their own reputations.[18] And in his mature writings he consistently subscribed to a view of human sensation according to which people projected their own subjective responses onto the world and mistook them for objective properties; as we will see, he viewed evaluative judgments as analogous to sense impressions in this respect. Taken together, these beliefs conspired to make traditional rhetoric seem a dangerous art, through which men sought to impress one another by insisting on the truth of their subjective reactions to the world.

Nothing in *Leviathan* or any of his later writings suggests that Hobbes gave up this set of beliefs about rhetoric.[19] In fact, *Leviathan* itself should be read as an effort to carry out the explicitly antirhetorical program announced in *Elements*. There Hobbes had argued that the errors of sense and language through which rhetoric had grown powerful—the errors which explained why "*ratio*, now, is but *oratio*"—could only be rectified by "beginning anew from the very first grounds of all our knowledge, sense; and, instead of books, reading over orderly one's own conceptions: in which meaning I take *nosce teipsum* for a precept worthy the reputation it hath gotten."[20] In *Leviathan* Hobbes began in precisely this way, citing the same dictum, *nosce teipsum*, in the introduction and starting with a chapter called "Of Sense."[21] The opposition to controversy and to the dispersal of judgment that gave rise to it was a constant feature of Hobbes's writings. He continued to associate eloquence with the tumultuous character of popular assemblies in *Leviathan*, and, in *Behemoth*, written well afterwards, he continued to blame orators for having stirred up the civil war. Indeed, in the latter work he offered a strikingly bitter retrospective on what should have been done to silence the orating preachers: "Had it not been much better that those seditious ministers, which were not perhaps 1000, had been all killed before they had preached? It had been (I confess) a great massacre; but the killing of 100,000 is a greater."[22] Moreover, as Richard Tuck points out, Hobbes published his earlier, more geometrical Latin works together with his Latin version of *Leviathan*, suggesting that he saw no fundamental contradiction between them. His willingness to utilize the techniques of rhetoric in *Leviathan* must be understood in light of the constancy of his substantive views about the sources of controversy and the best means of avoiding it.[23]

Skinner's account is puzzlingly silent about Hobbes's stance toward controversy in the later works. When describing the humanist rhetorical tradition in which the young Hobbes was educated, Skinner highlights the importance that the tradition placed on the practice of *controversia* and therefore on the knowledge of how to argue both sides of any question. He notes that for Cicero arguing *in ultramque partem* was "the most important skill of all" and that "the same assumptions occur with even greater emphasis in the Renaissance."[24] Further, Skinner indicates that the dialogical character of this practice is what might make it attractive to theorists today.[25] But when arguing for Hobbes's return to the humanist rhetorical tradition, Skinner does not consider Hobbes's view of controversy; he notices only his use of tropes and figures. Could Hobbes really have returned to the rhetorical tradition without embracing its central practice? It is true that he invoked a traditional humanist formula about the marriage of wisdom and eloquence in the "Review and Conclusion" of *Leviathan*. But there he was only offering new wine in an old cask. The modern science that Hobbes proposed was different from the older *scientia civilis* in ways that made it fundamentally antagonistic to the tradition of rhetorical controversy. Because Hobbes "returned" to rhetoric without coming to value controversy and without abandoning the epistemology, psychology, and politics that fueled his suspicion of controversy in the first place, the rhetoric he deployed in *Leviathan* is fundamentally different from the rhetoric he learned as a student and later attacked. Hobbes's use of rhetoric was meant to consolidate, not reverse, his effort to put politics on a scientific foundation. Anyone wanting to support a more deliberative or dialogical mode of political discourse would have to reject not only the Hobbes of the *Elements* but also the Hobbes of *Leviathan*.[26]

In the rest of this chapter I will first discuss how Machiavelli and the Tacitists paved the way for Hobbes's attack on rhetoric and then turn back to the contrast between Hobbes and the Ciceronian-humanist tradition. I argue that when Hobbes made the alienation of judgment central to his notion of consent he was aiming to undermine the appeals to judgment that had been at the heart of Aristotelian and Ciceronian rhetoric. He considered such appeals dangerous because of the intransigent character of appeals to conscience in the Puritan rhetoric of the early seventeenth century. We will see that Puritan orators and rhetoricians often described the insights of conscience with analogies to vision and hence opened the door to Hobbes's peculiar approach to politics, which began with reflections on the senses. In arriving at the beginning of Hobbes's theory in this way, I hope to show how his distinctive uses of rhetoric and metaphor are best understood as an attack on the Ciceronian rhetorical tradition rather than a return to it.[27]

Silencing Cicero

The foundation on which Hobbes built his attack was laid down by an earlier challenge to the Ciceronian tradition, a challenge put forth by Machiavelli and disseminated by the Tacitists. Machiavelli sought to focus the attention of the princes on the "effectual truth" rather than on the ambiguous, duplicitous claims of partisans, and he sought to draw their attention away from speeches or "professions" and more toward deeds.[28]

In the *Discourses* Machiavelli indicated his scorn for the soft, studied eloquence of classical persuasion by juxtaposing Cicero's failure and Julius Caesar's success. Caesar's bold actions had easily triumphed over Cicero's orations.[29] Machiavelli did not deny that princes had to be concerned with the opinions of the citizens, but he thought it best to control opinion through extraordinary and violent acts that left lasting impressions rather than through speeches. He suggested that public executions every ten years might have saved Rome from corruption; no political founding was complete, he wrote, without "a memorable execution against the enemies of the present conditions."[30] In this way he implicitly approved of the one deed for which Cicero was usually condemned, his order in 63 B.C. to execute five of Catiline's coconspirators without trial. Whether trying to preserve a tyranny or a free state, Machiavelli taught that it was always necessary to "kill the sons of Brutus."[31] The function of the executions was to rekindle in the hearts of the citizens "that terror and that fear" promoted obedient citizenship. Sensational deeds would silence words.

Against the tremendous force of this attack the art of rhetoric could defend itself only by arguing that words themselves could be deeds. While humanists who felt the power of Machiavelli's argument did not suddenly abandon their interest in rhetoric, they increasingly focused on the "effectual truth" of the spoken word, on the power that speech could wield rather than the arguments it could articulate. They adjusted their humanism by turning their attention away from Cicero and toward Tacitus, the classical historian whose realism seemed friendlier to (and yet more acceptable than) the Machiavellian point of view.[32] Jean Bodin, the French writer who was largely responsible for introducing Tacitus into later Renaissance political thought, associated Tacitus with Machiavelli and offered a response to their skepticism about rhetoric.[33] Bodin recommended Tacitus over Cicero and the other staples of Renaissance humanism because only Tacitus spoke about "secrets of state."[34] Elsewhere in the same text he noted that Machiavelli was able to "rightly give a decision [concerning] . . . the secrets of princes."[35] While Bodin criticized the republican parts of Machiavelli, he seemed to exempt *The Prince* from his criticism, and the reasons he gave for doing so echoed the reasons he gave for preferring Tacitus.[36] In contrast to the most prominent earlier use of Tacitus, Leonardo Bruni's oration spurring Florence on toward a republican ideal, Bodin's appropriation emphasized the techniques a prince could use to consolidate his rule. He admired Tacitus's realism. The realistic lessons about rhetoric were, first, that its arguments could seldom be trusted—Bodin called it "the art of successful lying"—and, second, that it nevertheless had enormous effective power.[37] To illustrate this crucial point, Bodin referred to an image from Lucian in which Hercules was portrayed as an orator whose words could be more powerful than armies:

> Our forefathers portrayed the Celtic Hercules as an old man, trailing after him a crowd of people fastened by the ears with chains issuing from his mouth. They thus intimated that the powers and armed forces of kings and princes are not so potent as the vehemence of an ardent and eloquent man.[38]

Though Bodin followed Tacitus in warning that this power could be used to stir up faction and civil war, Bodin immediately went on to recommend that princes learn how to use that power to consolidate their own rule.

This is the line of thought that Hobbes drew out in his own work on Tacitus. In an early essay, "A Discourse upon the Beginning of Tacitus," Hobbes conceded Machiavelli's lesson about the beginnings of cities, admitting that Rome's leaders had founded their empire on force. Like Machiavelli, Hobbes admired Caesar more than Cicero because Caesar had recognized that actions trumped words. Echoing chapter 25 of *The Prince*, he wrote, "But Caesar knew the Republic to be feminine, and that it would yield sooner to violence, than flattery." Nevertheless, Hobbes also suggested that "though violence cannot last, yet the effects of it may; and that which is gotten violently, may be afterwards possessed quietly, and constantly." Augustus, he argued, had found ways to keep what he had attained by "politic provisions" that mollified the angry and allured the weak, and Hobbes reminded his readers that "in a multitude, seeming things, rather than substantial, make impression." He emphasized mistakes that had been made by mishandling matters of public perception and implied a managerial task for rhetoric when arguing about Augustus's skill: "And now having power over the bodies of the people, he goes about to obtain it over their minds, and wills, which is both the noblest and surest command of all other." Like Bodin, the early Hobbes suggested a way for rhetoricians to defend themselves against the Machiavellian attack on their tradition. If words could supplant the striking violence of Machiavellian deeds, a new, more manipulative rhetoric could perform some of the actions necessary to establish and maintain a state.[39]

At least two of the most widely read English rhetoricians of the later sixteenth century, Thomas Wilson and Henry Peacham, had tried to address
the Machiavellian or Tacitist challenge from within the Ciceronian tradition. In the prologue to his *Arte of Rhetorique* Wilson paraphrased a well-
known scene from Cicero's *De inventione,* in which the orator was portrayed
as a founder of a commonwealth who assembled scattered individuals together and persuaded them to submit to just rule.[40] Following Cicero
closely, Wilson described a natural state in which men were "wild savages"
and credited rhetoric with the capacity to tame men, to convince them to
accept equality, and thus to draw them into civil society. The prominence
Wilson and Peacham gave to their paraphrases of this passage indicated
their continuing loyalty to Cicero, but the way in which they focused on
and adapted the passage suggests that they were in some sense aware of the
Machiavellian challenge and that they were trying to respond to it from
within the traditional Ciceronian corpus. In doing so, they were stretching
the Ciceronian tradition far from its original spirit. Cicero's own conception
of rhetoric did not focus as much on the problem of founding as this one
passage, taken out of context, would suggest. Cicero had written that his
own arguments in *De inventione* had been immature, and in *De oratore,* his
later work on rhetoric, he had considered orators' practice of arguing on
both sides of various questions at least as much as their role in forming
cities.[41] Earlier humanists had focused on the controversial element of Cicero's rhetoric, stressing the importance of arguing *in ultramque partem.*[42]
Wilson and Peacham, in contrast, both emphasized the motivating, effective
power of speech. And even within the motivational model they departed
from Cicero. Where Cicero had written of an orator persuading men to
"submit to justice," Wilson indicated that the work of oratory was to persuade subjects to do a monarch's work and fight his wars. What is most
interesting in Wilson is the way in which he tried to integrate the traditional
Ciceronian image with the very different one that we have already seen
Bodin using, the image from Lucian in which Hercules was portrayed as an
orator whose power consisted of chaining men into groups and dragging
them about. After weaving the Ciceronian passage together with this one,
Wilson went on to emphasize the effects that powerful speech could produce. Without rhetoric, he asked, "who would dig and delve from morn till
evening? Who would travail and toil with the sweat of his brows? Yea, who
would for his king's pleasure adventure and hazard his life, if wit had not so
won men?"[43] In dealing with the same passage from Cicero, Henry Peacham

suggested that oratory could make a person "the emperour of mens minds & affections."[44] Thus the Ciceronian image that originally gave orators credit for instituting republican government was presented by Wilson and Peacham as proof that rhetoric could be a useful tool for monarchs who wanted to control their subjects.

Far from showing the continuity of the Ciceronian tradition, the use that Wilson and Peacham made of this passage from Cicero suggests that they were aware of the great change in the understanding of the function of rhetoric that was required to defend the art against the challenge that had been brought forth by Machiavelli and the Tacitists. Their paraphrases of the *De inventione* passage seem to anticipate Hobbes's *Leviathan* in that they describe natural men as savages who need to be brought out of a state of nature into civil society. From this perspective Hobbes's theory itself might also be seen as a response to the Machiavellian challenge to Ciceronian rhetoric.

The character of Hobbes's response, however, was different from that of the rhetoricians in whose writings he had been schooled. While Wilson and Peacham followed Cicero in making orators responsible for leading men out of the savage state, Hobbes made orators responsible for leading men further into it. He listed oratory as one of the principal causes leading to the dissolution of commonwealths. And when Hobbes made use of Lucian's image of Hercules as an orator leading chained men around by their ears, he cleverly modified the depiction and revised its meaning. Whereas the original image had revealed the muscular power of an orator, Hobbes's version demonstrated how a sovereign would prevent orators from wielding that power. Hobbes described the sovereign's opinions, expressed in civil laws, as "artificial chains" that the people "themselves, by mutuall covenants, have fastned at one end, to the lips of that Man, or Assembly, to whom they have given the Soveraigne Power; and at the other end to their own Ears."[45] In this picture the citizens each chained themselves individually to the sovereign's mouth and so could not be chained together into a faction by any other speaker. By granting the sovereign a monopoly of attention, Hobbes sought to immunize the citizens against the preaching rebels. An orator looking for an audience in a Hobbesian commonwealth would find the subjects' ears already fastened to the lips of the sovereign and many of their opinions dictated by the sovereign. Of course, Hobbes's version of the image seemed to make the sovereign himself a master orator, but it also insisted that the chains by which he bound his subjects were not speeches but laws. Thus while Hobbes adopted images and concerns from the earlier rhetoricians, he nevertheless rejected their efforts to rescue Ciceronian rhetoric from the Machiavellian attack. As we shall now see, Hobbes was closer to the spirit of that attack than to those who resisted it.

Alienating Judgment

At the heart of the Ciceronian rhetorical tradition was the view that politics required citizens to appeal to one another's capacity for practical judgment.[46] While an orator might learn figures of speech and structures of argument, while he might try to move the passions, the ultimate purpose of these techniques was to make his arguments more persuasive to his audience members' judgment. Judgment was the faculty that drew upon perception, passion, and reason to determine what to think and do in any particular situation; it was the faculty in which the various sense impressions, memories, and reasons somehow came together, drawn from their plurality into one active mind.[47] Because judgment was thought to draw on sensation and passion as well as reason, orators used images, metaphors, and similes, and they incited strong feelings, such as anger, gratitude, or jealousy. These sorts of appeals were not always seen as efforts to corrupt judgment; they could instead be legitimate efforts to engage judgment. Although Aristotle and Cicero recognized that practical judgment was imprecise and often unreliable, they also recognized that the art of rhetoric ultimately rested upon some sort of confidence that an audience could judge well when engaging in public deliberations.[48] Aristotle ended his *Rhetoric* in the way that he thought an orator must effectively end every speech—by laying himself at the mercy of his audience: "I have done. You have heard me. The facts are before you. I ask for your judgment."[49] The strong link between rhetoric and practical judgment persisted throughout the Renaissance, so that when the Italian professor of rhetoric Giambattista Vico defended his subject against the Cartesians, he explained that defending humanist rhetoric was the only way to defend the realm of practical judgment.[50]

Such confidence in judgment seemed too optimistic to Hobbes, who thought most men were superstitious, intellectually lazy, easy to manipulate, and obstinate in their ignorance. Especially sensitive to the dynamic of pride in public assemblies, Hobbes held out no hope that public debate would draw out good judgment from the participants. "What can that large number of debaters contribute to policy with their inept views but a nuisance?" he asked when discussing deliberations about foreign policy in

De Cive.[51] Convinced that orators aimed primarily at gaining reputations for themselves and that their audiences had access to no shared standard of judgment on which to base an agreement, he argued that public speeches and debates tended to produce violence rather than deliberation. "In all debates of what kind soever," he argued, it was necessary to appoint an external arbitrator. If disputing parties instead tried to persuade one another by appealing to reason or judgment, they would reach one of only two outcomes: "Their controversie must either come to blowes, or be undecided."[52] The speed with which citizens moved from disagreement to violence in Hobbes's political theory demonstrates how deeply he mistrusted rhetorical appeals to judgment.

The depth of his suspicion of judgment can be seen in his explanation of why the state of nature was unbearable. He moved quickly from the fact that in the state of nature every person had a right to judge what posed a danger to his self-preservation to the conclusion that everyone had a "right to all things."[53] What Hobbes assumed in making this move was either that individuals could not be trusted to be reasonable about what their self-preservation required or that no practical criterion of reasonableness existed. Whereas both scholastics and humanists had referred often to a criterion of "right reason," Hobbes assumed that people would simply call "right" whichever reason seemed best to them.[54] Throughout his writings on politics Hobbes made it clear that the problem in the state of nature arose from the absence of an external judge to decide controversies. In assuming that a judge had to be brought in from outside, he implicitly denied that public judgment could arise from the people themselves. But that idea had been precisely the presupposition of the classical and humanist traditions of rhetoric.

With this in mind, it is easier to see how Hobbes's view of consent was distinctive and why it undermined the tradition we have been discussing. According to what might be called the natural meaning of consent, a government should be responsive to the opinions of its citizens. Puritans and republicans using the language of consent clearly meant that the king should be responsive to the opinions expressed by the parliament. They used the language of consent to attack absolute authority. Against such reformers Hobbes introduced a second, more artificial meaning of consent. He asked every citizen to transfer his right of judging the best means to preserve his life to one sovereign, "and therein to submit their Wills, every one to his Will, and their Judgements, to his Judgment."[55] This second meaning of consent was, in a sense, the opposite of the first. Rather than encouraging citizens to press their opinions about particular laws or policies on government, Hobbes's use of "consent" explained to citizens why the government could legitimately disregard their opinions.

In Hobbes's theory the locus of political decision-making was not once but twice removed from the ordinary deliberative judgment of citizens. First, Hobbes sought to replace the Aristotelian conception of practical judgment, in all its indefiniteness, with a clearer and more definite criterion. Whereas Aristotle had proposed the doctrine of the mean as a heuristic to help guide men's judgment, Hobbes offered a more concrete, more easily applicable standard—the necessity of seeking peace. He dismissed Aristotle's notion of the mean as the dangerously vague view that the goodness of the various virtues lay "in a mediocrity of passions: as if not the Cause, but the Degree of daring, made Fortitude; or not the Cause, but the Quantity of a gift, made Liberality."[56] The problem with this understanding of virtue was that it was susceptible to manipulation by orators, who took advantage of the uncertainty implicit in it through the technique of redescription, or *paradiastole*. They would redescribe a virtue as its neighboring vice, or vice versa, as when they called a courageous man "rash." By offering a clearer criterion for the virtues, Hobbes aimed to disrupt this rhetorical strategy.[57]

Even having replaced Aristotle's doctrine of the mean with a clearer criterion of practical judgment, however, Hobbes still did not believe that people would avoid dangerous controversy. He recognized that the natural law to seek peace, while clear, nevertheless left room for different judgments about what would best assure peace in particular situations, such as during the ship money case of the 1630s.[58] Therefore, he thought it necessary to introduce a second stage of distance between citizens' judgments and the opinions by which a government was ruled. Citizens would agree to let a sovereign judge for them what did and did not promote peace. In fact, the sole decision that citizens made when using the grounds of natural law that Hobbes introduced before the political covenant was the decision to alienate their judgments and wills to a sovereign. Once inside political society, Hobbes's citizens found themselves twice removed from their own judgments—once because the natural law told them what criterion was relevant and a second time because they were not allowed to use that criterion themselves. In disregarding their own judgments, they would become immune to the efforts of orating preachers to influence their judgments. Convinced that orators appealing to private judgment had stirred the people to rebellion, and persuaded that he had no means of acting against the orators themselves, Hobbes sought to inoculate the citizens against their influence.[59]

If orators played such an important role in the problem that Hobbes addressed, however, one might think that the best solution would be to try to protect individual judgment rather than alienate it. For if the political dilemma arose from the influence of demagogues, then it arose not so much from individuals making judgments for themselves as from their failing to do so, from their willingness to mindlessly follow the preachers who led them into factions and turned their loyalties against the state. Richard Tuck points out that Hobbes actually seemed to favor a dispersal of private judgment when he praised the Protestant independency of the "Primitive Christians," in which individuals had been free from the influence of priests and churches. Hobbes remarked that in that state men had been free "to follow Paul, or Cephas, or Apollos, every man as he liketh best: Which, if it be without contention, and without measuring the Doctrine of Christ, by our affection to the Person of his Minister . . . is perhaps the best." He went on to claim that "there ought to be no Power over the Consciences of men, but of the Word it selfe" and that it was unreasonable "to require of a man endued with Reason of his own, to follow the Reason of any other man, or of the most voices of many other men."[60] But Hobbes offered this idea as something of an aside, and the two stipulations that he attached to his support of such a dispersal of judgment—that it not produce contention and that it not involve taking one's point of view from a minister—were not ones that he thought could be met for any significant length of time. Perhaps he did regard the deepest commitments of an individual as beyond the reach of a sovereign, but the key point for his political theory is that he did not think that individuals' private judgments could serve as a viable basis for ongoing deliberation or governance. Independency was valuable for Hobbes principally because it brought citizens closer to the war of all against all, which was the necessary precursor to adopting his more permanent political solution. Independency dissolved religious factions and so set every individual against every other, at least potentially; it reduced the sphere of religion to a state of war and so created the need for the sovereign.[61] The structure of argument here parallels the structure of Hobbes's argument about how to deal with prophecies. He argued that individuals should use their natural reason to discern true from false prophecies but almost immediately concluded that natural reason would decide to use the sovereign's determinations as criteria.[62] Hobbes's admiration for independency, and for the dispersal of independent judgment it brought, demonstrates his estimation of its relative standing against the alternative of religious factionalism but not its viability as a permanent political solution. In Hobbes's view, the one crucial judgment that independent individuals made in the political realm was that they should alienate their private faculty of judgment to the sovereign.

None of this meant that a Hobbesian sovereign could not allow his subjects wide latitude to judge many matters for themselves in practice. In fact, Hobbes sometimes suggested that it would be wise for a sovereign to introduce a fairly liberal and tolerant regime for the sake of stability. The crucial point, however, was that citizens could only act on their private judgments at the pleasure of the sovereign. Once they had consented to be governed, their opinions had no independent claim to constrain the sovereign. The most liberal regime would come about not because the state respected the independent legitimacy of individual judgment but because the sovereign might choose, as a matter of prudent policy, to give back to the citizens part of the judging power they had ceded to him.[63] Thus, even citizens of a very liberal Hobbesian state would find that their own judgments had a status fundamentally altered by their consent. Their judgments would return to them only indirectly, filtered by the sovereign.

Why did Hobbes mistrust men's judgment so? One part of the answer is that he did not think that people had access to a natural or shared criterion of judgment; he took skepticism seriously.[64] But Hobbes was not the first to have recognized or worried about the lack of a clear criterion on which to base practical judgments. We should not imagine that humanist rhetoricians were unaware of the uncertainty and subjectivity inherent in human judgment. As followers of Cicero, they could hardly have ignored Academic skepticism. Erasmus, for instance, referred to the sort of argument that Hobbes would later use against the reliability of our senses, remarking on "those who have remained a long while in the sun, so that whatever they should see thereafter appears in that brilliant hue which they themselves bear within the eyes damaged by cataracts."[65] But whereas Hobbes used such arguments to suggest why citizens should allow a sovereign to judge for them, Erasmus thought that one could take the lessons of skepticism as reasons to avoid dogmatism and to try to improve one's own judgments.

Noticing the moderate character of Erasmus's response to skepticism helps to demonstrate the radical nature of Hobbes's solution. Erasmus adopted the view that opinions in practical matters had the epistemic status of "probable" rather than "certain" beliefs and thus thought they were subject to revision and compromise in the course of deliberations. He thought that skepticism could moderate our attachment to beliefs without undermining our judgments entirely; he never asked his readers to do anything as drastic as alienate their judgments to an external sovereign. He linked skepticism to the Christian virtue of humility, which required open-mindedness and a willingness to submit one's judgments to deliberation, usually in the forums of the Catholic Church. He articulated this view clearly when responding to Luther, arguing that controversial questions were best resolved over a period of time in church assemblies, among "senates of learned men," who would construct, through deliberation, a general consensus about the most probable and practical truth. In echoing Cicero's emphasis on the senate and the *consensus omnium*, he illustrated the classic humanist faith that controversies arising from the uncertainties of judgment could be managed by deliberation in appropriate institutional settings.[66] Thus in the example of Erasmus we find a skeptic perfectly at home with the sort of deliberative controversy that Hobbes seems to have thought could only devolve into war.

The humanist sort of deliberation in which Erasmus placed his faith required that opinions be susceptible to revision and improvement. If Hobbes did not allow for that possibility, it was in part because he adopted a deeper Pyrrhonist skepticism that would call into doubt the basis on which one might claim that some views were more "probable" than others. But he also thought that few people were likely to view their own opinions as merely "probable." Hobbes viewed men as proud and obstinate in their judgments; they were "children of pride," who could only be subdued by a Leviathan. When he asked citizens to alienate their judgment to a sovereign, he was asking them to accept not the mild Academic skepticism of Cicero or Erasmus but a more radical self-alienation. To see why he thought this alienation was politically necessary, we have to notice not only that he thought private judgment was subjective but also that he thought it was obstinate. What we still have to investigate, then, is why he thought people tended to remain so dogmatic in their private judgments.

The Dogmatism of Conscience

When Hobbes wrote about the dangers of "private judgment," he often had a particular sort of private judgment in mind—the private judgment of conscience.[67] Appeals to conscience were the regular form of public preaching among the Puritan ministers so important to seventeenth-century politics in

England. A claim of conscience was a claim that one's judgment or opinion was inviolable, even if the magistrate should demand otherwise. Hobbes viewed appeals to conscience as subversive efforts to incite sedition. One of his targets may have been the books and influence of William Perkins (1558–1602), whose *The Art of Prophecying* taught the politically active Puritan ministers of the seventeenth century how to write their sermons and whose works on conscience helped to shape their moral reasoning.[68] In addition to speaking of preaching as a form of "prophecy," Perkins had clearly required that, in a case where the magistrate's demands conflicted with those of God (as known by conscience), the latter should take precedence.[69] Perkins had called conscience "a little God sitting in the middle of men['s] hearts, arraigning them in this life as they shal be arraigned for their offences at the tribunal seat of the everliving God in the day of judgement."[70] Moreover, Perkins's etymology of the word "conscience" will be familiar to any reader of *Leviathan*, for Hobbes offered a very similar etymology in chapter 7. Perkins had traced the origin of the word in this way:

> And hence comes one reason of the name of conscience. *Scire*, to know, is of one man alone by himselfe: and *conscire* is, when two at the least knowe some secret thing; either of them knowing it together with the other.[71]

Perkins had argued that since only God could know men's thoughts, conscience was only possible between a man and God. In *Leviathan* Hobbes offered a similar etymology but complained that claims of conscience had been expanded, by means of rhetoric and metaphor, to include arguments that had no particular connection with God at all:

> Afterwards, men made use of the same word metaphorically, for the knowledge of their own secret facts, and secret thoughts; and therefore it is Rhetorically said, that the Conscience is a thousand witnesses. And last of all, men, vehemently in love with their own new opinions, (though never so absurd,) and obstinately bent to maintain them, gave those their opinions also that reverenced name of Conscience.[72]

Two features of Hobbes's response stand out. He viewed claims of conscience as unjustified attempts to make one's private judgments sacred, and he viewed metaphor as the tool by which the word conscience had been turned into a justification for obstinacy.

Hobbes did not think that calling our opinions "dictates of conscience" granted them any special status. He argued that conscience was simply another term for private judgment and therefore that his theory, in which citizens alienated their judgments to a sovereign, applied also to conscience.[73] Thus, a person who followed the laws in a Hobbesian commonwealth was by definition acting according to the dictates of conscience, since he had transferred the right of determining "the publique conscience" to the sovereign: "The law is the public Conscience."[74] Of course, many questions would arise about which the laws were silent, in which case one's private conscience could be followed. But when the laws spoke, Hobbes argued, no one who had consented to be governed could claim conscience as a reason for disobedience:

> The conscience being nothing else but a man's settled judgement and opinion, when he hath once transferred his right of judging to another, that which shall be commanded, is no less his judgement, than the judgement of that other; so that in obedience to laws, a man doth still according to his conscience, but not his private conscience. And whatsoever is done contrary to private conscience, is then a sin, when the laws have left him to his own liberty, and never else.[75]

Hobbes's theory thus seems to have been arranged precisely as a way of neutralizing the sort of claims that Perkins and like-minded Puritans had made central to the practice of preaching. The divine certainty to which they sought access through conscience was, to Hobbes, often little more than a guise under which they asserted the inviolability of their own opinions, and the preaching in which they proclaimed the dictates of conscience was a dangerous threat to civil peace. Perkins's book on rhetoric was titled *The Art of Prophecying;* Hobbes insisted that claims to prophecy were veiled attempts to rule:

> And consequently men had need to be very circumspect, and wary, in obeying the voice of man, that pretending himself to be a Prophet, requires us to obey God in that way, which he in Gods name telleth us to be the way to happinesse. For he that pretends to teach men the way of so great felicity, pretends to govern them; that is to say, to rule, and reign over them.[76]

Insofar as the reformers of the first half of the seventeenth century were influenced by the Puritan rhetoric of conscience and prophecy, they would not have viewed their own opinions with the mild skepticism that Erasmus had thought necessary to public deliberations of any kind. Though Puritan reformers may have invoked theories of republicanism, they voiced their substantive opinions in a language too dogmatic for the deliberation that republicanism demands. Aristotle wrote that if anyone was clearly superior to the rest of the citizens, he would have to either be made king or be exiled; he could not fit into the regular politics of a city.[77] The Puritan rhetoric of conscience implicitly claimed such superiority. It followed the classical tradition in one respect, for it appealed to the judgment of its audience. But it failed to recognize that deliberation occurred within the realm of uncertainty and probability that Aristotle and Cicero had emphasized in their accounts of judgment. The rhetoric of conscience thus helped to set the stage for Hobbes's attack, by making a return to the Ciceronian rhetorical tradition seem impossible. When that tradition's facilitation of controversy was combined with the dogmatic character of opinions based on conscience, the result was a form of republicanism that encouraged controversy without encouraging the mild skepticism necessary to make controversy deliberative.

It was in response to prophesiers using the language of conscience that Hobbes used the phrase "publique reason." Immediately after his chapter attacking those citizens who used prophecy to "bewitch" their fellows into rebellion and civil war, Hobbes confronted the question of how citizens should decide whether to believe in miracles. He argued that in practice this question always resolved itself into another question: how should they decide whether to believe a person who claimed to have seen or produced a miracle? Hobbes cast doubt on such prophesiers in general by comparing them to jugglers, ventriloquists, conjurers, and con artists, and he noticed that ignorance and gullibility made most men easy targets for such "enchanters," whose words more often deceived people than produced legitimate miracles. To protect citizens from being taken in by such deceivers, Hobbes introduced the term "publique reason." The question that citizens usually faced was whether the report of a miracle was the truth or a lie:

> In which question we are not every one, to make our own private Reason, or Conscience, but the Publique Reason, that is, the reason of Gods Supreme Lieutenant, Judge; and indeed we have made him Judge already, if wee have given him a Soveraign power, to doe all that is necessary for our peace and defence.[78]

Hobbes went on to concede that a private citizen would always be free to believe the claims of a prophesier in his own heart if he saw fit. When it came to professing that belief in public, however, he would have to take the public judgment as his own: "But when it comes to confession of that faith, the Private Reason must submit to the Publique, that is to say, to Gods Lieutenant."[79] Thus, it would be the sovereign who would judge whether someone claiming to have produced or witnessed a miracle should be believed. This sovereign authority would in turn prevent citizens from being persuaded to follow a charismatic leader on the strength of his supposed connection to miracles, a danger that Hobbes repeatedly worried about in *Leviathan*. Indeed, Hobbes argued that the purpose of miracles was to bring citizens to follow certain men, such as Moses, by providing evidence that they were indeed the messengers or prophets of God. But claims about miracles were, Hobbes pointed out, liable to be abused by pretenders.[80] Hobbes introduced the notion of public reason to immunize citizens against the alluring but politically destabilizing rhetoric of false prophets. Public reason was the public conscience, which was in turn the sovereign's laws, which we have already seen Hobbes describe as chains binding each citizen's ears directly to the mouth of the sovereign. "Publique reason" was thus introduced to political thought as a chain meant to secure citizens against the stirring eloquence of Puritan reformers preaching the revolutionary rhetoric of conscience.

The Great Deception of Sense

In addition to its dogmatism, the Puritan rhetoric of conscience may have influenced Hobbes in a second way—by emphasizing an important analogy between opinions and sense impressions. When preachers appealed to conscience, they often likened the faculty of conscience to the senses, especially to vision. This analogy may help explain how Hobbes would have thought about the problem of political controversy. He had devoted a great deal of attention to the question of how to found a reliable natural science while granting that virtually everything we perceive through our senses is in fact a projection of our own minds. If the unreliability and dogmatism of our opinions was analogous to that of our sense impressions, the approach that Hobbes had used to establish a reliable foundation for a science of optics would also yield a stable foundation for politics.

Of course many writers prior to the Puritans had likened knowledge to sense data, but the Puritans seem to have put new emphasis on that analogy. Calvin himself often used vision as a metaphor to describe the directness with which he could know divine matters, and Puritans used images of vision to describe the directness with which they claimed to know the dictates of their consciences. Perry Miller's classic work *The New England Mind* is a good guide and source for examples. Miller shows how the analogy between opinion and sight received emphasis in the work of Petrus Ramus, the sixteenth-century French writer whose reform of logic and rhetoric aimed to eliminate the realm of uncertainty in which classical rhetoric had done its work (and whose method influenced William Perkins significantly): "In a metaphor—worked to the limit by his followers—[Ramus] said that as the eye perceives colors, so the mind sees arguments without needing any other demonstration"[81] "'For as sight [is] in the eyes,' wrote one Ramist, 'so is intelligence in the spirit.' When reason perceives a color, it forms an 'argument' of it, so that an argument is 'the image of a thing formed in the soul.'"[82] The Ramist notion that opinions were known with the certainty of sense impressions became a dominant trope in seventeenth-century Puritan oratory. Perhaps this is why the analogy appears in Hobbes's translation of Aristotle's *Rhetoric*. Hobbes titled several chapters by equating "colours" with "common opinions," as in chapter 6: "Of the Colours, or common opinions concerning Good and Evil."[83] Hobbes would have been especially prone to viewing political opinions this way, since he wrote his political theory as an interruption to his work on *De Homine*, in which the senses and especially vision played an important role.

In the realm of optics Hobbes aimed to found a science impervious to the problem of skepticism about the validity of what is seen. He admitted that the many qualities we think we see in the world exist only as motions in our own minds. He conceded that we are trapped within our own sense impressions and that we have no reason to think that those impressions share any characteristics with the motions that cause them; we have no reason to think they are accurate representations of an external world. Nevertheless, Hobbes suggested that a reliable science could be built on our ability to reflect on the activity of sensing itself, regardless of the specific content of our sense impressions. We simply have to notice that our impressions exhibit change over time and, thus, that sensing involves motion. All motion must have a cause, and there is no source of such motion inside us. Therefore, Hobbes thought it safe to conclude that an external world does exist and that it is a world of objects in motion. Upon this basis alone a science could be built whose foundation would not be undermined by the subjectivity and deceptiveness of our senses.[84]

A fundamental premise of this argument was what Hobbes called "the great deception of sense":

> Whatsoever accidents or qualities our senses make us think there be in the world, they be not there, but are seeming and apparitions only: the things that really are in the world without us, are those motions by which these seemings are caused. And this is the great deception of sense, which is to be by sense corrected: for as sense telleth me, when I see directly, that the colour seemeth to be in the object; so also sense telleth me, when I see by reflection, that colour is not in the object.[85]

Hobbes regarded this insight as his own contribution to the sciences, insisting on its originality at least twice, and it is difficult to overestimate the influence the point had on the rest of his thought. He reaffirmed it near the beginning of each of his major works and applied the form of argument well beyond the field of optics. The general point demonstrated by the great deception of sense was that "men measure, not onely other men, but all other things, by themselves."[86] Again and again throughout his writings Hobbes undermined opinions by showing them to be nothing more than projections of internal conceptions onto the external world.

Hobbes used this strategy to especially devastating effect when he described religion. Men, he wrote early in *Leviathan*, "stand in awe of their own imaginations" and make "the creatures of their own fancy, their Gods. By which means it hath come to passe, that from the innumerable variety of Fancy, men have created in the world innumerable sorts of Gods. And this Feare of things invisible, is the naturall Seed of that, which every one in himself calleth Religion." Throughout the second half of *Leviathan*, when arguing against the existence of spirits, angels, demons, and other religious entities, he frequently claimed that they were phantasms of the mind to which men mistakenly attributed external existence. He began the chapter on demons with a full paragraph reminding the reader of his theory of sensation, so that he could show that demons were projections of the imagination. He argued that it was his insight into the deception of sense which distinguished him from the ancients: "This nature of Sight having never been discovered by the ancient pretenders to Naturall Knowledge; much lesse by those that consider not things so remote (as that Knowledge is) from their present use; it was hard for men to conceive of those Images in the Fancy, and in the Sense, otherwise, than of things really without us." The deception of sense argument was so central to Hobbes's treatment of religion that he mentioned an optical lens or "Looking-Glass" at two key moments in his argument about Christianity.[87]

Perhaps the most famous instance in which Hobbes used this argument to discredit religion was the slandering of the Catholic Church as a "Kingdom of Fairies," after he had defined fairies as visions which "have no existence, but in the fancies of ignorant people." But Hobbes closed the final chapter of *Leviathan* by remarking that not only the Catholic spirit but also "an Assembly of Spirits worse than he" might pose a danger to the commonwealth, "for it is not the Romane Clergy onely, that pretends the Kingdome of God to be of this World, and thereby to have a Power therein, distinct from that of the Civill State." Protestant reformers and their prophetic rhetoric of conscience could also be disposed of with the deception of sense argument. Hobbes dismissed prophecy as nothing more than a dream or disturbance of the mind:

> For when Christian men, take not their Christian Soveraigne, for God's Prophet; they must either take their owne Dreames, for the Prophecy they mean to bee governed by, and the tumour of their own hearts for the Spirit of God; or they must suffer themselves to bee lead by some strange Prince; or by some of their fellow subjects, that can bewitch them . . . and by this means destroying all laws, both divine, and humane, reduce all Order, Government, and Society, to the first Chaos of Violence, and Civill warre.

The deception of sense thus helped Hobbes to undermine the "arte of prophecying" taught by William Perkins and practiced by the Puritan orators. Insofar as they used the language of vision, they fell easily into Hobbes's trap: "To say [someone] hath seen a Vision, or heard a Voice, is to say, that he hath dreamed between sleeping and waking: for in such manner a man doth many times naturally take his dream for a vision, as not having well observed his own slumbering."[88]

At the heart of the deception of sense argument was the distinction between the activity of sensing and the objects of sense. The scholastics had followed Aristotle's *De Anima* in assuming that when we see, we receive some true information about the objects we are seeing. Hobbes flatly rejected their view early in *Leviathan:* "Some say the Senses receive the Species of things, and deliver them to the Common-sense; and the Common Sense delivers them over to the Fancy, and the Fancy to the Memory, and the Memory to the Judgement, like handing of things from one to another, with many words making nothing understood."[89] Hobbes's objection was not merely that the scholastic account was obscure. If a "species" or form really was transferred through sight and if some judgment was involved in the very act of seeing or in a "common-sense" that unified various perceptions before they were cognized, then it would not have been easy to dismiss an object of sight as nothing more than an apparition. If vision transferred forms, then it would indeed convey knowledge of what the world was really like; the impression in the wax, to use Aristotle's analogy, really would "re-present" the shape of what had made the impression. Hobbes attacked this understanding of vision because it undermined a crucial axiom of his science: the assertion that the images people saw in their minds, while caused by motion in the external world, did not represent to them what that world was like.[90]

Hobbes took a parallel approach in the realm of moral and political opinion. He conceived of a moral science that began by considering the passions separately from their objects. Just as people tended to call objects red when the redness in fact resided in their minds, Hobbes argued, they also tended to call an object "good" when the positive quality actually came from their own minds and desires. In the *Elements* Hobbes introduced his account of the passions by referring back, in Euclidean style, to the earlier section in which he had introduced the great deception of sense. By a phenomenon parallel to the deception of sense, he thought, people tended to mistakenly attribute objectivity to their subjective responses, thinking their desire for an object responded to some quality inhering in it.[91]

With this in mind, Hobbes could envision a basis for his political science that was analogous to the foundation he had provided for the natural sciences. In the introduction to *Leviathan* he asked his readers to notice that their own passions were the same as those of everyone else. By this observation he meant that while they might have felt attracted and repelled by different objects, the activity of feeling attraction and repulsion was the same in them as it was in all other people. The distinction between passions and their objects allowed one to catch sight of a similarity, an equality, in all men:

> I say the similitude of the Passions, which are the same in all men, desire, feare, hope, &c; not the similitude of the objects of the Passions, which are the things desired, feared, hoped, &c: for these the constitution individuall, and particular education do so vary, and they are so easie to be kept from

our knowledge, that the characters of mans heart, blotted and confounded as they are, with dissembling, lying, counterfeiting, and erroneous doctrines, are legible only to him that searcheth hearts.[92]

The three passions that Hobbes named here—desire, fear, and hope—reappeared in a crucial passage later in the text. At the end of the thirteenth chapter Hobbes presented them as the means of escaping war: "The Passions that encline men to Peace, are Feare of Death; Desire of such things as are necessary to commodious living; and a Hope by their Industry to obtain them."[93] Aside from the change of order in Hobbes's list, which indicates the priority of fear in his solution, the most obvious contrast between these passions and the ones listed in the introduction is that in this later list they came with objects attached. The particular objects were crucial, for Hobbes showed that the same passions attached to different objects—fear of invisible spirits, desire for power, and hope of eternal salvation—led to war. Somehow Hobbes's theory had to move his readers from the observed similitude of objectless passions to a consensus on the objects specified in chapter thirteen. The general strategy for making this change was to show that if one were to reflect upon the structure and nature of the passions themselves, considered without objects, one would discover emerging from their structure alone higher-order passions for certain general objects—for power, reputation, and, above all, security. It was these higher-order desires that grounded the laws of nature.[94] The "similitude of the passions" on which Hobbes asked his readers to focus in the introduction to *Leviathan* thus pointed to certain shared objects of desire. This similitude also revealed the respect in which all people were equal. But that equality would only be recognized once the distinction between passions and their objects was brought to light. Thus much of Hobbes's rhetoric in *Leviathan* aimed to dramatize this distinction. In optics, he pointed to the phenomena of reflection and refraction, through which one could make an object appear to be somewhere that it was not, thus proving that the object was separate from its appearance. The analogous phenomenon in morals—moral refraction, we might call it—occurred when something that was once called "good" as an object of desire later became an object of aversion, with no explanation other than one's changed mood.[95] By emphasizing the subjectivity of our moral language, and thus revealing the distinction between passions and their objects, Hobbes meant to bring to light a fundamental human similitude or equality.

At least one of Hobbes's contemporaries noticed the central importance of the distinction between passions and their objects in Hobbes's theory and objected to it. The constitutional royalist Edward Hyde, Earl of Clarendon (1609–1674), complained that few people were capable of appreciating this distinction and that those who could do so would not come any closer to knowing what other people were feeling by contemplating their own passions. He further maintained that people's physical constitution and education affected not only the objects of their passions, but the passions themselves: "If a Sanguine, and a Melancholic man hope the same thing, their hopes are no more alike each others, then their complexions are . . . so little similitude there is in the passions themselves without any relation to their objects." The distinction between passions and their objects seemed to Hyde characteristic of Hobbes's artificially scientific approach to human affairs, an approach that culminated in "an imaginary Government by his Rules of Arithmetic and Geometry, of which no Nation hath ever yet had the experiment." Hyde had little faith that Hobbes's "speculative" approach would yield better counsel than a careful study of practical histories. Throughout his reply to *Leviathan* he mocked Hobbes's attempt to apply a geometrical method to politics. Since the objectless passions were the axioms of Hobbes's system, the earl viewed his own refusal to consent to the distinction between passions and their objects as a fundamental disagreement.[96]

Hyde was right. If people could not be persuaded of that distinction, Hobbes's new science would lose its foundations. A fundamental goal of Hobbes's rhetoric was therefore to persuade citizens that they could trust neither their senses nor their passions to give them information about the outside world. The great deception of sense not only undercut prophetic claims to divine guidance but also undermined the ordinary opinions by which people oriented themselves in the world. The ideal subject of Hobbes's rhetoric would become mistrustful of his senses and unencumbered of his passions for particular objects; the disorientation brought on by this consciousness of his subjectivity would humble him and make him ready to submit to a sovereign. Persuaded that images or representations in his mind did not represent the world, he would be ready to consent to a political "representative" who did not represent his views.

The Rhetoric of Representation

Hobbes seemed to take some pleasure in concluding from his reflections on sense that a person might not know whether or not he was dreaming. It is a commonplace that this sort of skepticism about the veridical nature of sensation leaves individuals isolated within their own minds, divided from both the world and their fellows. But Hobbes's distinctions between seeing and objects of sight and between passion and objects of passion dissolved not only community but also the continuity of an individual's experience of his own life. For if sense impressions were subjective, if objects appeared differently according to one's current state of mind and body, as Hobbes argued, then there was no reason that one would call "good" today what he had approved of last week. For this reason, Hobbes followed his reflections on sensation with chapters dwelling on the problem of how easily an individual's train of thoughts could become incoherent.[97] In *Leviathan,* he twice used this inconstancy within an individual to illustrate why it was unreasonable to think one could find concord between different individuals:

> And because the constitution of a man's Body, is in continuall mutation; it is impossible that all the same things should alwayes cause in him the same Appetites, and Aversions; much less can all men consent, in the Desire of almost any one and the same Object.[98]

And later, more explicitly:

> Good, and Evill, are names that signifie our Appetites, and Aversions; which in different tempers, customes, and doctrines of men, are different . . . Nay, the same man, in divers times, differs from himselfe; and one time praiseth, that is, calleth Good, what another time he dispraiseth, and calleth Evil: From whence arise Disputes, Controversies, and at last War.[99]

In these passages Hobbes noticed the difficulty that individuals faced in maintaining a stable orientation of beliefs or opinions. He pointed out that their views tended to shift with changes in circumstance or bodily constitution; he saw that human beings were moody and fickle creatures. In light of this inconstancy, what could provide their psyches with any degree of unity and consistency over time? Whereas an Aristotelian conception of the soul suggested that our various senses all presented their data to one unified faculty of judgment, which drew that data together into cognizable objects for one coherent mind, Hobbes's psychology seems to have lacked that unifying faculty.[100] His account left individuals awash in changing sensations and judgments, always susceptible to irrationality and madness.[101] The deception of sense cast doubt on more than the validity of prophecies and claims of conscience. It yielded a suspicious, skeptical stance not only toward the claims of others but also toward one's own judgments about the character of the world and about moral qualities. To separate passions and senses from their objects was to introduce into the human psyche a dramatic disunity.

Of course, introducing that disunity was Hobbes's goal. He cast each individual back upon fragmented and unsteady imaginations, leading him to doubt even his own interpretation of his sense impressions. Hobbes did not thereby eliminate the need for the unifying faculty of judgment that the Aristotelians had discussed, the faculty of judgment to which the senses had presented their data. He simply removed that faculty from the individual soul. He thereby left citizens in need of a way to unify their psyches from the outside. The conclusion of Hobbes's science was the need for external sovereignty. The sovereign was a creation designed to perform the function of judgment and thus to bring unity to individuals. Because the sovereign's judgment was external, it could impose the same unity on more than one individual and so bring unity to the commonwealth as well. Hobbes announced this aspiration when he described the product of sovereignty as "more than Consent, or Concord; it is a reall Unitie of them all, in one and the same Person."[102] Through authorizing this artificial person, citizens found a way to present themselves to themselves; they found a way to be represented.

It is in the passage on authorizing this external locus of judgment that we find some of Hobbes's greatest metaphors: the commonwealth is a person, and also a great whale, and also a mortal God. But the greatest of Hobbes's metaphors was the one depicted in the frontispieces, the one all the others were meant to reinforce—it was the doctrine of representation itself, through which he managed to identify citizens with their sovereign even as he subjected them to its will and judgment. There is no doubt that this doctrine was an impressive feat of eloquence and rhetoric, but it did not signal a return to the classical-humanist tradition of rhetoric that Hobbes had learned in school. Hobbes's rhetoric of representation was a rhetoric against rhetoric. Instead of teaching citizens how to address one another as if each had a faculty of judgment within, Hobbes taught them to avoid such appeals and accept judgments from without. In portraying political controversy as a conflict of passions, he demonstrated his distance from classical and humanist rhetoricians. He did not admire the pull and sway of political debate; he did not see in the exchange of spirited argument the political judgment that distinguishes men from animals, and he did not aim to equip ambitious citizens to succeed in such debate. Pressed upon by the dogmatic quality of religious and political opinions in his time, he deployed metaphors and wit in an effort to reconstitute citizens so deeply that they would put aside their opinions and those supplied to them by orators and rely instead on the judgments of an external sovereign. Hobbes used rhetoric to persuade citizens to seek a politics immune from controversy and thereby to eliminate the need for the art of controversy.

CHAPTER 2

Persuading without
Convincing: Rousseau

But as men . . . have made an Artificiall Man, which we call a
Common-wealth; so also have they made Artificiall Chains, called
Civill Lawes, which they themselves by mutuall covenants, have
fastned at one end, to the lips of that Man, or Assembly, to whom
they have given the Soveraigne Power; and at the other end to their
own Ears.

> —Hobbes, *Leviathan,* chapter 21

Man was born free, and everywhere he is in chains . . . How did
this change occur? I do not know. What can make it legitimate?
I believe I can answer this question.

> —Rousseau, *Social Contract* 1.1

Since the legislator is therefore unable to use either force or
reasoning, he must necessarily have recourse to another order
of authority, which can win over without violence and persuade
without convincing. This is what has always forced the fathers
of nations to have recourse to the intervention of heaven and
to attribute their own wisdom to the Gods.

> —Rousseau, *Social Contract* 2.7

In aspiring to legitimate our chains rather than free us from
them, Jean-Jacques Rousseau accepted and deepened Hobbes's attack on the
politics of persuasion. He pointed the way toward a new sort of rhetoric
against rhetoric, a prophetic language of conscience and community that
would go even further in closing off the realm of controversy than Hobbes's
efforts had. Those are the claims of this chapter. I must defend them against
a set of considerations that might lead one to think that Rousseau was

friendly to classical rhetoric, such as his famous nostalgia for ancient city-states, his explicit praise of ancient eloquence, his harsh criticism of those Enlightenment thinkers who "use reason in too unadorned a form, as if men were all mind," his own considerable rhetorical prowess, and, finally, most crucially, his observation in the *Social Contract* that the legislator's special talent is the ability "to persuade without convincing."[1] In addition, we must take into account the fact that Rousseau was above all a republican thinker who prized active political engagement by all citizens, who deposited sovereignty firmly in their hands and who denied that it could legitimately be represented by any ruler or assembly. In light of these features of his thought, can he really have followed in the footsteps of Hobbes, who defended absolutist kings, opposed popular sovereignty and sought to represent the people through an external sovereign? At least since Tacitus, the art of rhetoric has been associated with the republicanism that Hobbes attacked. In what way can it be said that Rousseau, perhaps the figure most responsible for the modern revival of republicanism, adopted Hobbes's attack on rhetoric?

The link between Hobbes and Rousseau lies in the notion of sovereignty. While Rousseau objected strenuously to the idea of submitting oneself to an external sovereign, he did not dissent from Hobbes's requirement that citizens endorse one set of authoritative public judgments. No less than in Hobbes, we shall see, the public conscience that Rousseau described was meant to construct one sovereign source of judgment and thus guard citizens against the corrupting, divisive voices that sought to lure them into faction. But Rousseau was more determined than Hobbes was to naturalize this authoritative perspective, to eliminate the citizens' feeling of being chained to it, and so to reduce any sense of alienation that might arise from the relinquishing of judgment involved in its adoption. Thus the authorization of a sovereign that we saw in Hobbes became in Rousseau's hands a much more complex process of psychological transformation. Rousseau explored what it would take to make the sovereign perspective penetrate deeply into citizens' psyches in such a way as to thoroughly reconstitute them, reorienting their wills from within and giving new content to their consciences. He sought a way to produce judgments that would be felt privately in the heart of each citizen and yet also be fully congruent with those of every other citizen. These judgments would comprise a public conscience that could be accessed, not by looking up at a looming image of the ruler nor out through his eyes, as depicted in the frontispieces of *Leviathan*, but instead by looking deep within one's own soul.

If sovereignty could be internalized in this way, no external representative would be necessary. Rousseau could gain the harmony of a Hobbesian commonwealth without risking the oppression of a Hobbesian monarch. Moreover, if the sovereign public point of view came from within each individual, Rousseau suggested that it could be seen as a source of freedom, where freedom was understood as living according to a law one gave to oneself. Certain features of the internalized sovereign point of view—its generality of concern, its distance from one's natural private inclinations, and its self-legislative activity—pointed toward the "moral freedom" or autonomy that Kant so admired in Rousseau's writings. Insofar as we emphasize the way in which those features of sovereignty were devised to undermine the power of orators preaching private interests, we find ourselves describing moral autonomy in a new and surprising way—as immunity to controversial rhetoric.

In addition to bringing out the way in which Rousseau adopted and transformed Hobbesian sovereignty and the attack on rhetoric implicit in it, I also aim to show in this chapter that it was precisely that adoption and transformation that led Rousseau to propose the need for the legislator to find a language that could "persuade without convincing." It was because Rousseau saw the need to reconstitute individuals from within that he sought a language of persuasion with a deeper and more immediate impact than anything found in Hobbes's own rhetoric against rhetoric. This language would have to be a primitive, musical, and melodious sort of speech that would provide immediate access to prerational sources of communal feeling. Rousseau offered the alluring and prophetic chanting of charismatic religious figures such as Moses and Muhammad as examples, and he openly admitted the link between such nonrational forms of persuasion and fanaticism. I suggest that both features of the language that would "persuade without convincing"—both its musicality or nonrationality and its prophetic and potentially fanatical character—arose in response to the demands of the internalization of sovereignty. The musicality was meant to produce the generality of concern that the sovereign perspective required, and the prophetic quality was meant to preserve the sense of freedom in those citizens whose wills were being transformed. Insofar as the internalized sovereign represented a project to disarm controversial rhetoric, these characteristics of the legislator's persuasive speech also arose from that project. It was the effort to minimize the politics of rhetorical controversy that led Rousseau to propose an affecting and potentially dangerous form of nonrational persuasion, musical and prophetic in character. "Persuading without convincing" was a new form of rhetoric against rhetoric.

In the following text I first show why Rousseau's nostalgia for persuasion is not admiration for the classical or humanist arts of rhetoric and then look more closely at how he appropriated the attack on those arts by transforming Hobbes's external sovereign into an internalized public conscience. After describing in more detail both Rousseau's agreement with Hobbes and his departure from him on this point, I explore how Rousseau's position led him to propose the need for a mode of persuasion with both musical and prophetic qualities, a mode of persuasion that might be called the rhetoric of prophetic nationalism.

In suggesting that both Kantian moral freedom and the rhetoric of prophetic nationalism emerged from Rousseau's effort to internalize Hobbesian sovereignty, I aim to shed light on a potentially puzzling feature of Rousseau's political thought: how it has inspired two projects that seem different and even opposed to one another. John Rawls finds in Rousseau the basic framework for the Kantian-liberal project of constructing a legitimate state around the consent of morally autonomous individuals united in a conception of public reason.[2] But others find in the same political theory arguments for a more romantic politics in which strong and prerational passions—patriotic and nationalistic sentiments of belonging—play a central role.[3] These are just the sort of unreasonable and local passions that are suspicious to those interested in Kantian-liberal theories of justice. How can Rousseau's thought inspire both perspectives? In looking at this puzzle through the lens of rhetoric, we will find that the two projects are in fact more closely related than we usually recognize. Both projects arise as parts of an effort to found politics on a basis separate from and more unified than the ordinary judgments and opinions that private individuals naturally entertain; both projects tend to view those opinions as partial, prejudiced, and corrupt, often born of self-interest and pride and liable to lead individuals toward controversy, factionalism and inequality; therefore, both projects decline the classical political work of trying to weave competing opinions together into a differentiated, organized whole. This is simply to say that both Kantian-liberal theories of justice and ideologies of nationalism aim to avoid what we have been calling the politics of persuasion. Both arise out of the effort to leave behind rhetorical controversy; both are products of the attack on rhetoric.

Mute Eloquence

When Rousseau railed against the Enlightenment reliance on reason, he often voiced nostalgia for the ancients. Statements such as the following might lead us initially to think that in giving "persuasion" pride of place in his theory, Rousseau was turning back to the classical tradition:

> One of the errors of our age is to use reason in too unadorned a form, as if men were all mind . . . I observe that in the modern age men no longer have a hold on one another except by force or by self-interest; the ancients, by contrast, acted much more by persuasion and by the affections of the soul because they did not neglect the language of signs.[4]

But we should not allow this nostalgia to lure us into the belief that Rousseau's love of "persuasion" was an effort to introduce into modern politics ancient rhetoric or its engagement with political opinion. While he may have agreed with the ancient rhetoricians that men were not "all mind," his criticism amounted to much more than a call for renewed attention to the passions. His mention of the "language of signs" points toward the way in which he differed from the classical tradition of rhetoric. In the first chapter of his *Essay on the Origin of Languages* he criticized "long discourses" in favor of what he called a "mute eloquence."[5] He cited the story of the Levite of Ephraim, who stirred the tribes of Israel into avenging his wife's death, not by delivering a speech but by dividing her body into twelve pieces and sending them out to the tribes. While Rousseau went on to argue that such visual signs were not as effective as sounds in rousing interests or stirring the passions, he remained interested in the immediacy and impact that a language of visual signs could have. He told of "Salaam" cultures in which the sending of ordinary objects, such as a fruit or a ribbon, conveyed particular and immediate meaning and also of "the mutes of the Grand Vizier" who successfully communicated with one another. He often associated the "persuasion" of the ancients with a dramatic language of signs, such as when Tarquinius lopped off the heads of the tallest poppies in his garden to send a message to kill the most prominent of his enemies. But while he used ancient examples, his admiration for the efficacy of spectacle was Machiavellian and might remind us of similar accounts in the *Discourses on Livy* and *The Prince*—Brutus killing his own sons, or Cesare Borgia having his minister Remirro d'Orco deposited in pieces in the public square, leaving the people "satisfied and stupefied."[6]

Like Machiavelli, Rousseau praised the Roman prejudice against the effeminate and ineffectual arts of oratory and philosophy. He ended the *First Discourse*, itself a prize-winning work of eloquence, by calling upon his fellow citizens to prefer acting well to speaking well.[7] In this spirit he preferred Marc Antony to Cicero, who Rousseau thought had been softened by Greek intellectualism. In the *First Discourse* he complained that Rome had been corrupted when it "filled up with Philosophers and Orators" and had turned to "the frivolous eloquence that is the object of study and delight of futile men."[8] In the chapters on Rome in the *Social Contract* he took issue with Cicero's greatest triumph, his exposure of the conspiracy of Catiline. While admitting that it was only fair to honor Cicero as the liberator of Rome, Rousseau criticized Cicero for his methods. Rousseau suggested that in choosing to simply make speeches, Cicero had shied away from the boldest and surest action, that of claiming dictatorship for himself.[9] Against the verbose and ornate Ciceronian ideal, Rousseau insisted that ancient eloquence had been most persuasive "when the orator spoke least."[10] He noted, "the Jews' Prophets and the Greeks' Lawgivers who frequently presented visible objects to the people, spoke to them better with these objects than they would have done with long discourses, and the way in which, according to Athenaeus, the orator Hyperides got the courtesan Phryne acquitted without urging a single word in her defense, is yet another instance of a mute eloquence that has at all times proven effective."[11]

Rousseau's interest in "mute" eloquence can be contrasted with the famous passage we have already noticed in Cicero's *De inventione*, in which the Roman gave orators credit for having drawn scattered, savage men together into society: "To me, at least, it does not seem possible that a mute and voiceless wisdom could have turned men suddenly from their habits and introduced them to different patterns of life."[12] A number of elements in Cicero's account could fit neatly into the speculative history that Rousseau gave in the *Second Discourse*. Cicero had imagined men in a natural, prepolitical state; he had imagined that they were scattered from one another in that state; and he had portrayed them as "savages" needing to be "transformed" into beings willing to accept equality, "to be put on a par with those among whom [each] could excel." But in rejecting long speeches in favor of the mute language of signs, Rousseau indicated that he did not accept Cicero's praise of eloquence. Rousseau's version of the scene that Cicero depicted—of an orator delivering a speech to draw men into political society—was not an admiring one. In the second half of the *Second Discourse*, Rousseau described such a speech as delivered by a member of "the rich, under pressure of necessity," who "easily invented specious reasons to bring [others] over to his purpose." The speech that Rousseau put into the mouth of the orator speaking for the rich was full of plausible-sounding arguments about justice, peace, and mutual duties, but its effect was not the glorious founding of political society that Cicero had lauded: "Much less than the equivalent of this Discourse was needed to sway crude, easily seduced men . . . All ran toward their chains in the belief that they were securing their freedom." In the final analysis, the speech, so full of noble words, "henceforth subjugated the whole of Mankind to labor, servitude and misery."[13] Rousseau thus undermined the image that had always embodied the value of Ciceronian oratory, linking it to subjugation rather than republican freedom. The "persuasion" that Rousseau admired was something very different from the Ciceronian ideal.

The mute language of visual signs was not in fact Rousseau's final replacement for that ideal, but his interest in it reveals both his suspicion of traditional forms of eloquence and his admiration for forms of communication that were more immediate. Without keeping this attitude in mind, we cannot understand what he meant when he described the legislator's task in the *Social Contract* as one of "persuading without convincing." In an early draft of the passage about the legislator's persuasion, Rousseau had mentioned "superhuman eloquence" *(une éloquence . . . plus qu'humaine)*, but he removed even this mention of "eloquence" in the final version, leaving only "persuade without convincing."[14] As Jean Starobinski points out, the change is significant. When asked about his own considerable eloquence, Rousseau responded in a letter by carefully distinguishing persuasion from eloquence: "Do I have some true talent for writing? I do not know. A lively persuasion has always taken the place of eloquence for me and I have always written cowardly and badly when I have not been strongly persuaded."[15] Rousseau thus took care to distinguish whatever skill he himself possessed from the skill at argument that was taught in the schools as part of the Ciceronian heritage. Even in *Émile*, where Rousseau did allow that his student should be educated in the art of eloquence, he immediately clarified that the taste to be instilled in Émile was one that would set "little store by words" and that would prefer simple, direct, and brief speech to Ciceronian fullness: "Drawn by the masculine eloquence of Demosthenes, he [Émile] will say, 'This is an orator.' But in reading Cicero, he will say, 'This is a lawyer.'"[16]

At the end of his *Essay on the Origin of Languages* Rousseau did nostalgically invoke the image of a people gathered in a public square to listen to an orator, but he did not think that this noble example could be recovered simply by turning to the techniques of eloquence taught in the schools. In modern times, when politics was a realm of interests and force, eloquence was "useless."[17] The "persuasion" that Rousseau called for in the legislator was not a return to the eloquence of the ancients but was instead meant to "take the place of eloquence" in a modern political world in which languages had been so far corrupted as to be incapable of regenerating themselves and in which most efforts at eloquent public speech devolved into the dangerous demagogy of factionalism or the agonized and empty sermons of preachers.[18]

The most famous moment of mute eloquence in Rousseau's political thought is his insistence in the *Social Contract* that among virtuous citizens "there is no question of intrigues nor of eloquence to pass into law what each has already resolved to do as soon as he is sure that others will do likewise." Rousseau went even further, suggesting that ideally citizens should have not only no eloquence but "no communication" among themselves.[19] In this image of a silent citizenry Rousseau displayed not so much his admiration for mute eloquence but something even more radical—an effort to silence eloquence. Instead of deliberating together aloud in a public assembly, the virtuous citizens of Rousseau's ideal city look inward before voting. They search for the general will not by presenting arguments for the various sides of controversial questions to one another but rather by seeking the final and comprehensive answer to questions about the public good in their own consciences.

The Sovereign Within

In asking citizens to look to their consciences for the general will, Rousseau might seem to have found a means of silencing rhetoric very different from what we saw in Hobbes, who thought that voicing one's opinions in the language of conscience produced dangerous controversy. But Rousseau's turn to conscience was not a reinvigoration of private judgment, and he did not regard vigorous debate among citizens with different views as a sign of healthy republican politics. On the contrary, he argued, "the more harmony there is in the assemblies, that is, the closer opinions come to obtaining unanimous support, the more dominant as well is the general will. But long debate, dissensions, and tumult indicate the ascendance of private interests and the decline of the State."[20] In asking citizens to look inward, Rousseau did not disagree with Hobbes about the desirability of finding a common source of judgment about controversial matters. Nor did he disagree with Hobbes about the sovereign status that judgments made from that perspective should have. The conscience that Rousseau asked citizens to consult was a version of Hobbes's sovereign written into the heart of each individual. Ultimately this sovereign within was closer to what Hobbes called the "publique conscience" than it was to the private judgment that Puritan ministers such as William Perkins had encouraged their parishioners to consult or to the *bon sens* that Descartes had invoked when encouraging individuals to judge for themselves. In *Émile* Rousseau made a famous appeal to a more private sort of conscience as part of an effort to form a moral person, but when he was concerned with forming citizens, he presented conscience as a voice of public reason, and it functioned to quell controversy and silence rhetoric in much the same way that Hobbes's sovereign did.[21]

It is true that Rousseau located popular sovereignty firmly in the hands of the people, that he insisted they could never allow their sovereignty to be represented, that they should be assembled periodically, and that when they assembled, no voice could substitute for their own. In all these ways he might seem to have opposed precisely the alienation of judgment that was so central to constructing sovereignty in Hobbes. But we cannot understand these undeniably democratic aspects of his thought without taking note of the standpoint from which he asked citizens to exercise their sovereign judgment and consult their consciences—the standpoint of citizens. It is in the psychological and moral change required to adopt this perspective that we find something like an alienation of private judgment in Rousseau's theory. Instead of agreeing to abide by the judgments of a representative person or body, Rousseau's citizens agreed to abide by the judgments made from the standpoint required by the general will. In spite of his democratic commitments, Rousseau cannot be said to have favored each individual exercising his natural reason and judgments in legitimating the state, for Rousseau agreed with Hobbes and Locke that "each man being his own judge" would lead directly to a state of civil disorder. Properly understood, "the sovereign alone is the judge of what matters," and each individual's own reason could not, before it took on this public or sovereign standpoint, be the unique arbiter of public duties. Thus one of the reasons that Rousseau gave in *Political Economy* for distinguishing political rule from the familial rule of fathers was that fatherhood could be performed well simply by following one's natural inner voice, through which one could accurately intuit one's duties. For citizens, however, the natural voice of the heart would not be a good guide. Nor would a citizen's own reason: "Even his own reason should be suspect to him, and he should follow no other rule than the public reason, which is the law." When later in the same article Rousseau dealt with the problem of how to distinguish the general will from private interests, he again recommended consulting "the precepts of public reason" that emerged from the law as a "celestial voice." While Rousseau wrote that this voice taught citizens to act according to their own judgments, the force of this assertion was directed against their tendency to capitulate to the voices of other interested parties. The judgments that citizens were taught to consult were those they made for themselves once they had adopted the standpoint of the general will. Public reason and the general will constituted for Rousseau a sovereign point of view with all the unity and authority that sovereignty and "publique reason" had in Hobbes. As in Hobbes, the sovereign source of judgment was meant to anchor citizens against the lures of oratory and faction.[22]

We can most easily catch sight of the Hobbesian aspect of Rousseau's views about rhetoric in the various passages where Rousseau worried about the dangers of "partial associations" or factions. In *Political Economy* he explained that such associations "modify in so many ways the appearance of the public will by the influence of their own." The interest of each faction appeared to be a kind of general will for its members but it was a particular will with respect to the larger society, and for this reason the interest of the faction distorted citizens' view of the general will of the whole. Such distortion was heightened by the rhetoric of the ambitious men who led the factions and thereby corrupted democratic deliberations:

> Nor is it impossible for the council of a democracy to pass bad decrees and condemn innocent men. But that will never happen unless the people is seduced by private interests that some wily men have been able to substitute for its own. Then the public deliberation will be one thing and the general will a completely different thing.

Rousseau interpreted the influence of these "wily men" as evidence that a seeming democracy—Athens is the one he named—could in fact be a "highly tyrannical aristocracy, governed by learned men and orators." He thus echoed Hobbes's charge that democracies often degenerated into "aristocracies of orators." In a letter Rousseau endorsed the thesis that "all Historians unanimously maintain, that the corruption of the Athenians' morals and of their government were due to the Orators."[23]

Rousseau voiced the same worry about the potential vices of democratic deliberation in the chapter of the *Social Contract* on the question of whether the general will could ever make a mistake. The general will was always right, he argued, but popular deliberations were not. The problem was not so much that the people as a whole might be corrupt as that they might be "fooled" into voting as members of their particular associations rather than as individuals. Though he did not here specify who would do the fooling, he indicated the role of public speech by suggesting that the danger could be avoided if the citizens did not speak with one another:

> If, when an adequately informed people deliberates, the citizens were to have no communication among themselves, the general will would always result from the large number of small differences, and the deliberation would always be good. But when factions, partial associations at the expense of the whole, are formed, the will of each of these associations becomes general with reference to its members and particular with reference to the State. One can say, then, that there are no longer as many voters as there are men, but merely as many as there are associations . . . Then there is no longer a general will, and the opinion that prevails is merely a private opinion.

Later in the *Social Contract* Rousseau returned to the danger that democratic deliberations could be ruined when citizens were "fooled." He took note of cynical theorists who "laugh when they imagine all the nonsense that a clever swindler or an insinuating talker could put over on the people of Paris or London." At this point in the text he maintained the possibility that some peoples would in fact resist such talkers. The virtuous citizens of small cities such as Berne and Geneva, he suggested, would have "condemned to hard labor" clever rhetoricians like Cromwell, who appeared again later in the book in the same guise—as an ambitious and clever speaker able to trick citizens into civil disorder, using Christianity as a tool. Rousseau here provided the utopian image of peasants governing themselves by gathering under an oak tree, noting that such simple, unsubtle citizens were "hard to fool" and "not even clever enough to be duped." Among such peasants new laws would be adopted without debate and there would be no need for eloquence; long debates were a sign of corruption. The chief threat that faced democratic deliberations was, in this view, that clever orators could distort the public good by fooling citizens into allowing the interest of some partial association to claim their loyalties rather than thinking of the good of the whole.[24]

In the dedicatory letter to the *Discourse on Inequality* Rousseau implored his readers, "Consult the secret voice of your conscience." But it is instructive to notice what he thought their consciences would tell them. It would reveal the moderation and wisdom of their magistrates and their laws and so help them resist the arguments of those who might try to persuade them to disobey. The paragraph advising readers to consult their consciences ends with this advice: "Above all, and this will be my last Advice, beware of ever heeding sinister interpretations and venomous discourses, the secret motives of which are often more dangerous than are the actions they are about."[25] Protecting the state against orators and the partisan controversies they inflame by substituting a public, unified reason or conscience for ordinary private judgment was Rousseau's strategy as much as it was Hobbes's.

Against Theater and Sword

But of course Rousseau was not Hobbes, and the argument about the similarity between them that I have just given must immediately be qualified so as not to present a deceptive portrayal of both theorists. Rousseau, concerned more than Hobbes was with the subjective feeling of unfreedom that came from being subjected to the wills of other people, emphasized more than Hobbes did the importance of naturalizing the sovereign point of view by internalizing it in citizens' hearts and minds. The process of authorization in Hobbes became, in Rousseau, one of deep, psychological transformation. One way of seeing this difference is to focus on the way in which Rousseau opposed the theatricality of Hobbesian sovereignty.

Hobbes's sovereign represented the people by "personating" them, and Hobbes had explicitly taken the language of personation from the world of theater:

> The word Person is latine: instead whereof the Greeks have πρόσωπον, which signifies the Face, as Persona in latine signifies the *disguise,* or *outward appearance* of a man, counterfeited on the Stage; and sometimes more particularly that part of it, which disguiseth the face, as a Mask or Visard: And from the Stage, hath been translated to any Representer of speech and action, as well in Tribunalls, as Theaters. So that a *Person,* is the same that an *Actor* is, both on the Stage and in common Conversation; and to *Personate* is to *Act,* or *Represent* himselfe, or an other; and he that acteth another, is said to bear his Person, or act in his name; (in which sence *Cicero,*

useth it where he saies, *Unus sustineo tres Personas; Mei, Adversarii, & Judicis,* I
beare three Persons; my own, my Adversaries, and the Judges;) and is
called in diverse occasions, diversly; as a *Representer,* or *Representative,* a *Lieutenant,* a *Vicar,* an *Attorney,* a *Deputy,* a *Procurator,* an *Actor,* and the like.[26]

When Hobbes wrote that the sovereign must "bear the person" of the multitude in a commonwealth, he was extending this analogy from the theater.
Even if a citizen identified deeply with the sovereign point of view in a
Hobbesian commonwealth, he was identifying with the view of someone
playing a role or wearing a mask. Citizens in a Hobbesian commonwealth
resembled the audience at a theater. Each individual was focused on the
persona being presented before his eyes, united with other spectators not
directly by looking at or talking to them, but indirectly, by allowing himself
to live through the same theater or, as Hobbes might have thought while
working on *Leviathan* in France, the same *représentation*. The frontispiece to
Leviathan portrayed each individual citizen as captivated by the spectacle of
sovereignty, looking not at his fellow citizens but only at (or through) the
sovereign's persona. With only a few changes the frontispiece might be depicting precisely the scene that Rousseau criticized in his *Letter to d'Alembert,*
when he described people leaving aside their private concerns of family and
neighbors to visit the stage: "people think they come together in the theatre, and it is there that they are isolated."[27] While Rousseau agreed with
Hobbes that some artificial means of producing social unity was necessary,
given man's natural unsociability, he could not rest satisfied with the self-
consciously theatrical character of Hobbes's solution.

Hobbes described the sovereign as an artificial person. In internalizing the
sovereign, Rousseau could be said to have democratized the artificiality, allowing every citizen to be an artificial person. But whereas Hobbes proudly
drew attention to the artifice involved in his approach, proclaiming in
the introduction to *Leviathan* that the commonwealth was a work of art,
Rousseau was a great enemy of artificiality, who criticized the "assemblage
of artificial men" produced by society and who lamented the need to live
outside oneself and adopt masks for the purposes of social interaction.[28]
Rousseau's dilemma thus arose from his wanting obedience to an internal
sovereign to feel natural, and yet knowing that such obedience could not
arise from nature. He resolved, or it is better to say he confronted, this
dilemma by insisting that the artificiality of sovereignty was not necessarily
an obstacle to its naturalness: "One must use a great deal of art to prevent

social man from being totally artificial."[29] It might be true that sovereignty introduced an artificial, public sovereign standpoint, as Hobbes proposed, and that this perspective arose only when men gave up the more natural private point of view from which they were accustomed to exercising their judgment. But this new artificial standpoint could still be made into a role in which a person could feel natural and whole. This was the hope expressed in Rousseau's *Social Contract* and especially in the famous passage about the task of psychological transformation that the legislator found himself confronting, the task of "changing human nature, so to speak; of transforming each individual, who by himself is a perfect and solitary whole, into a part of a larger whole from which this individual receives, in a sense, his life and his being."[30]

Rousseau objected to the theatrical character of Hobbes's theory not simply because of its metaphorical implications and not only out of an instinctive distaste for artificiality in the abstract. More fundamentally, he objected to the very real separation that Hobbes's solution created between citizens and their sovereign. In Hobbes the distance between citizens' private judgments and the "publique reason" was institutionalized in their ruling themselves only through an external sovereign, someone who could, and in practice often did, turn against them. It was the artificiality of the covenant through which citizens ruled themselves that explained why Hobbes thought a sword and the awe it produced was necessary to make sovereignty work. Knowing that the process of authorization was a sort of theater or role-playing, citizens never succeeded in alienating their judgments entirely. Indeed, Hobbes insisted that citizens retain enough of that capacity to judge, at the very least, that they possessed the "liberty of subjects" that lay in the "silence of the laws" and that they were not required to lay down their lives for the commonwealth.[31] Because they remained conscious of the distinction between themselves and the personas borne by the sovereign, citizens sometimes needed to be reminded that they had agreed to identify the two. Their agreement was contrary to their natural passions of partiality, which was why Hobbes thought that "covenants, without the sword, are but words." The agreement, he wrote,

> is by Covenant only, which is Artificiall: and therefore it is no wonder if there be somewhat else required (besides Covenant) to make their Agreement constant and lasting; which is a Common Power, to keep them in awe, and to direct their actions to the Common Benefit.[32]

It was the self-conscious artificiality or theatricality of Hobbes's external sovereign that created the need for his sword.

Internalizing the sovereign point of view eliminated both the theatricality and the sword. The individual envisioned himself as sovereign, not through the theater of representation, but by becoming a citizen with his whole being, leaving the role of private individual behind. One could not be both a man and a citizen, Rousseau suggested, without splitting one's soul in a way that made happiness impossible. Rousseau's language about what was required in becoming a citizen was therefore more radical than Hobbes's ever had been, as for example in *Émile:* "Good social institutions are those that best know how to denature man, to take his absolute existence from him in order to give him a relative one and transport the *I* into the common unity, with the result that each individual believes himself no longer one but a part of the unity and no longer feels except within the whole."[33] To no longer even so much as feel except within a whole is to internalize sovereignty to a degree that Hobbes never seems to have explicitly contemplated. Hobbes did once mention the possibility that a multitude of men might consent to observe justice without a common power to keep them in awe, but he described that possibility in the conditional tense as if to dismiss it as a fantasy that would also have removed the need for government itself, "because there would be Peace without subjection."[34] What Rousseau aimed to describe in the *Social Contract* was precisely a way of understanding what would be required to produce "peace without subjection" or sovereignty without the sword.

The irony for anyone concerned with freedom is that it was precisely the theatricality of Hobbes's solution that tied his theory to liberalism. Because the citizens' identification with the sovereign took place through an external representative, citizens in a Hobbesian commonwealth could continue to exercise their judgments separately from the sovereign so long as they agreed to adopt public personas in public dealings and to let the sovereign decide what was "public." In fact, it was the distinction between the persona and the real person that allowed for moments, perhaps many moments, during which citizens could forget about their public personas and relax in the privacy of their homes. These were the moments that comprised "the liberty of subjects" found in "the silence of the laws." While the distinction between the real person and the artificial gave rise to the need for the sword in Hobbes's theory, it also gave rise to the slice of private liberty found there. Rousseau did not find it possible to eliminate the sword without also eliminating this trace of liberalism.

Of course, Rousseau claimed that with the sacrifice of private judgment came new and higher forms of freedom, the "civil freedom" defined by the general will and the "moral freedom" that came from distancing oneself from one's natural passions and from obeying only laws one prescribed for oneself.[35] The individual who enjoyed these types of freedom, the autonomous individual, became the centerpiece of a new generation of liberalism after Kant. The generalized will at the heart of this conception of the person was the perspective of the internalized sovereign, and the sacrifice of private liberty involved in internalizing and naturalizing this perspective offers a reminder of what was lost in creating the autonomous individual.[36] What is more, we have seen that the function of sovereignty was in part to offer citizens a source of judgment separate from their own shifting and unreliable opinions and therefore to protect them against the mass of declaiming preachers and orators vying to influence those opinions. Insofar as the autonomous individual was one who adopted the perspective of the internalized sovereign, he can also be described as one who gained the immunity to rhetoric that such a perspective provided. The very idea of an autonomous individual, the conception of the person around which Kantian liberalism was framed, thus incorporated deep within itself an effort to neutralize the power of classical rhetoric.

The Musical Language of Moral Needs

When Rousseau turned to the question of how to create such an individual, he raised the need for the legislator and for the language of persuading without convincing. Many readers have pointed out the irony that Rousseau advocated rhetorical persuasion by the legislator even as he sought to make rhetorical eloquence unnecessary in the polity he created.[37] But it is important to notice that the character of the persuasion Rousseau endorsed was very different from that of the rhetoric he sought to eliminate. The Ciceronian rhetoric of controversy was the language of argument clothed in eloquence, while Rousseau's persuasion was something altogether different—a musical, prophetic language of accent and enthusiasm that did not embellish or ornament reasonable argument so much as seek to replace it altogether. Even more interesting than the contrast between these two linguistic strategies, I want to argue here, is that the need for the nonrational form of persuasion arose precisely from the ambition to produce citizens immune to the more argumentative or rational sort.[38] Rousseau thought that such immunity would arise from the internal sovereign only if the sovereign perspective was general rather than particular in its scope of concern, and he thought this generality of concern could only be produced by a language that left argument or "convincing" behind altogether.

In the *Social Contract* Rousseau ended the chapter on the generality of legislation by noticing the threats that particularity posed to the general will and suggesting that those threats pointed to the need for the legislator. The legislator, in turn, had to resort to the language of persuading without convincing that Rousseau thought great founding fathers such as Moses and Muhammad must have used. The way the argument progresses suggests what may be a surprising thesis: Rousseau thought the legislator's need to use a nonrational form of persuasion arose because only such language could instill in the hearts of citizens the generality of concern that characterized the internalized sovereign. The nonrational, passionate character of the legislator's language was tied to the project of combating particularity. This thesis is surprising because a more intuitive understanding of Rousseau's turn to persuasion tends to associate the appeal to passions with a concession to human particularity. In this view, reason is linked to generality or universality, and the passions invite particularity and concreteness.[39] It seems to me, however, that part of what is so interesting about Rousseau's account is the way in which he reversed this conventional view and suggested that it was only through a certain sort of passionate appeal that one could hope to reach beneath the particular interests that ordinarily motivated individuals and to find the seeds of a disposition to will generally in the way required by the standpoint of the internalized sovereign. Rousseau's position thus brings to light a surprising connection between the liberal understanding of an autonomous individual and a kind of rhetoric often thought to be the nemesis of liberalism, the rhetoric of unreasoned, passionate appeals to communal identity.

Rousseau referred to a language that could "persuade without convincing" not only when describing the legislator's speech in the *Social Contract* but also when describing in the *Essay on the Origins of Languages* what the earliest human language must have been like: "Instead of arguments it would have pithy sayings; it would persuade without convincing, and depict without demonstrating."[40] He imagined a primitive language full of images and figures of speech, comprised of metaphors rather than literal descriptions. He described it as a form of speech characterized by many accents or changes in pitch but few articulated consonants. It would have

been appealing to the ear, he thought, abounding in images and ono-
matopoeia. Above all, he thought it would have been a lyrical and musical
language; "men would sing rather than speak."[41] He made the connection
between this description of early language and the project of legislation not
only by repeating the phrase "persuade without convincing" but also by asserting in several places that the first laws were songs. The ancient Greeks
spoke in a highly accented and musical language, he noticed, and he concluded that the ancient Greek legislators had led their assembled communities in song.[42]

The melodic character of the language of persuasion was important because one of Rousseau's primary goals in the *Essay* was to argue that
melodic music had a special power over men's souls, greater than that possessed by other arts or by the harmonic music being made popular by Jean-
Philippe Rameau and his followers in France at the time. Rousseau
described the primitive, melodic language as one of "passion seeking to
communicate itself." He suggested that its power came from its ability to imitate the passions directly:

> One of the great advantages the musician enjoys is that he can paint things
> that cannot be heard, whereas the Painter cannot represent things that
> cannot be seen . . . [T]he musician's art consists in substituting for the im-
> perceptible image of the object, that of the emotions which that object's
> presence excites in the beholder's heart. It will not only churn up the sea,
> fan the flames of a conflagration . . . but it will also depict the desolation of
> dreadful deserts, dusk the walls of a subterranean dungeon, appease the
> storm, clear and still the air and, from the orchestra, spread renewed fresh-
> ness through the woodlands. It will not represent these things directly, but
> it will excite in the soul the very same sentiments which one experiences
> upon seeing them.

What was at stake for Rousseau in arguing for the special power of melody
to touch the passions was a far-reaching point against materialist reductionism. The thrust of his argument in the *Essay* was to resist efforts to explain the social passions, or "moral needs," by reducing them to physical
terms or processes. Against Étienne Bonnot de Condillac, he insisted that
languages could not have arisen simply from interests, which he called
"physical needs." Against Rameau, he argued that music could not be reduced to the harmonic vibrations on a sounding board. Against Isaac
Newton and his followers, he argued that sounds could not be described by

their physical characteristic (frequency of vibration) as as colors could. The common thread in all of these quarrels was Rousseau's effort to avoid reductionism. He devoted a full chapter of the *Essay* to making sure that his readers did not miss this theme, beginning, "Note how everything constantly brings us back to the moral effects about which I have spoken, and how far the musicians who account for the impact of sounds solely in terms of the action of air and the excitation of [nerve] fibers are from understanding wherein the power of this art consists. The more closely they assimilate it to purely physical impressions, the farther away they remove it from its origin." The "moral effect" could be accounted for when sounds were considered not only as physical vibrations but as signs of affections and sentiments.[43]

For our purposes what is most interesting is the way in which Rousseau carried this concern with "moral needs" into debates about the origin of society itself. In the *Essay,* as in *Émile* and the *Second Discourse,* he denied that men could have been led into lasting political societies by "physical needs," meaning self-interest, alone.[44] He asserted that such needs would by themselves tend to disperse individuals rather than bring them together.[45] Nor could the social spirit be inculcated by reasoning from within the language of those physical needs. Arguing from self-interest to social virtue simply would not be successful unless one recognized "a moral good" as an irreducible part of the argument from the beginning.[46] In both the *Second Discourse* and *Émile,* Rousseau rejected even the simple maxim of reason, "Do unto others as you would have them do unto you," as the source of good and moral action. Whereas Hobbes had suggested that an inverted version of this maxim could make the laws of nature "intelligible even to the meanest capacity," Rousseau asserted that even this simple golden rule rested on a premise that one could not take for granted.[47] It rested on a willingness to see oneself as fundamentally similar to others. This crucial habit of identification lay at the foundation of society, and Rousseau did not think that it could be instilled by reasoning from within the language of interest. It was ultimately a matter of feeling. "Do not get lost in fine reasonings intended to prove to the adolescent that he is a man like others and subject to the same weaknesses," Rousseau warned in *Émile.* "Make him feel it, or he will never know it."[48] In Rousseau's thinking, the source of our ability to identify with others lay not in our physical needs or interests but in our moral needs or passions.[49]

Rousseau found the moral or passionate root of society in the prerational

sentiments of pity, "an innate repugnance to see his kind suffer," and commiseration, which "puts us in the place of him who suffers."[50] These sentiments would lead us to "identify" with others and "this identification must,
clearly, have been infinitely closer in the state of Nature than in the state of
reasoning. It is reason that engenders vanity, and reflection that reinforces
it." Pity offered a "gentle voice" that moderated our self-love and brought
us "without reflection" into good relations with others. Rousseau contrasted
the working of pity with the maxims of "reasoned justice":

> It is in this Natural sentiment rather than in subtle arguments that one has
> to seek the cause of the repugnance to evil-doing which every human
> being would feel even independently of the maxims of education. Al-
> though Socrates and Minds of his stamp may be capable of acquiring virtue
> through reason, Mankind would long ago have ceased to be if its preserva-
> tion had depended solely on the reasonings of those who make it up.[51]

In *Émile* the project of turning the boy into a moral being was one dominated by the inculcation and direction of pity.[52] Pity was a sentiment that
included two ideas: it recognized others as equal in their capacity to suffer,
and it regarded that capacity to suffer as more fundamental than qualities in
which people were unequal.[53] Only these two ideas together could lead
Émile to identify with others in as deep a sense as morality required, and
Rousseau indicated that what could bring one to identify so strongly with
one's fellows was the "strength of an expansive soul," a phrase like the one
he used to describe the legislator.[54] And when the purpose was a more political act—to form a citizen—a similarly deep sense of identification was
necessary, for in good social institutions each individual "no longer feels except within the whole," which is to say that he felt with others, through
compassion.[55] This strong identification with others, based in self-love and
expanded not through reason but through pity, characterized what it was
like to full-heartedly take as one's own the perspective of the general will,
in which "there is no one who does not apply this word *each* to himself, and
does not think of himself as he votes for all."[56]

Pity and commiseration were the sources of the human ability to "transport ourselves outside ourselves." Ultimately they developed into social passions such as clemency, humanity, benevolence, friendship and love. But in
the *Essay* Rousseau remarked that pity did not become an active moral or
social motive, enlarging the sphere of others considered like oneself beyond
the narrowest circle of family, until accidents of history brought people into

sustained contact with one another. Before this development there were in-stincts but not passions, an important distinction for Rousseau. It was the latter, feelings such as love rather than impulses such as lust, that were signs of man's irreducibly moral nature and of his innate capacity for social life.[57]

If the recognition that one was essentially similar to others was crucial to the development of the social passions, and if those passions were the true source of the human capacity to generalize the scope of their concern to a broad set of individuals, then it was precisely that recognition of similitude that the legislator's language had to convey. At the opening of the *Essay*, Rousseau indicated how closely he thought the development of social senti-ments was linked to the development of language itself: "As soon as one man was recognized by another as a sentient, thinking Being, similar to himself, the desire or the need to communicate to him his sentiments and thoughts made him seek the means to do so."[58] Rousseau introduced the *Essay* as a work not only about the origin of languages but also about the origin of nations. The fundamental feeling of belonging to a nation was one of identifying or commiserating with one's fellow citizens simply by virtue of a felt similarity with them.[59] That same feeling of identity gave rise to and was in turn deepened by early languages. Rousseau's argument was that nations, mutual recognition, and languages grew up together, intertwined and inextricable from one another.

An implication was that any effort to distinguish whether society or lan-guage came first would run into tremendous difficulties. This was precisely the puzzle to which Rousseau called attention and which he despaired of resolving in the *Second Discourse*, of which the *Essay* was originally meant to be a part. The question was, "which was the more necessary, an already united Society for the institution of Languages, or already invented Lan-guages for the establishment of Society?" Rousseau remarked that "speech seems to have been very necessary in order to establish the use of speech" and complained that Condillac's account of the origin of languages "as-sumed what I question, namely some sort of society already established among the inventors of language." The puzzle might also be viewed as a challenge to the famous image that we have already noted several times from Cicero's *De inventione*, that of an orator drawing scattered individuals together to found a community through speech. Cicero's model of the lin-guistic construction of a community presumed that men in their presocial state could understand and be motivated by the speech of the orator. But what language would he speak to them?[60]

The puzzle about the chronology of the development of language and society arose, in turn, out of a more fundamental quandary about the origin of languages that Rousseau also highlighted in the *Second Discourse*. This was the question of the relation between speech and thought and especially between speech and general ideas. Rousseau again posed the puzzle in its most vexing, circular form: "if Men needed speech in order to learn how to think, they needed even more to know how to think in order to find the art of speech."[61] General ideas, he noticed, could enter the human mind only with the help of language, for the more natural way of perceiving and cataloguing the world was to name particulars, such as different oak trees, with different names, since they appeared each in their particularity to one's imagination. Only words, with their abstraction, introduced generality into one's thoughts. Rousseau moved quickly in his argument from this problem to the difficulty about how language could have been established without society, or vice versa. The connection seems to lie first, in the notion that the meaning of abstract words would have to be set by social convention, and second, in the idea that the mutual identification implicit in society rested on individuals' ability to abstract or generalize, to see not only different oak trees as essentially similar but also different humans in that way. In posing these puzzles and declaring himself unable to resolve them, Rousseau drew attention to the close tie between the emergence of language, of nations, and of the more fundamental human capacity to generalize.

The crucial point that emerged from the close relation between language, society, and the capacity for generalization was that one could not easily translate the basis of a truly social spirit into languages if it was not found within them already. The languages of the "north," French in particular, had over time developed in a way meant to express private interests; they were suited to saying "give money." Interestingly, the issue of translation appeared in Rousseau's explanation of why the legislator had to find a language of persuading without convincing. If we look in more depth at the relevant passage from the *Social Contract*, we find that this language of persuading was introduced as a response to the difficulty of translating between the language of private interest and that of more general ideas:

> Another difficulty deserves attention. Wise men who want to use their own language, rather than that of the common people, cannot be understood by the people. *Now there are a thousand kinds of ideas that are impossible to translate into the language of the people.* Overly general views and overly remote ob-

jects are equally beyond its grasp. Each individual, appreciating no other aspect of government than the one that relates to his private interest, has difficulty perceiving the advantages he should obtain from the continual deprivations imposed by good laws . . . Since the legislator is therefore unable to use either force or reasoning, he must necessarily have recourse to another order of authority, which can win over without violence and persuade without convincing.[62]

Knowing how thoroughly Rousseau had reflected on questions of language, we can suggest that in asserting the difficulty of translation, he had in mind the view of language implicit in the *Essay*—language was not an arbitrary system of signs representing one universal and preexisting substrate of thoughts or ideas. Instead, language helped to constitute one's thinking, defining and delimiting its character and range. People were, to a much greater extent than they realized, trapped in patterns of thought and feeling that their languages imparted on them.

Thus the problem of translation as Rousseau would have seen it was close to what we might today discuss as the problem of cross-cultural understanding. In contrast to animals—some of whom could communicate through a "natural language" that they were born knowing, that did not develop or change, and that was the same for all in a species—human language was conventional and therefore varied according to the community and its history. So deep did Rousseau think these differences among humans ran—over both time and geography—that he ridiculed those who expected to be able to translate ancient Greek eloquence or music into a modern language or notation. In this context he gave a striking metaphor:

I have read that American Indians, seeing the amazing effects of firearms, used to pick musket balls up off the ground and, after hurling them with a loud outcry, were utterly surprised to find that they had not killed anyone. Our orators, our musicians, our scholars are like those Indians. The wonder is not that we no longer achieve with our music what the Greeks achieved with theirs; the wonder would, rather, be that the same effects could be produced with such very different instruments.[63]

Rousseau's point was not only to contrast the weakness of modern language and music with the strength of ancient arts but also to highlight the difficulty of translating between them. He made the argument most explicitly with regard to music, noting that the melodies that most impressed modern Europeans seemed "but an empty noise to the ear of a Carib," that "an

Italian requires Italian tunes, a Turk would require Turkish tunes," and that "Bernier's Cantatas are said to have cured a French musician of the fever; they would have given one to a musician of any other nation."[64] The idea that music might be a universal language was tied for Rousseau to the notion that its effects could be explained by its physical properties, the impingement of vibrations in the air on human ears, which was the theory of music propounded by Rameau. The difficulties in cross-national or cross-cultural understanding that Rousseau delighted in pointing out provided evidence, he thought, that such a reductionist view of music and language could never account for its "moral effects," its ability to reach within the hearts of individuals and arouse the social passions.

This is why Rousseau's effort to undermine rhetorical, controversial politics calls upon a linguistic strategy so different from Hobbes's similar effort. Hobbes's strategy was one of translation or redefinition of words. Even in *Leviathan,* his most rhetorical writing, much of the argumentative work was accomplished in the carefully constructed definitions of key terms such as *power, honor, covenant, person, liberty,* and so on. Indeed, whole chapters take the form of a series of definitions, the import of which only comes to light when one sees how Hobbes used them, as, for example, when he pointed out that according to his carefully constructed definition of liberty, a covenant entered into because of fear was nevertheless entered into freely. What permitted Hobbes to arrange his definitions so carefully, in turn, was his view of language itself, a view that must have been natural to someone who spent much of his time working as a translator. In contrast to Rousseau, who spent a great deal of time copying music as a way to earn money, Hobbes devoted his attention to translating classical texts, most famously the works of Thucydides, Aristotle, and, at the end of his life, Homer. Implicit in the very possibility of this work of translation lay the same presumption about language that made possible the redefinition of terms within one language, the presumption that there was a substrate of thought or meaning existing independently from the words themselves that could be attached, in principle, to any word so long as one was clear about what one was doing. For Hobbes the function of speech was to name thoughts.[65]

This view of language in turn made possible Hobbes's understanding of scientific reasoning: "nothing but reckoning (that is, adding and subtracting) of the consequences of general names agreed upon for the marking and signifying of our thoughts."[66] The conventionality of language was also what permitted Hobbes's sovereign to settle disputes. The sovereign could, by simple assertion, provide fixed definitions for disputed terms—not only for traditional words of moral evaluation, such as the names of virtues and vices, but even for other sorts of terms, such as those describing units of measurement. The simple assertion of these definitions echoes the simple assertions by which the commonwealth itself could be instituted, the words of authorization, which themselves echo the fiat "Let us make man" of divine creation.[67] All were possible because words were themselves nothing more than signs, and languages nothing more than systems of signs, with no inherent link between any particular word and the world it represented. The view of language that lay beneath Hobbes's rhetoric of redefinition or translation presumed the same skepticism about our direct knowledge of the external world that his view of sensation did. Hobbes thus found the distinction between representer and represented not only in the "great deception of sense" that we explored in the previous chapter but also in his view of language. And this view of language helps to explain the character of Hobbes's own rhetoric against rhetoric; he sought to put his metaphors and other rhetorical techniques in the service of a science that in turn worked by redefinition or translation.

The strikingly different character of Rousseau's rhetoric against rhetoric, its much deeper departure from rationality as evidenced in its musical character, can now be understood as a necessary consequence of several ideas. First, Rousseau desired to reconstitute citizens from the inside in a much deeper way than Hobbes had, so as to instill within the heart of each individual the shared perspective of sovereignty, which was in part a disposition to give one's will a certain generality. Second, Rousseau believed that such generality of concern arose in humans not through reason so much as through the development of certain social passions. Third, he thought that those passions developed only as part of language itself, that they could not be translated into a language of private interests in which they were not already implicit. Together these ideas suggest that Rousseau's reason for making the legislator's language nonrational and musical was not, as it is often supposed, that he thought only such a language could meet the challenge of tying particular people to particular loyalties or land. That explanation would be comforting to interpreters made uneasy by his turn to nonrational persuasion, because the dangers of such persuasion could be tied exclusively to the particularist aspects of Rousseau's thought and dismissed with them. But the ideas I have traced out here suggest that the need for such persuasion arose from the special difficulties involved in generalizing people's wills rather than from the challenge of particularizing them, and therefore that the need to persuade without convincing emerged as a part of the project of internalizing the sovereign perspective and creating the autonomous individual. If we add that thought to what has already been argued, we can say that the call for nonrational persuasion emerged out of the project to create individuals immune to the more traditional forms of persuasion recommended by rhetoricians.

The Rhetoric of Prophetic Nationalism

The nonrational or musical character of the legislator's language is not the only feature that needs explanation. Another is its prophetic character. One final look at the passage on persuading without convincing will serve to remind us of this trait:

> Since the legislator is therefore unable to use either force or reasoning, he must necessarily have recourse to *another order of authority,* which can win over without violence and persuade without convincing. *This is what has always forced the fathers of nations to have recourse to the intervention of heaven and to attribute their own wisdom to the Gods;* so that the peoples, subjected to the laws of the State as to those of nature . . . might obey with freedom.[68]

Rousseau suggested that it was through the invocation of "another order of authority" and by "attributing their own wisdom to the Gods" that legislators could wield the influence necessary to accomplish their task. The examples of good legislation that he went on to give were the Jewish and the Islamic law, and elsewhere he cited Moses and Muhammad as exemplary political founders or legislators. In the *Essay* Rousseau had imagined the effect of Mohammed's founding speeches in this way:

> Because he can read a little Arabic, a man smiles as he peruses the Koran; if he had heard Mohammed himself proclaim it in that eloquent rhythmic language, in that rich and persuasive voice which seduced the ear before it did the heart, constantly infusing his succinct sayings with the accent of enthusiasm, he would have prostrated himself and cried: *Great Prophet, Messenger of God, Lead us to glory, to martyrdom; we want to conquer or to die for you.* Fanaticism always appears ludicrous to us, because it has no voice to command a hearing among us.[69]

Mohammed could thus do what the legislator had to do—"make the Gods speak or be believed when he declares himself their interpreter"—and he did it with a musical and seductive form of speech that inspired not only loyalty but also, to use Rousseau's word, fanaticism.

Rousseau was certainly aware of the dangers of fanaticism. In the chapter on civil religion in the *Social Contract* and in an earlier version of that work, he dwelt on precisely these dangers, remarking, "the whole earth would be covered with blood and the human race would soon perish if philosophy and laws did not hold back the furies of fanaticism and if the voice of men was not louder than that of the Gods."[70] In the *Second Discourse* and in *Émile*, however, his emphasis was different. He suggested a link between the powerful passions of religious zealotry and the social passions that were necessary to any society, and he raised the possibility that fanaticism could be redirected to serve the purposes of politics:

> [Fanaticism,] although sanguinary and cruel, is nevertheless a grand and strong passion which elevates the heart of man, makes him despise death, and gives him a prodigious energy that need only be better directed to produce the most sublime virtues. On the other hand, irreligion—and the reasoning and philosophic spirit in general—causes attachment to life, makes souls effeminate and degraded, concentrates all the passions in the baseness of private interest, in the abjectness of the human *I*, and thus quietly saps the true foundations of every society. For what private interests have in common is so slight that it will never outweigh what sets them in opposition.[71]

Rousseau thus valorized the seductive persuasiveness of legislators such as Mohammed because he heard in their language an antidote to the lure of private self-interest, a means of countering "the abjectness of the human *I*" and reconstituting individuals from the inside in the way that the creation of citizens required.

But there was also another reason why Rousseau thought the legislator should appear to be a prophet and why he should attribute his wisdom to the gods. Rousseau thought the prophetic character of language like Mohammed's would help to preserve the citizens' sense of freedom. Only if citizens believed the laws issued by the legislator came from a nonhuman source would they be able to "obey with freedom." To understand this argument, we can turn to *Émile*, where the tutor's primary charge was to maintain control over the child without making him feel unfree. Rousseau's advice there was to "keep the child in dependence only on things":

> There are two sorts of dependence: dependence on things, which is from nature; dependence on men, which is from society. Dependence on things,

since it has no morality, is in no way detrimental to freedom and engenders no vices. Dependence on men, since it is without order, engenders all the vices, and by it, master and slave are mutually corrupted.

The child's freedom thus consisted in never finding his wishes opposed by the will of another person. The mute resistance of objects taught him to moderate his desires to match his capacities, restraining him without producing either resentful defiance or imperious claims to authority over other people. Even while growing up under the watchful eye of his tutor, Émile never found himself up against the tutor's authority. When the tutor needed to teach a lesson, for instance against lying, he did not do so by giving lectures but rather by arranging the environment in such a way that Émile found himself against external obstacles. To prevent Émile from becoming a liar, the tutor insured that "the lie attracts evil to [Émile] which he sees as coming from the very order of things and not from the vengeance of his governor." What preserved Émile's sense of freedom was that he saw restraints arising only from "the very order of things," that he never encountered a human will directly opposed to his own. While the tutor's will was always at work behind the lessons, arranging the "things" that Émile encountered and cloaking his efforts with a veil of nature, Émile did not see his artful work. Rousseau's advice to the tutor was to "let him [Émile] always believe he is the master, and let it always be you who are. There is no subjection so perfect as that which keeps the appearance of freedom. Thus the will itself is made captive."[72]

Rousseau suggested that in politics as in education, arranging matters so that people confronted things of nature rather than the authority of men was the best way to preserve freedom. The application to politics emerged in the same paragraph in which he introduced the distinction between depending on things and depending on wills:

If the laws of nations could, like those of nature, have an inflexibility that no human force could ever conquer, dependence on men would then become dependence on things again; in the republic all of the advantages of the natural state would be united with those of the civil state, and freedom which keeps man exempt from vices would be joined to morality which raises him to virtue.[73]

With this passage in mind, and recalling that Rousseau published *Émile* in the same year as the *Social Contract*, we can reasonably interpret the legislator's turn to religion as a strategy parallel to the one adopted by Émile's tutor. In presenting his laws as divine in origin, the legislator hid his art, made his laws seem to emerge from "the very order of things," and so aimed to preserve the citizens' subjective sense of freedom.

The language that persuades without convincing thus combined two features. First, it instilled in its listeners a disposition to will generally, by tapping into nonrational social passions that encouraged primal feelings of sympathetic identification among fellow citizens. Second, it preserved a sense of freedom in those it influenced, by presenting the human or artificial source of its authority as a manifestation of natural or divine will. These two features together characterize a form of rhetoric that is still familiar in the modern world of nation-states, a rhetoric of prophetic nationalism. Rousseau himself cannot be blamed for the emergence of such a rhetoric, nor did he explicitly write about it. But in the dynamics of his thought we can see how the call for a rhetoric of prophetic nationalism might emerge out of the effort to internalize and naturalize a shared authoritative perspective on controversial issues. We have tied that effort in turn to Hobbes's campaign against controversy and controversial rhetoric. Rousseau's turn to a language of persuading without convincing thus demonstrates how the modern attack on rhetoric, devised initially to disarm dangerous forms of dogmatic religious speech, can itself produce new and equally threatening forms of fanaticism.

CHAPTER 3

The Sovereignty of Scholars: Kant

Our age is, in especial degree, the age of criticism, and to criticism everything must submit.

—Kant, *Critique of Pure Reason*, A xii

Seen from the viewpoint of politics, truth has a despotic character.

—Hannah Arendt, "Truth and Politics"

In the last two chapters I have argued that both Hobbes and Rousseau sought to suppress the politics of persuasion, and that they did so by asking citizens to alienate their capacity for private judgment to a unitary and authoritative source of public judgment. In this chapter I will argue that Kant followed in their footsteps. When Kant defended the "public use of reason" he was implicitly attacking the public use of rhetoric. Critical reason played the role of sovereign, immunizing those who used it against rhetorical appeals to their particular judgments. While Kant was interested in vindicating a certain faculty of judgment, his interpretation of that faculty ultimately severed it from the realm of prudence, probability and practice. Kant's defense of judgment was in fact an attack on the sort of practical judgment that the rhetorical tradition had prized.

At one time an argument showing that Kant's thought did not do justice to this sort of practical judgment might not have been a very interesting one to make, since it was widely assumed that Kant's emphasis on universal rules and maxims did not offer a useful perspective for theorists interested in the capacity to deal with particulars. A new generation of sympathetic readers of Kant, however, has now shown that this interpretation of his writings is inadequate. These readers have highlighted parts of his thought—

primarily his anthropology and his aesthetics but also previously underexplored parts of his epistemology and moral theory—in which perception, emotions, virtue, and judgment all play more significant and more legitimate roles than was acknowledged by the older understanding of him as a philosopher of rules and duties. What is more, a number of recent theorists have proposed not only that Kant's thought does not ignore such matters but that it is in fact an especially promising place to look for an account of judgment and its connection to politics. Thus there is renewed debate on the potential contribution of Kantian thought to our understanding of these issues and new reason to consider Kant's relation to the tradition of thought in which judgment was central.[1]

Hannah Arendt deserves credit for stimulating some of this reevaluation of Kant. She was herself intensely interested in exploring the phenomenon of judgment and in reviving the politics of persuasion, and it was she who first suggested that Kant's thought might be mined for such purposes. While others had paid attention to Kant's third critique, the *Critique of Judgment*, for its contribution to aesthetics, she made the original claim that we could find in that work a "nonwritten political philosophy" in which practical and political judgment finally received its due from the moderns.[2] Her own interest in the theme had begun much earlier. In "The Crisis in Culture" she had already indicated her sense of what was at stake, writing, "The capacity to judge is a specifically political ability . . . Judgment may be one of the fundamental abilities of man as a political being insofar as it enables him to orient himself in the public realm."[3] She noticed that judgment was linked to persuasion, a form of speech that she described as distinctively political because it aimed to influence and yet refrained from coercing in the way that dialectical reasoning did when it asserted truths. In this early essay these ideas led her to defend a form of humanism. She drew explicitly from Cicero's writing on rhetoric to identify connections between practical judgment and modes of argument appropriate for political action.[4] Her later lectures on Kant's *Critique of Judgment* pursued the same interests in a new way. The project of showing how practical judgments might claim a sort of validity distinct from the truth-claims of philosophic or scientific statements seemed to her to fit into the larger program of defending the sphere of persuasive but noncoercive political argument.[5]

In this chapter I accept much that Arendt wrote about the importance of the *Critique of Judgment* to Kant's political thought, but I do not adopt her view of its implications. Instead I find that Kant did not generously give judgment a book of its own so much as shunt it off into its own realm, stranding it from the substantive moral and political functions that it had in earlier thought and subordinating it to a conception of reason that was, as critics have always charged, overly formalistic. The recent wave of interest in the *Critique of Judgment* reveals a growing awareness among political philosophers that contemporary forms of political theory often fail to find a place for judgment, but it is a mistake to look to Kant for a remedy.

A telltale sign of Kant's final position with regard to practical judgment is his quick dismissal of persuasion and rhetoric. When he mentioned rhetoric, he objected to it as a threat to enlightenment and free thought. But, as we shall see, Kant's conception of freedom required self-discipline, and in the invention of an authority to mete out this discipline there was a deep similarity between Kant's thought and Hobbes's. The construction of a sovereign authority to settle disputes was central to both thinkers; both objected to rhetoric because it dispersed judgment and so posed a threat to that authority. In this chapter I will suggest that Arendt's attempt to draw a political theory out of ideas about sociability and the *sensus communis* in the *Critique of Judgment* did not adequately address the fundamental question of sovereignty or authority at the deepest levels of Kant's thought.

Arendt aimed to find in Kant a political theory compatible with the Ciceronian humanism she admired, a theory compatible with the controversial back-and-forth of argument that she viewed as the realm of true "politics."[6] But as we shall see, Kant explicitly opposed the Ciceronians of his time, the so-called "popular philosophers" who denied the possibility of finding or constructing a certain and incontrovertible, authoritative standard from outside the world of experience that could settle disputes once and for all. Unlike the popular philosophers, Kant never deferred to the "common sense" to be found in existing opinions. In metaphysics, in morals, and in politics, he always aimed to provide an authoritative criterion based outside those opinions. Recent commentators who defend Kant's critical reason as an authority we all participate in constructing do not address the more fundamental question of whether such a unitary authority is necessary or possible. Nor do they acknowledge the practical outcome of asserting the sovereignty of reason—the dominion of professional reasoners or scholars. The latter part of this chapter will turn from Kant's "non-written" political philosophy to his written political thought. In evaluating Kant's republicanism, a republicanism without rhetoric, we will in the end have to weigh the threat posed by an aristocracy of orators against that posed by the sovereignty of scholars. First, however, we must begin with Kant's few brief mentions of rhetoric itself.

The Machinery of Persuasion

When Kant quickly touched upon the art of rhetoric in the *Critique of Judgment*, he mentioned it only to distinguish it from poetry, which he ranked first among the arts. In articulating the reasons for poetry's superiority, Kant emphasized its association with freedom, its spirit of playfulness, and its honesty. Poetry "strengthens the mind by making it feel its faculty—free, spontaneous, and independent of natural determination," and it exercises this freedom in a playful spirit, without intending any particular consequence and without intending to deceive or manipulate its audience.[7] It was precisely in this way that poetry differed from oratory, which aimed to produce a definite result and therefore lacked a playful spirit and threatened the freedom of its audience. Kant offered the following revealing reflections in a footnote:

> I must admit that a beautiful poem has always given me a pure gratification, while the reading of the best discourse, whether of a Roman orator or of a modern parliamentary speaker or of a preacher, has always been mingled with an unpleasant feeling of disapprobation of a treacherous art which means to move men in important matters like machines to a judgment that must lose all weight for them on quiet reflection.[8]

He described rhetoric as "the machinery of persuasion, which, since it can be used equally well to beautify or to hide vice and error, cannot quite lull the secret suspicion that one is being artfully overreached."[9]

Kant thus likened both persuasion itself and the audience caught in its grasp to machines. In Kant's thought machinery and mechanism in general raised the threat of determinism. The last words of his famous essay "What is Enlightenment?" described the enlightened citizen as someone "who is *more than a machine*."[10] Machinery was thereby linked to the "immaturity" from which enlightenment rescued us, an "inability to use one's own understanding without guidance from another."[11] This guidance included requiring "a spiritual advisor to have a conscience for" the individual, one of the most visible roles for rhetoric in Kant's time.[12] The courage to think for oneself—the root of Kant's notion of autonomy and of enlightenment—was a virtue that served to safeguard one from the influence of orators, who would "deceive" and "captivate" the mind. Kant's principal reason for objecting to rhetoric was the threat it posed to free judgment:

> Rhetoric, in so far as this means the art of persuasion, i.e. of deceiving by a beautiful show *(ars oratoria)*, and not mere elegance of speech (eloquence and style), is a dialectic which borrows from poetry only so much as is needful to win minds to the side of the orator before they have formed a judgment and to deprive them of their freedom; it cannot therefore be recommended either for the law courts or for the pulpit.[13]

Kant's sense that rhetoric aimed to win minds "before they have formed a judgment" can be contrasted with Aristotle's notion that rhetorical speech should be seen as winning minds by appealing to the faculty of judgment.

Kant may have linked the manipulative potential of rhetoric to machinery in part as a response to the efforts of some rhetoricians to adapt to Cartesian mechanistic psychology. In "What is Enlightenment?" he alluded to La Mettrie's *L'homme Machine* (1748), but in these passages on the machinery of persuasion Kant may also have had in mind works offering mechanistic explanations of how rhetoric influenced the mind. Rhetoricians had tried to incorporate Cartesian mechanism into their theories of how speech moves men at least since the work of Hobbes's nemesis John Wallis (1616–1703). Wallis's work had been picked up by Bernard Lamy in his *L'art de parler* (1676) and probably helped encourage the elocutionary movement in eighteenth-century England.[14] The mechanistic explanations of rhetoric had been prevalent enough even in Jonathan Swift's time to merit satire in a volume of Swift's that Kant cited.[15]

Regardless of where Kant received his notion that rhetoric sought to "move men like machines," he clearly worried not so much about its political effects as about its pernicious influence on habits of mind. Even when an orator aimed at praiseworthy ends, his involvement "spoiled" the maxims and dispositions of his listeners by discouraging them from thinking independently. Kant's argument was that rhetoric prevented individuals from thinking for themselves in the way that enlightenment demanded.[16]

The Sovereignty of Critique

Kant's objection to rhetoric seems at first to be very different from the objection we have seen in Hobbes. Whereas Hobbes objected to rhetoric in the name of authority or sovereignty, Kant objected in the name of freedom. Beneath this apparent difference, however, is an underlying similarity, one that we can see by considering more carefully how Kant understood free thought.

To think for oneself was first and foremost to reject the authority of other people, of tradition, and of prejudice. But Kant's view of freedom, whether in the realm of thought or of morality, was not merely negative in content. Freedom could not be achieved simply by rejecting external authority, for Kant thought that a mind without any authority at all was little more than an unorganized mass of sensations, prone to fall victim to any promise of direction that came its way. Thought could be free only if we could find a way of guiding it without resting on any external authority or source of discipline. He thought we had to find or create a source of authority from within reason itself. This is why he viewed the task of freeing reason as identical to the task of teaching reason to discipline itself. As in his moral theory, freedom was found not in the absence of restraint but rather in following laws one gave to oneself:

> Freedom of thought . . . signifies the subjection of reason to no laws other than those *which it imposes on itself;* and its opposite is the maxim of the **lawless use** of reason . . . [I]f reason does not wish to be subject to the law which it imposes on itself, it must bow beneath the yoke of laws which someone else imposes upon it; for nothing—not even the greatest absurdity—can continue to operate for long without some kind of law.[17]

As this passage makes clear, there were only two options for Kant—discipline from outside or self-discipline.[18] If we did not find a way of disciplining our thoughts, if we allowed ourselves to indulge in what Kant called a "merely random groping," then we would fall victim to the dogmatic arguments of polemicists, and ultimately to zealotry, superstition, and atheism.[19]

Reason could discipline itself, Kant suggested, through a special practice of criticism. In the preface to the second edition of the *Critique of Pure Reason* Kant likened criticism to police who secured order in a commonwealth: "To deny that the service which the Critique renders is positive in character, would thus be like saying that the police are of no positive benefit, inasmuch as their main business is merely to prevent the violence of which citizens stand in mutual fear, in order that each may pursue his vocation in peace and security."[20] He pressed this analogy to peacekeeping further in the section "The Discipline of Pure Reason." There he explained the need for criticism in terms supplied by Hobbes. The comparison is so surprising that it is worth quoting at length:

> The critique of reason can be regarded as the true tribunal for all disputes of pure reason . . . In the absence of this critique reason is, as it were, in the state of nature, and can establish and secure its assertions and claims only through *war*. The critique, on the other hand, arriving at all its decisions in the light of fundamental principles of its own institution, the authority of which no one can question, secures to us the peace of a legal order, in which our disputes have to be conducted solely by the recognized methods of *legal action*. In the former state, the disputes are ended by a victory to which both sides lay claim, and which is generally followed by a merely temporary armistice, arranged by some mediating authority; in the latter, by a *judicial sentence* which, as it strikes at the very root of the conflicts, effectively secures an eternal peace. The endless disputes of a merely dogmatic reason thus finally constrain us to seek relief in some critique of reason itself, and in a legislation based upon such criticism. As Hobbes maintains, the state of nature is a state of injustice and violence, and we have no option save to abandon it and submit ourselves to the constraint of law, which limits our freedom solely in order that it may be consistent with the freedom of others and with the common good of all.
>
> This freedom will carry with it the right to submit openly for discussion the thoughts and doubts with which we find ourselves unable to deal, and to do so without being decried as troublesome and dangerous citizens. This is one of the original rights of human reason, which recognizes no other judge than that universal reason in which everyone has his say.[21]

The force of this drawn-out analogy with the state of nature lay in its emphasis on the need for a sovereign judge whose authority "no one can question" and whose judgments offer "relief" from "endless disputes." The disputes Kant had in mind were those metaphysical controversies about issues such as freedom of the will that he discussed elsewhere in the first critique, rather than the more political disputes that had concerned Hobbes. But the analogy suggests that Kant viewed the problem of thinking for oneself as analogous to the political problem that Hobbes had raised—thinking for oneself required that we construct an authority to settle disputes.

Kant sometimes also spoke of this same project as one of inuring us against illusions, deceptions, and precipitous judgments. Indeed, he explained the need for discipline by noticing that "the temptation to judge is great" and that we were, in the realm of metaphysics, liable to fall into "a whole system of illusions and fallacies."[22] The way out of such uncertainties was to see behind each side's "illusions and prejudices," to put aside their "sophistical arguments," often made in a "falsified form" motivated by "mere personal vanity," and to refer instead to an accepted standard on the basis of which controversy could be arbitrated.[23] Once in possession of that standard of critical reason, one "begins to feel his own capacity to secure himself against such injurious deceptions, which must finally lose for him all their illusory power."[24] In a footnote on enlightenment in the *Critique of Judgment* Kant noticed that "self-legislative" thought was difficult both because we would be tempted to overreach in our judgments and because there were always people "who promise with much confidence that they are able to satisfy our curiosity."[25] In this line of thinking we can again find echoes of Hobbes, who had constructed sovereignty as a standard that could help individuals avoid being misled by illusions of sense and by seductive arguments of polemicists. In Hobbes, individuals were protected against the arguments of orators by allowing their ears to be chained to the lips of the sovereign. In Kant, the attachment to the sovereign judgments of critical reason protected individuals from the dogmatic polemicists on both sides of metaphysical disputes and against the popularizers who translated such polemic into "*materialism, fatalism, atheism, free-thinking, fanaticism, and superstition.*"[26]

From this perspective we can see that Kant's objection to rhetoric was actually closer in character to Hobbes's than one might think on first reading. It is true that Kant objected to rhetoric in the name of free thought while Hobbes objected in the name of sovereign authority. But Kant's notion of freedom required the sovereign authority of critique. Rhetoric posed a threat to free thought in Kant because it challenged the authority of the critique of reason. In Kant as in Hobbes, rhetoric was dangerous because it threatened to insubordinate the sovereign.

Constructivism and Legitimacy

If we seek to prosecute Kantian critique on the charge of seizing sovereignty for itself, however, its defenders will object that critique can be authoritative without being authoritarian—that its sovereignty is legitimate. Onora O'Neill makes this case by drawing our attention to Kant's insistence that "reason has no dictatorial authority; its verdict is always simply the agreement of free citizens, of whom each one must be permitted to express, without let or hindrance, his objections or even his veto."[27] In this passage O'Neill finds the suggestion that the authority of reason is one that we construct for ourselves, simply by reflecting on standards implicit in the practice of trying to reason with other people. Elaborating on ideas from Arendt's *Lectures,* O'Neill argues that the constructed character of critical reason legitimates its authority. Since we participate in constructing the standard, we can hardly view it as alien or imposed. Kant wrote that there was "no other judge than that universal human reason *in which everyone has his say.*"[28] Rather than subjecting us to a standard imposed from outside ourselves, O'Neill insists, Kant would have us submit only to a standard that arises from the "agreement of free citizens."[29]

The political analogy that O'Neill emphasizes is meant to draw upon the legitimizing power of consent, the device by which authority and freedom can be made to coexist. As O'Neill writes, "Reason, on this account, has no transcendent foundation, but is rather based on agreement of a certain sort."[30] In advancing this interpretation, O'Neill draws our attention to the long passage I have quoted from *Critique of Pure Reason* in which Kant likened critique to Hobbes's sovereign. O'Neill emphasizes the fact that reason's authority is constructed rather than imposed, but in making the analogy, she does not mention the absolute character of Hobbes's sovereign. If Kant did construct reason on the model of Hobbes's sovereign, that fact in itself is not necessarily an argument for accepting reason's legitimacy. After all, we do not accept Hobbes's claim that virtually absolute monarchical rule would be legitimate if it were constructed.

Still, the hypothetical contract that is said to ground critique is different from the covenant found in Hobbes's theory. The agreement Kant imputed to us was meant to be one to which we were already a party, whether we realized it or not, whenever we made reasonable appeals to other people. If we reflect on what we do when we debate and argue, O'Neill suggests, we will see that we cannot help but implicitly invoke a standard of reasonability meant to be understood by all other reasonable creatures. The standard of reason "cannot be questioned because intelligible questioning presumes the very authority it seeks to question."[31] Thus the original hypothetical contract imputed to us by Kant was different from Hobbes's covenant because Kant's contract was one that we did not have to be persuaded to enter; we were already committed to it.

O'Neill follows Arendt in connecting this idea to the notion of "universal communicability" found in the *Critique of Judgment.* Expanding the scope of Kant's argument from aesthetic judgments to all reasonable appeals, O'Neill and Arendt emphasize Kant's view that when people assert their views "everyone expects and requires from everyone else this reference to universal communication, as it were from an original compact dictated by humanity itself."[32] From the fact that every reasonable appeal seems to presume the possibility of some shared standpoint of reason, Arendt and O'Neill derive the possibility of a universally shared standpoint—a standpoint that is authoritative or sovereign for every reasonable creature. They suggest that the construction of the sovereignty of critical reason arises from within the practice of argument itself.

The allure of this view lies in its promise to bring together the aspirations of Kantian philosophy with those of Arendt's political thought. If reason itself is constructed through the process of argumentation and controversy, it is related to the sort of politics that Arendt recommends, the back-and-forth of debate and the practice of persuasion that she links with Ciceronian humanism.[33] Arendt referred to Cicero again in her lectures on Kant's *Critique of Judgment,* citing the account of judgment in *De oratore* when explaining the relevance of Kant's "universal communicability," and she aimed to find in that notion of communicability a modern resource for defending some variant of the politics of persuasion.[34]

It is at this point that Arendt's thesis deserves closer scrutiny. As we shall see, Kant thought that his notion of sovereign critique was opposed to the Ciceronian humanists of his day, the "popular philosophers" who were concerned with communicability in a more traditional rhetorical sense and who denied both the need for and the possibility of the universal sovereignty of critical reason that Kant aimed to establish. Looking at Kant's thought in this context will help show that Kant would not have shared Arendt's interpretation of his thought. It will also suggest that the driving motivation of his thinking can in some ways be traced to his opposition to these Ciceronian popular philosophers. The difficulty in Arendt's project of reconciling Kantianism with Ciceronian humanism is that, in some sense, an opposition to the attempt to revive such humanism constituted the very heart of Kant's critical thought.[35]

Against Popular Philosophy

Most histories of philosophy explain Kant's "critical turn" as a response to the debate between rationalists and empiricists. Kant, however, positioned

himself slightly differently. He suggested that his critique was an alternative
to the reigning reaction to that metaphysical debate, a reaction he characterized as "indifferentism."[36] The writers that Kant had in mind were those
theorists known as "popular philosophers" *(popularphilosophen),* who wrote
between the 1750s and 1780s and who sought to revive a humanistic approach to knowledge. While they endorsed a modern program of "enlightenment" based on recent advances in philosophy, they sought to reverse
what they saw as a trend toward scholasticism in German thought. To
counter this trend they self-consciously emulated the Renaissance humanists, producing new translations of Cicero along with new commentaries
and following the Roman orator in emphasizing the moral import and popular impact of philosophy.[37] While the popular philosophers followed with
great interest the controversies between Wolffians and Lockeans, and while
they allowed themselves to be provoked by Hume and attracted by the
Scottish theorists of common sense, they sought to negotiate these contemporary debates in a humanistic fashion. For this reason Hegel placed them
in the category of "Ciceronian philosophy" alongside Petrarch, Erasmus,
and Montaigne; more recently Johan van der Zande has characterized them
as "deliberately rhetorical in nature."[38] The popular philosophers were "Ciceronian" and "rhetorical" not only because they concerned themselves
with writing in an accessible way but also because they approached theory
in a prudential spirit. They adopted Cicero's eclectic approach to philosophical controversies, taking plausible elements from competing schools; they
were more concerned with piecing together a pragmatic and prudent form
of enlightenment than with establishing the absolute authority of any one
system.[39] Like Cicero, they sought beliefs that were probable, certain
enough for the moment but always revisable. Because they took this pragmatic stance toward the status of knowledge, the popular philosophers
tended not to probe too deeply into the ultimate foundations of reason.
But it was a sense of crisis about these foundations, arising initially from
Descartes's rejection of the probable and subsequent endorsement of radical
doubt, which fueled Kant's Copernican revolution.[40]

Kant may have felt some sympathy with the popular approach at a certain point in his career. John Zammito has suggested recently that Kant
even considered taking the path of a popular philosopher himself. Known
as an engaging teacher and an eloquent writer in his precritical days, Kant
was actually considered for a professorship in rhetoric at Königsberg University in 1764.[41] But however seriously he may have taken this option at

one point, by the time that he introduced his notion of critique, the path of popular philosophy was clearly the road he had chosen not to take. He offered his notion of critique precisely as an alternative to the popular philosophers' approach. Characterizing their moderate eclecticism as "indifferentism," he described it as a philosophically inadequate response to metaphysical disputes:

> But it is idle to feign indifference to such enquiries, the object of which can never be indifferent to our human nature. Indeed these pretended indifferentists, however they may try to disguise themselves by substituting a popular tone for the language of the Schools, inevitably fall back, in so far as they think at all, into those very metaphysical assertions which they profess so greatly to despise. None the less this indifference, showing itself in the midst of flourishing sciences, and affecting precisely those sciences, the knowledge of which, if attainable, we should least of all care to dispense with, is a phenomenon that calls for attention and reflection. It is obviously the effect not of levity but of the matured judgment of the age, which refuses to be any longer put off with illusory knowledge. It is a call to reason to undertake anew the most difficult of all its tasks, namely, that of self-knowledge, and to institute a tribunal which will assure to reason its lawful claims, and dismiss all groundless pretensions, not by despotic decrees, but in accordance with its own eternal and unalterable laws. This tribunal is no other than the *critique of pure reason*.[42]

While Kant did not simply dismiss the popular philosophers, he also did not regard their stance as one worthy of philosophical engagement. He regarded their responses as feeble efforts to paper over difficult problems.[43] Popular philosophy, he wrote, was not a philosophical position but a cultural phenomenon among scholars, a "prevailing mood" that could be overcome by adopting the right method. That method required the creation of a sovereign "tribunal." The political metaphors and the notion of critique entered Kant's thought together as a means of escaping the humanistic rhetorical approach to controversy endorsed by the popular philosophers.

The popular philosophers, many of whom had admired Kant's precritical writings, found themselves leading the charge against his critical philosophy. The first review of the *Critique of Pure Reason* was written by Christian Garve and heavily edited by Johann Georg Heinrich Feder, both leading *popularphilosophen*.[44] Published anonymously in a Göttingen journal, the review seems to have provoked Kant primarily through two of its arguments:

it suggested that his theory was a version of Bishop Berkeley's idealism rather than anything very new, and it criticized the book for its inaccessible and unnecessarily technical prose style that "strains [the reader's] attention to the point of exhaustion" and "fight[s] against this commonly accepted language."[45] Though seemingly unrelated, the two criticisms in fact were linked by their hostility to Kant's project of establishing reason as an authoritative standard wholly independent of ordinary experience. Kant responded to the review in the second edition of the critique and in the *Prolegomena to Any Future Metaphysics*. His responses help to clarify the ways in which his theoretical aspirations differed from those of the popular philosophers and thus the way in which he rejected their Ciceronian or humanistic approach.

Most accounts of the Garve-Feder-Kant philosophical exchange devote attention to sorting out the extent to which Kant's idealism was different from Berkeley's.[46] But it is also worthwhile to look at the criticism of Kant's style. Kant's *Critique of Pure Reason* was an ugly work of philosophy, written in a specialized, technical jargon and in a schematic fashion that Kant himself recognized few would have the patience to endure.[47] The first reviews did not fail to comment on this ugliness.[48] Even when Garve wrote to Kant disclaiming much of Feder's edited review, the one part that he did not recant was the criticism of Kant's style: "My opinion, perhaps mistaken, is still this: that your whole system, if it is really to become useful, must be expressed in a popular manner, and if it contains truth then it can be expressed."[49] Kant himself was acutely conscious that his first critique was written without the elegance necessary to appeal to a wide public.[50] Though he sometimes expressed regret about this, and suggested in letters that he could have smoothed over the rough edges if he had taken more time, he also defended the inaccessibility of his works. He argued that philosophers who engaged in critique rather than in dogmatic philosophy would always and of necessity remain behind the scenes, wielding their influence mostly against the dogmatism of other scholars. A pleasing style was necessary, he wrote, "only from a popular point of view; and this work can never be made suitable for popular consumption." He dismissed "that loquacious shallowness, which assumes for itself the name of popularity."[51] He thought the work of critique was to be done by philosophers behind the scenes to produce new principles of scientific certainty.

Lurking just behind this seemingly superficial disagreement about style was a deep point about the status of ordinary opinion. Garve argued not simply that Kant's philosophy was difficult to understand but also that if it contained truth, it should have been translatable into more familiar language.[52] In making this point, Garve presumed the link between opinion and truth that grounded Aristotelian dialectic and rhetoric. This link gave a philosopher faith that sorting through common opinion and language would bring him closer to truth. The popular philosophers' position was not that one could not distinguish opinion from truth, but that elements of truth resided in opinion. Thus, while the popular philosophers did support "enlightenment," they thought it necessary to proceed more slowly than Kant and to be more respectful of reigning opinion or prejudice. Moses Mendelssohn, in his answer to the question "what is enlightenment?", warned that responsible scholars would hesitate to attack particularly useful prejudices:

> If certain useful and—for mankind—adorning truths may not be disseminated without destroying prevailing religious and moral tenets, the virtue-loving bearer of enlightenment will proceed with prudence and discretion and endure prejudice rather than drive away the truth that is so closely intertwined with it.[53]

Mendelssohn's notion of enlightenment, unlike Kant's, included a role for rhetoric and eloquence.[54] Written independently from (rather than in reaction to) Kant's famous essay on the same topic, Mendelssohn's piece on enlightenment was different precisely in his argument for rhetorical prudence. At the heart of the disagreement was not only a different estimate of the political danger of destroying prejudice but also a divergence of opinion about the epistemic value of prejudice. Where Kant saw only error, Mendelssohn saw a "truth . . . so closely intertwined with it." Elsewhere Mendelssohn warned of a "sham enlightenment . . . where everyone ridicules prejudices, without distinguishing what is true in them from what is false."[55] Kant's refusal to grant credence to popular opinion, evident in both the content and the style of his critiques, rejected this deeply rhetorical element of the popular philosophers' approach. In spite of the critical thinker's lack of popularity, Kant wrote, he "still remains the sole authority in regard to a science which benefits the public without their knowing it, namely, the critique of reason. That critique can never become popular, and indeed there is no need that it should."[56] In Kant's preface to the *Metaphysics of Morals* he explicitly raised Garve's requirement that "every philosophic teaching be capable of being made popular . . . if the teacher is not to be suspected of being muddled in his own concepts." Kant accepted this opinion in part, but denied its application to the critique of reason or ideas dependent on that critique, which he again argued could "never be made popular."[57]

Common Sense

Leaving the matter of style aside, the popular philosophers' more substantive responses to Kant echoed the rejoinder that Thomas Reid, the Scottish common sense theorist, had made to Berkeley.[58] In the introduction to *An Inquiry into the Human Mind on the Principles of Common Sense* Reid had disputed the notion that philosophic reason should have authority over ordinary opinion or "common sense":

> [T]he votaries of this [idealist] Philosophy, from a natural prejudice in her favour, have endeavoured to extend her jurisdiction beyond its just limits, and to call to her bar the dictates of Common Sense. But these decline this jurisdiction; they disdain the trial of reasoning, and disown its authority; they neither claim its aid, nor dread its attacks.[59]

To the contrary, Reid argued a bit later, the principles that most people used in ordinary life "are older, and of more authority, than Philosophy."[60] In Germany the popular philosophers similarly rejected Kant's effort to subject those principles to the jurisdiction or "tribunal" of critique. Having likened Kant's *Critique of Pure Reason* to Berkeley's idealism, the popular philosophers applied Reid's arguments against Berkeley directly to Kant.[61] The last paragraph of the Göttingen review suggested that Kant's approach did violence to more moderate and natural ways of thinking, and both Garve and Feder indicated in other reviews that they viewed common sense as the alternative to Kant's criticism. Feder attacked Kant in the name of the "Simple and Secure Grounds of Common Sense."[62] Garve, in his original (unedited) review of the critique, dramatically demonstrated the popular philosophers' attachment to common sense when, in the midst of a fairly sober summary of Kant's arguments, Garve confessed that he had shed tears when he had come upon Kant's more familiar description of moral goodness:

> This reviewer cried when he arrived at this part of the book! After having stumbled over each small stone that he encountered on the path of specu-

lation, he jumps over entire rocks and cliffs as soon as the stronger interest of virtue calls him back to the cleared road of common sense.[63]

And yet Garve went on to wonder whether it was possible to maintain this moral feeling if one had accepted the rest of Kant's theory and thereby "abandoned" nature. He closed his review with the striking assertion that Kant's theory, even if true, was irrelevant. Since people naturally took objects to really exist rather than as mere representations, and since they could not live without doing so, it was more reasonable to use the language and concepts closer to their natural understandings: "[I]t is completely irrelevant whether we reduce things to ideas, or transform ideas into things. The latter is more in accord with our nature—and is so much a part of our language that we cannot express ourselves in any other way."[64] Like Reid, both Garve and Feder wished to restrain overzealous theoreticians from undermining natural ways of thinking that people simply could not live without.

Noticing Reid's influence on Kant's reviewers explains why Kant took the trouble to criticize Reid and his followers (James Oswald and James Beattie) by name in the *Prolegomena*. In Kant's view, Reid and, by implication, the popular philosophers who translated and praised him, failed to grasp the challenge that Hume's skepticism posed to ordinary beliefs:

> It is positively painful to see how utterly his [Hume's] opponents, Reid, Oswald, Beattie, and lastly Priestly, missed the point of the problem . . . The question was not whether the concept of cause was right, useful, and even indispensible for our knowledge of nature, for this Hume had never doubted; but whether that concept could be thought by reason *a priori,* and consequently whether it possessed an inner truth, independent of all experience . . . This was Hume's problem.
>
> But to satisfy the conditions of the problem, the opponents of the great thinker should have penetrated very deeply into the nature of reason, so far as it is concerned with pure thought—a task which did not suit them. They found a more convenient method of being defiant without any insight, viz., the appeal to *common sense.*[65]

Kant challenged others to show how a science of metaphysics was possible without adopting his critique, and he insisted that they not resort to two strategies: first, "trifling about probability," which he thought could have no role in a science designed to arrive at "perfectly certain judgments"; and second, "a decision by means of the magic wand of so-called common sense."[66] Common sense could not serve as the foundation for a science of metaphysics because it was grounded in experience, and metaphysics aimed at concepts that were valid "outside the conditions of experience."[67] In practice, Kant thought, common sense tended to serve as an unphilosophical resort to popular opinion. He suggested that Reid and his followers failed to see the import of Hume's challenge and that their appeal to common sense was a "convenient" way of escaping or ignoring the real problem:

> To appeal to common sense when insight and science fail, and no sooner—this is one of the subtle discoveries of modern times, by means of which the most superficial ranter can safely enter the lists with the most thorough thinker and hold his own. But as long as a particle of insight remains, no one would think of having recourse to this subterfuge. Seen in a clear light, it is but an appeal to the opinion of the multitude, of whose applause the philosopher is ashamed, while the popular charlatan glories and confides in it.[68]

When Kant objected to common sense as "an appeal to the opinion of the multitude" of the sort in which only a "popular charlatan" would indulge, he offered an argument that would have been familiar to the Socrates of Plato's *Gorgias*—it is the classic argument against rhetoric. It is not surprising that common sense theorists would draw upon themselves the criticisms formerly leveled at orators. Rhetoricians of the time certainly saw the notion of common sense as one that helped to provide philosophical grounding to their art, and works on rhetoric were among the important sources for Reid's formulation of common sense. Reid cited the third book of Cicero's *De oratore* as one source for his understanding of common sense and Claude Buffier, author of *Traité de l'éloquence* (1728), as another.[69] George Campbell, a member of Reid's philosophic circle in Aberdeen and author of the highly influential *The Philosophy of Rhetoric* (1776), immediately saw the relevance of Reid's notion of common sense for rhetoric and adopted it in his work.[70] Orators had always been taught to appeal to their audience's capacity for judgment; common sense provided a way of defending that capacity against the post-Cartesian theories that questioned its adequacy. Given this link between rhetoric and common sense, Kant could hardly attack one without also calling the other into question. Kant's dismissal of common sense as an "appeal to the multitude" was an attack on the rhetorical tradition as it appeared in the work of the Scottish theorists and their German followers.

We should include in Kant's attack on common sense not only the passages cited above but also the seemingly more conciliatory passages on the topic—including the passages from the *Critique of Judgment* to which Hannah Arendt drew attention. Though there are hints of reconciliation in the *Prolegomena*, Kant most obviously tried to present himself as a defender of common sense in section 40 of the *Critique of Judgment* on the *sensus communis*. He offered to save the notion from the "vulgar" connotations of the word "common" and the experiential connotations of the word "sense." He aimed to portray criticism as an investigation into the grounds of common sense rather than a rejection of it. From this perspective, common sense was closely related to the activity of reasoning, and so was in need of the same discipline and authority that gave reason its autonomy. Kant proposed that we understand the *sensus communis* as a faculty of judgment that operated independently of experience and sensation:

[The faculty of judgment] takes account *(a priori)* of the mode of representation of all other men in thought, in order, as it were, to compare its judgment with the collective reason of humanity, and thus to escape the illusion arising from the private conditions that could be so easily taken for objective, which would injuriously affect the judgment. This is done by comparing our judgment with the possible rather than the actual judgments of others, and by putting ourselves in the place of any other man, by abstracting from the limitations which contingently attach to our own judgment. This again is brought about by leaving aside as much as possible the matter of our representative state, i.e. sensation, and simply having respect to the formal peculiarities of our representation or representative state.[71]

Kant outlined three "maxims of common human understanding," which, if followed, allowed us to escape the illusions of our private judgments, to abstract from the limitations of our personal situation, and to put ourselves in the place of all other reasoning people.[72] The first of these maxims was the slogan of enlightenment, "to think for oneself," which Kant explained as avoiding the "passivity" of prejudice and superstition. The second maxim was "to put ourselves in the place of everyone else." The third maxim, the one specific to "reason," was "always to think consistently." The second maxim, which concerned judgment especially, led Kant to speak admiringly of "a man of enlarged thought" who "disregards the subjective private conditions of his own judgment . . . and reflects upon it from a *universal standpoint*."[73] Thus Kant turned common sense into a way of raising the idea of "universal communicability," which was the regulative idea governing judgments of taste and which pointed to man's natural sociability. Together the three maxims were meant to articulate the necessary preconditions of universal communicability. If we thought for ourselves, from a universal standpoint and consistently, we would honor the "contract" we found ourselves in simply by virtue of being rational and sociable creatures.

These three "maxims of understanding" can be contrasted with the "maxims of common sense" or *"regulae philosophandi"* that Reid had mentioned at the beginning of *An Inquiry of the Human Mind*. Reid's maxims were taken from Newton, and they aimed to describe a process by which we tended to "trace particular facts and observations to general rules, and to apply such general rules to account for other effects, or to direct us in the production of them." Reid insisted "that there is but one way to the knowledge of nature's works—the way of observation and experiment."[74] Kant's maxims of common understanding were opposed to Reid's notion of common sense insofar as they directed our attention away from experience. From Kant's perspective, Reid's approach was a form of naturalism, which lacked the authority to ground a truly scientific sort of knowledge.[75] From Reid's perspective, Kant's project of judging experience in front of some tribunal or sovereign led only to the danger of what Reid had called "metaphysical lunacy."[76] Instead of regressing on the necessary conditions of communicability, Reid surveyed experience and arrived at general propositions that all reasonable men seemed to acknowledge. Thus he and other common sense theorists looked at languages as they were actually spoken. They focused on communication rather than communicability.

Arendt suggested in her lectures that Kant's notion of common sense could be renamed "community sense." People would disagree in their judgments, she noticed, and one could not force others to judge a particular way: "[O]ne can only 'woo' or 'court' the agreement of everyone else. And in this persuasive activity one actually appeals to the 'community sense.' In other words, when one judges, one judges as a member of a community."[77] In this passage Arendt came close to describing the classical-humanist understanding of rhetoric, in which persuasion was the activity of appealing to fellow citizens' judgments. Citing a passage from Cicero's

De oratore, she seemed to want to draw Kant toward endorsing a politics of persuasion.

From the perspective of Reid or of a rhetorician such as Campbell or of the popular philosophers, Arendt's linking of Kant and Cicero would seem perplexing. Reid, the author whose notion of common sense Kant had singled out for criticism, had quoted precisely the same passage from Cicero to support his view.[78] Reid's use of Cicero is more convincing than Arendt's because Reid and Cicero were both concerned with actual communities in a way that Kant was not. To call Kant's notion of *sensus communis* the "community sense" ignores the fact that Kant insisted the *sensus communis* was independent of any particular community. Kant's concept is perhaps better called *the idea of a community sense*, since its content is abstracted from any actual society.[79] In fact, Kant elsewhere used "communicability" as a criterion of truth without any mention of community or *sensus communis* at all. In the *Critique of Pure Reason*, in section 3 of "The Canon of Pure Reason," Kant introduced universal communicability as the criterion by which we could distinguish true belief, or conviction, from the "mere illusion" of "persuasion": "The touchstone whereby we decided whether our holding a thing to be true was conviction or mere persuasion was therefore external, namely, the possibility of communicating it and of finding it to be valid for all human reason."[80] Persuasion here referred to "merely private validity" or private opinion, and Kant suggested that it was indistinguishable from illusion except by reference to this hypothetical shared standard of communicability. One could call "true" only propositions that could garner agreement from all reasonable creatures. Kant made no reference to any particular community other than the hypothetical "everyone."

Kant was most concerned to put the weight of argument against resting satisfied with private opinion.[81] Arendt followed his lead in this way, remarking that "the less idiosyncratic one's taste is, the better it can be communicated."[82] But then her argument seems to have made an unwarranted leap. She rightly pointed out that "one can communicate only if one is able to think from the other person's standpoint" but wrongly concluded from this idea that Kant's notion of "enlarged thought," which asked us to judge from a universal standpoint, was therefore a precondition of communication.[83] Her argument ignored that there is an intermediate range of perspectives between a solipsistic standpoint and one that is universal. While it is true that an individual with a wholly private and idiosyncratic set of tastes could not communicate with others (if such an individual can even be imagined to exist), it is also true that an individual who completely abstracts from the idiosyncrasies that he shares with his audience will find it difficult to communicate with them as well. For that reason, one of the central lessons of the art of rhetoric has always been to study those idiosyncrasies, attending to them carefully and learning their structure. Kant's dismissal of common sense as a "magic wand" that "does not convince everyone but accommodates itself to personal peculiarities" could describe, without prejudice, precisely the skill that orators were once taught to use.[84] Recognizing the "personal peculiarities" of one's audience was thought to be necessary to communication. Communication presumes generality, not universality. At times it seems that Arendt realized this; she went so far as to translate "general" where most translators use "universal" in the relevant passage from Kant (as Ronald Beiner notices), describing the product of enlarged thought as a "general standpoint" rather than a universal one.[85] Her actual description of that standpoint, however, seems to have followed Kant's in its aspiration to universality. Thus one can respond to her position, as to Kant's, by noticing that the precondition of communication is not only impartiality or disinterestedness but also attention to the particular prejudices and beliefs of one's interlocutors. For communication, sympathy is necessary as well as detachment.[86]

If few things are universally communicable, if communication must adapt itself to an audience that is not universal but merely general, then techniques of adaptation are necessary. Those techniques comprise the art of rhetoric. To search for the preconditions of universal communicability is to search for the means by which rhetoric might be made unnecessary. The project of redefining "common sense" in this way, the project that Arendt found in Kant's *Critique of Judgment* and magnified in her lectures, was fundamentally opposed to the Ciceronian rhetorical tradition and to the argumentative controversy that Cicero, and often Arendt herself, viewed as an integral part of political life. In asking us to consider the "possible rather than the actual judgments of others," to leave aside the "matter" of our position and consider only its "formal" properties, Kant emptied the notion of common sense of much of its content. Therefore, finding a political philosophy in Kant's version of the *sensus communis* would not in fact change very much our conception of his political thought, for he redefined *sensus communis* in such a way as to make it fit into the rest of his thought. As we will see next, the purely formal idea of community at work in his revised notion of common sense echoed the formal idea of a social contract at work in his theory of republicanism.

The Rhetoric of Public Reason

If we turn at last from what Arendt called Kant's "nonwritten" political thought to his explicit writings on politics, we find an emphasis not on communicability but on the analogous concept of publicity, which was central to the transcendental formula of public right announced in "Perpetual Peace": "All actions affecting the rights of other human beings are wrong if their maxim is not compatible with their being made public."[87] Just as communicability provided a standard for reasonable statements, publicity provided a standard for legitimate political action. And just as communicability did not necessarily require successfully communicating one's ideas to others in practice, Kant's use of publicity did not require actually gaining the approval of the public. As O'Neill notes, it was really "publicizability" that Kant valued as a criterion.[88] Like communicability, the notion was meant chiefly to help us engage in a thought experiment, a procedure through which each could determine for himself whether an action was just. Publicity was a formal quality of maxims, meant to "provide us with a readily applicable criterion which can be discovered *a priori* within reason itself."[89] As a criterion that was a priori, Kant's principle of publicity made no reference to actual experience, including the opinions of any actual public. In particular, it would not lead us to ask whether a particular population actually had consented to a particular constitution or law through any actual contract. What publicizability modeled was the idea of a contract "which would not exist as a fact . . . but only as a rational principle for judging any lawful public constitution whatsoever."[90]

To illustrate the workings of this principle, Kant applied it to the question of whether a people could ever rightfully rebel from a tyrant. The question might ordinarily give rise to a great debate, but Kant proudly announced that "the transcendental principle of publicness . . . can get round such long-winded discussion."[91] Because a people could never publicly admit its intention to rebel in certain situations without undermining the foundation of the state they meant to protect, he argued, rebellion was never justified. Using the principle of publicity exposed the particularity or exceptionality of rebellion. Political justice was the rule of law, and law by its nature could not allow for exceptions.

But Kant did not always emphasize publicity when explaining why rebellion could never be just. In "Theory and Practice" he instead accented the danger of dispersing judgment away from the sovereign, following the logic found in Hobbes. Even if a head of state had acted like a tyrant, there was no just cause to rebel, Kant argued, because citizens of a commonwealth had alienated their judgment to the sovereign:

> The reason [that there is no right to rebel] is that the people, under an existing civil constitution, has no longer any right to judge how the constitution should be administered. For if we suppose that it does have this right to judge and that it disagrees with the judgment of the actual head of state, who is to decide which side is right? Neither can act as judge of his own cause. Thus there would have to be another head above the head of state to mediate between the latter and the people, which is self-contradictory.[92]

If a subject believed that a piece of legislation would endanger his happiness, what could he do? Kant wrote, "There can be only one answer: nothing can be done about it, except to obey."[93] In a footnote Kant explained the need for a centralized arbiter by arguing that a group of individuals each judging for themselves without a sovereign would fall into anarchy and factionalism and thus be "devoured by ecclesiastics and aristocrats."[94] This statement might remind us of Hobbes's worry about an "aristocracy of orators." More generally, Kant's analysis of obedience in this passage followed Hobbes's argument in tracing the problem of politics to the dispersal of judgment.[95]

Here a puzzle arises. The two arguments that Kant gave against rebellion—the publicity principle and the need for concentrating judgment in one sovereign—seem to be in tension with one another. Publicity would seem to rely on dispersed judgment, or at least on the possibility of it. Making maxims public only exposes their injustice if others can judge them. But unified sovereignty seems to require that the people give up their right to judge. Kant escaped this dilemma by introducing what was essentially a distinction between two sorts of judgment, the sort that led to coercive action and the sort that did not. When coercion was at stake, "the people, under an existing civil constitution, has no longer any right to judge how the constitution should be administered."[96] But citizens in a commonwealth did retain for themselves the freedom to judge so long as they did not act on their judgments in a way that might threaten the sovereign. Thus Kant endorsed the infamous slogan, attributed to Frederick II: "*Argue* as much as you like and about whatever you like, *but obey!*"[97] In this respect Kant positioned himself "against Hobbes" in the subtitle to the second part of "Theory and Practice." Kant described as "terrifying" Hobbes's view that citizens should alienate their judgments of right and wrong to a ruler. He insisted that they be allowed to articulate their judgments in public by using "the freedom of the pen."[98] But he did not think the people could ever act on revolutionary judgments except through the hands of the sovereign itself. He reconciled publicity and sovereignty by severing judgment from action. He asked citizens to purchase the freedom of the pen by yielding their swords.[99]

The freedom of the pen was meant to both enlighten the people and advise the sovereign. It enlightened the people by making them accustomed to presenting their claims to others, instilling in them the habit of checking for communicability, the habit that itself helps to constitute the grounding of reason. Without the possibility of actual communication, the idea of communicability could not be understood and so could not perform its function of helping to construct the authoritative standard of reason. In the essay "What is Orientation in Thinking?" Kant argued against those who said that no external coercion could take away our freedom of thought:

> But how much and how accurately would we *think* if we did not think, so to speak, in community with others to whom we *communicate* our thoughts and who communicate their thoughts to us! We may therefore conclude that the same external constraint which deprives people of their freedom to *communicate* their thoughts in public also removes their freedom of thought, the one treasure which remains to us amidst all the burdens of civil life, and which alone offers us a means of overcoming all the evils of this condition.[100]

This freedom to publicly communicate one's thoughts—to make public use of one's reason—was all that was necessary to bring gradual enlightenment to the public, Kant claimed.[101] The freedom of the pen was meant to drive progress toward the time at which true popular sovereignty would be possible, the time at which the dictates of reason, which the sovereign ought to heed, would also be the dictates of the people. Publicity was meant to encourage reasoning, and the sovereign was meant to listen to reason. Kant's ideal republic would arise when the public and the ruler came together in recognizing the sovereignty of reason.[102]

But that time was not yet at hand. And whereas an older, Ciceronian style of political thought would have called upon orators to play the role of helping a people to come together in the way necessary to constitute a republic, Kant instead introduced two new ways in which people would be brought toward republican government. The first was the process of a providential history, which would guide even self-interested men toward the final ideal of pacific republicanism.[103] The second was the guidance of enlightened rulers. Kant hoped that rulers such as Frederick II would be ahead of their time; he hoped they would govern according to the republican idea even if they could not yet allow republican institutions: "Since it will be a considerable time before this takes place, it is the duty of monarchs to govern in a *republican* (not a democratic) manner, even though they may *rule autocratically*. In other words, they should treat the people in accordance with principles akin to the laws of freedom which a people of mature rational powers would prescribe for itself, even if the people is not literally asked for its consent."[104]

But how could a ruler know what laws a "mature" people would prescribe for itself? Arising to fill the gap between the people's present-day immaturity and their future sovereignty were the heroes of Kant's thought—not the orators but the scholars. Insofar as rulers allowed themselves to be advised by scholars and other independent thinkers, they might come closer to using reason as the standard with which to evaluate their policy.[105] Kant's pleas for state toleration of scholars, found throughout his writings and especially in his later essays, including "What Is Enlightenment?" and the "Contest of the Faculties," should be understood to reflect not merely his own growing troubles with the authorities but also the larger importance of theoreticians and intellectuals in the structure of his political thought. By scholars he meant most of all philosophers, who—unlike theologians and lawyers, the "higher" faculties in German universities who were subject to close state supervision—deferred to no authority other than that of critical reason. The higher faculties often "stir[red] up political struggles" and planted "the seeds of insurrection and factions." They were "self-appointed tribunes of the people . . . [who could] steer the judgment of the people in whatever direction they please[d]."[106] To protect the people, and especially the government, against the potential demagoguery of these higher faculties, Kant proposed that philosophers should be permitted special freedom. "The class of philosophers," he wrote in "Perpetual Peace," "is by nature incapable of forming seditious factions or clubs."[107] Their habit of critical reason made them men of "enlarged thought," as was described in his maxims of common sense, and this detachment made philosophers particularly well suited to divine the laws by which a mature people would rule itself. The free public use of one's reason that Kant defended in "What is Enlightenment?" was, in "Perpetual Peace," revealed to be a hidden means of allowing scholars to advise rulers without humiliating them.[108] In "The

Contest of the Faculties" Kant reassured authorities who were concerned about the effects of popular enlightenment that philosophers "[did] not address themselves in familiar tones to the people . . . but in respectful tones to the state, which [was] thereby implored to take the rightful needs of the people to heart."[109] The advice that philosophers gave to the sovereign included advice about war and peace. Kant remarked that one could identify an absolute monarch as one with the power to decide when to go to war. The only exception to the principle of publicity in "Perpetual Peace," the "secret article," concerned the role of scholars on precisely this point: "The maxims of the philosophers on the conditions under which public peace is possible shall be consulted by states which are armed for war."[110] Thus when exercising the key prerogative of sovereignty rulers were to listen to scholars, who advised them in the name of the people but from the perspective of reason. In Kant's republicanism policy was evaluated not by the people but by an independent and free class of scholars who, by publicizing their findings, secretly provided autocratic rulers with instruction on the dictates of reason.[111]

Kant could offer scholars this important role because he denied that any great difference existed between scholarship and statesmanship. The unifying theme of the three essays presented together in "Theory and Practice," highlighted in the introduction, was meant to refute the popular philosophers Garve and Mendelssohn. This unifying theme was the practicality of critical reason. Just as the artilleryman needed the mathematics of ballistics, Kant argued, the statesman needed the critical reason of academic philosophy.[112] In answer to the claim that practical experience brought its own sort of wisdom which theorists should not disregard, Kant wrote, "Such illusory wisdom imagines it can see further and more clearly with its mole-like gaze fixed on experience than with the eyes which were bestowed on a being designed to stand upright and to scan the heavens."[113] In Kant's lexicon "practical" did not refer to the traditional Aristotelian prudence that helped one derive from experience good judgments about how to act. Instead, the divide between practical and theoretical in Kant's thought concerned the way in which reason was deployed—practical reason was simply reason concerned with action. Thus in practice as well as theory, it was the scholars familiar with critical reason who knew best. From this vantage point Kant evaluated and judged familiar maxims about how to conduct international politics, subjecting them to the criterion of publicity and asserting, again against Garve, that so-called prudential wisdom was an "unwisdom and veiled injustice."[114] Prudence was a form of casuistry with the hidden agenda of excusing practical men from the demands of morality. The theoretical perspective of scholars, in contrast, derived its authority from its detachment from politics.

More generally, Kant's understanding of republicanism included the goal of institutionalizing some degree of the scholars' detachment. Just as Kant thought that philosophers should not become kings because "the possession of power inevitably corrupts the free judgement of reason," so too he thought that legislation should be separated from the executive power lest the exercise of rule corrupt the lawmakers.[115] The independence of reasoners was closely linked to the independence of legislation in Kant's ideal. In "Perpetual Peace" he divided all governments into two types, despotic and republican, and he made the distinction between the legislative and the executive the defining characteristic of republics: "*Republicanism* is that political principle whereby executive power (the government) is separated from legislative power."[116] While this requirement may sound in some ways like the separation of powers familiar from Montesquieu and *The Federalist Papers*, it actually arose from a different and contrary concern. Kant did not ask the legislature and the executive to check one another. Instead he separated the legislative power from the executive power so that the legislative power would not be corrupted. The legislative power had to be kept general and pure. In referring to the executive as "government," Kant drew on the similar distinction between sovereign and government in Rousseau's *Social Contract*. In Rousseau the distinction protected the general will from the particularity of the executive.[117] The activity of ruling required attention to the particular features of situations. The sovereign could maintain its generality only if it delegated the power to deal with particulars. Rousseau split ruling into legislative and executive functions to protect legislation from particularity. Kant's separation of powers proceeds from a similar motive, but he emphasizes more than Rousseau the link between legislation and reason.

Revealingly, Kant thought of the separation of powers as analogous to the parts of a syllogism. In "Perpetual Peace" he wrote,

> one and the same person can no more be at one and the same time the legislator and executor of his will (than the universal proposition can serve as the major premise in a syllogism and at the same time be the subsumption of the particular under it in the minor premise).[118]

The distinctive character of a major premise was its universality.[119] In presenting this analogy and making the executive the "minor" premise, Kant illustrated the secondary status that was implicit in the title of the executive, who did not rule but simply executed a law given by a higher authority. The separation of powers served to insure this hierarchy between generality (law) and specificity (execution); it distilled ruling into two parts and gave precedence to the former. And like the executive, the judicial power too served the legislative. The three powers of government seemed separate but were actually united in the image of a syllogism or, we might say, in the service of pure reason. It was reason that "legislated" and the legislature that ruled.

The need to maintain the purity and reasonability of legislative sovereignty, in turn, explains the importance of representation to Kant's republicanism. As in Hobbes, the concept of representation both hid and preserved the distance between ruler and ruled. Kant approvingly quoted Frederick II for taking the trouble to say that he was the nation's highest servant. Kant did not regard the statement as an attempt to cover authoritarian rule in the clothes of popular rule. Instead he saw in its mention of service the idea that the executive should be separate from the legislator. The defect of ancient republics, according to Kant, was their failure to insure this separation by utilizing representatives.[120]

Kant's modern republicanism aimed to create sovereignty without ceding rule to a particular person. Because governing requires dealing with particulars—and because responding to particulars is the work of a faculty of judgment that only particular individuals can exercise—governing might be thought to be necessarily the work of particular rulers. But Kant, following Rousseau, sought to avoid this necessity. He dissolved the activity of governing into the separate activities of legislating and executing, thereby purifying the legislative activity and putting the executive in service of what had been purified. This service was the "representation" at the heart of his republicanism. Therefore, Kant viewed democracy, not autocracy, as the chief enemy of republican government. In a democracy it was difficult to separate legislating and executing because "everyone . . . wants to be a ruler."[121]

A Kantian republic could not permit its citizens to actually rule unless it could trust that they could recreate the distance between the activities of legislation and execution within their own minds. They would have to allow reason to legislate even their own actions and insure that they remained uncorrupted by the peculiarities of perception or desire. They would have to become enlightened, autonomous individuals, disciplining themselves to follow neither their ordinary opinions nor their common sense judgments but instead the sovereign dictates of critical reason. It is true that those dictates emerged from a process of thinking that involved taking into account the possible judgments of other reasoners. Kant's critical reason was "public" in that sense. But this rhetoric of public reason should not obscure the fact that reason was also sovereign, meant to provide one authoritative perspective from which the disputes that arose between individuals exercising their precritical judgments could be definitively resolved. Insofar as public reason and the scholars best suited to exercise it were sovereign in Kant's thought, they diminished and displaced the prudential, experientially based faculty of judgment that both Arendt and more recent champions of humanism seem interested in reviving, the faculty so important to a politics of persuasion. Kant's thought is not the best place to look for an account of that sort of judgment. Instead, we should turn to the older tradition of rhetoric in which judgment played a central role.

PART II

For Rhetoric

CHAPTER 4

Drawing upon
Judgment: Aristotle

Each person judges well what he knows, and is a good judge about that.

—Aristotle, *Nicomachean Ethics* 1094b29

Since the modern suspicion of persuasive rhetoric is rooted in a crisis of confidence about the human capacity to use judgment in politics, any rehabilitation of rhetoric will have to address that crisis by offering a sympathetic account of judgment. Many theorists have turned to Aristotle's ethical writings on this topic, and for good reason. Unlike philosophers who approach ethics through rules or principles, Aristotle insisted that no general codes could fully capture what made human choices good. While he acknowledged that rules of thumb could be helpful, he assumed that the final determination of what was appropriate at any time fell into the domain of judgment, a human capacity that drew upon perception, emotion, and reason to respond to each situation in all of its particularity. In making practical judgment so central to his ethics, Aristotle found a way to recognize the importance of sensitivity, nuance, and insight—aspects of moral life that rule-based systems of ethics tend to ignore.[1]

Yet the Aristotelian account of ethics, however attractive, does not address the dangers that early modern thinkers located in judgment. Those dangers arose from the way that judgment was used, or left unused, in democratic politics. The question about the role of judgment in politics is distinct from questions about its role in individual ethics because it requires us to consider the social impact of many people exercising such an indefinite and fallible faculty when making decisions together. If practical judgment is a capacity to make decisions without reference to rules or laws, it seems to be defined largely by its lawlessness. When a polity admits the need to draw upon practical judgment, it tacitly admits that its laws are insufficient. In this way emphasizing the role of judgment may seem to weaken the rule of law. Given the potential lawlessness of judgment, the question that arises for us is how democratic polities can best draw upon the practical judgments of their citizens when making political decisions.

The threat posed by the unruliness of practical judgment seems especially acute in democracies. Aristotle suggested that judging well requires the sort of moral education that only organized societies friendly to aristocrats make possible. He also suggested that even properly educated people found it difficult to judge where the mean lay in any particular case. Even on Aristotelian grounds, then, it would be reasonable to think that democratic citizens encouraged to consult their own judgments will disagree about controversial matters and that if they remain attached to their various opinions, their disagreements may not be susceptible to easy resolution. We might conclude that while it makes sense to emphasize judgment in an account of ethics for individuals, political decisions in democracies should stand on firmer and more definite foundations.

This is the idea we found expressed most clearly by Hobbes, who viewed practical judgment as a weak faculty usually corrupted by republican politics. Public discourse and debate, he thought, tended to draw out not the practical wisdom of the multitude but the political ambition of the vainglorious few. Those few would become orators, using tricks of rhetoric to wield influence over their fellow citizens by appealing to private judgments or consciences. We saw that Hobbes went so far as to blame the judgment-corrupting orators for inciting the English Civil War. Persuaded he had no means of acting against the orators themselves, he sought to immunize citizens against their influence by asking citizens to alienate their judgments to a sovereign and to agree to abide by its determinations on controversial matters rather than judging for themselves. He asked them to disregard their own reasons and those supplied to them by orators and instead to take the sovereign's word as "publique reason."[2] Insofar as democratic theorists still invoke notions of public reason, they adopt something of Hobbes's approach to the political problems that arise when practical judgment is invited into politics without proper protection.

If we want to avoid alienating our judgment to a sovereign ruler or reasoner, if we want to find a way to bring the insights of citizens' practical judgment to bear on political decisions, we must offer some alternate way of addressing the problems that Hobbes raised. We cannot expect to give judgment a role in political decision-making without inviting efforts to influence judgment. Instead, we must show that efforts to influence judgment will not inevitably corrupt it. We must show, contra Hobbes, that political rhetoric or the art of persuasion can be turned into something other than a tool for manipulation and demagoguery.

Can we find the materials for such an argument in Aristotle? He could not address all the factors that made judgments seem so stubborn to Hobbes, for there was no ancient analogue to the Puritan rhetoric of conscience. Aristotle did, however, confront the political threat posed by the independence and detachment of judgment. He saw that citizens called upon to act as judges would often want to make their own verdicts supreme, setting themselves above the regime rather than viewing themselves as a part of it and subject to its laws. He remarked that if one person were ever to appear in the city who was obviously superior in virtue and wisdom to the rest of the citizens, that person would either have to be made king or be ostracized—he could not be integrated into the civic life of the city, "for such a person would likely be like a god among human beings."[3] One way to understand why Hobbes thought the Puritan rhetoric of conscience could not easily be integrated into a deliberative politics was that those who used it implicitly presented themselves as having such superior virtue and knowledge. Aristotle saw a related threat in the courts, where he thought sophistic demagogues invited the people to view themselves and their particular judgments as the final authority in the city.

The rhetoric of the courts was the most prominent sort of rhetoric practiced and taught by Aristotle's contemporaries. When Aristotle declared in the *Rhetoric* that his subject could be made an art *(techne)* only insofar as it focused on deliberation rather than forensics, he was arguing for a significant break from tradition.[4] In shifting the emphasis from judicial to deliberative rhetoric, he sought to focus rhetoricians' attention on a type of persuasion resistant to demagoguery, a rhetorical practice ultimately based upon and validated by its ability to tame the unruliness of practical judgment.[5] His treatment of rhetoric showed how public speech might draw private judgment into the activity of public deliberation and thereby take advantage of judgment's insight without capitulating to its independence. He outlined the art of rhetoric in such a way that those who mastered and practiced it would find themselves participating in a mixed regime, where deliberation was both necessary and possible. In the *Politics* the decision procedure associated with democracy was the drawing of lots. Election, or deliberative choice, was associated with aristocracy or oligarchy. Therefore, democracy could be combined with choice, or made deliberative, in a regime that mixed oligarchic and democratic elements.[6] Aristotle's art of rhetoric aimed to teach leading citizens of these deeply divided polities how to engage in controversy with one another in a way that would weave the city together through deliberation rather than tear it apart through demagogy.

At least two features of Aristotle's approach to deliberation should be especially interesting to theorists today. The first is that Aristotle did not rest his defense of deliberative rhetoric on moral injunctions about how speakers should and should not speak. As most readers of the *Rhetoric* have noticed, the book could never be mistaken for a work of political ethics. At the beginning Aristotle offered quick assurances that his readers should not worry about rhetoric's abuse, but these comments were brief; he dismissed the fear rather than addressing it in depth, dropping the subject entirely in the rest of the book.[7] Instead of examining ethical concerns directly, Aristotle focused on the extent to which rhetorical practice was susceptible to technical analysis.

It was by making rhetorical practice into an art or *techne*, I will argue, that Aristotle sought to indirectly address the problem of demagoguery. Rather than granting rhetoricians extraordinary powers and then asking them to impose external moral rules on themselves, he restricted the scope of their competence. He argued that rhetoric was most susceptible to technical analysis when it aimed at deliberative judgment and therefore that rhetoricians could only gain the technical mastery they desired if they focused their attention on this sort of appeal—if they viewed rhetoric as a technique of deliberation.

In proceeding this way, Aristotle sought both to defend rhetoric and to put it in its place. Its place was within the regime rather than above it. He aimed to integrate the practice of rhetoric primarily with one element of the regime, the deliberating part, and thus to give it a specified and delimited political function. In this way he opposed the sophists, who claimed to teach men to rule the city from outside its laws and practices. Sophist-trained rhetoricians viewed laws, the subject of political science, as material to be used rather than as conditions that defined their political role.[8] Aristotle's ambitious project was to make rhetoric a more modest art. He sought to reduce its dangerous political power by raising its intellectual status.

The second feature of Aristotle's approach to rhetorical deliberation that should interest theorists today is its reliance on two ideas that I will draw out and stylize as *situated judgment* and *deliberative partiality*. We shall see that Aristotle thought that citizens were worse judges when sitting as jurors in the courts than when sitting in a deliberative assembly and that this was the case because jurors in courts judged about matters that did not directly touch their own interests. He thought citizens tended to judge better in deliberative settings, where they were situated in their own perspectives and experiences and where their opinions and feelings about what would be good for them were relevant to the question before them. In Aristotle's opinion, they exercised their judgment best when they could draw upon structures of perception and value acquired throughout their lives. Even more surprising, perhaps, is that Aristotle thought that partialities and partisan political emotions could make citizens more rather than less susceptible to the sort of rhetoric that encouraged deliberation. If we are used to associating good judgment with detachment and impartiality, Aristotle's arguments will require a moment to digest. Implicit in his effort to reform rhetoric was the view that a certain situatedness and partiality could help make citizens' judgments more deliberative.

In the rest of this chapter I review the reasons for thinking that Aristotle associated judicial rhetoric with demagoguery and an exaggerated sense of judgment's independence. I explore his argument about why judgment tended to fail in the courts and why it improved when tied to deliberation. And I offer a more detailed investigation of the two ideas just introduced—that subjecting persuasion to technical analysis might combat demagogy and that appealing to situated and partial judgments might contribute to good deliberation. In the final section of the chapter I reflect briefly on the question of whether the notion of situated judgment implicit in Aristotle's approach allows for a rhetoric of reform.

Demagoguery and the Courts

Aristotle is often portrayed as having defended the art of rhetoric against the attack that Plato launched on it in the *Gorgias*. It is important to point out that this conventional view, while clearly true in some sense, is incomplete because it fails to notice the crucial points on which Aristotle agreed with Plato's attack. We cannot say that Aristotle defended the art that Plato attacked. Early in the *Rhetoric* Aristotle argued against the dominant trend in rhetoric as it was practiced and theorized by his contemporaries. When he subsequently defended rhetoric, he offered the sort of defense that sought to reform its subject. He defended not the practice that he saw so much as the practice he wanted to create.

The standard treatments of rhetoric that Aristotle argued against were those that focused on teaching students how to succeed in the courts. According to tradition, the first person to be paid for teaching rhetoric had been Corax, who advised citizens in Sicily how to sue for their land.[9] In Athens too, the rise of a professional practice of rhetoric was tied to litigation in the courts *(dikasteria)*. As these courts gained influence, so did the sophists who taught citizens how to succeed there. The special competence of rhetoricians like Gorgias was in teaching their students how to launch effective accusations and defenses.[10]

It makes sense that intellectuals wanting political influence would have focused their efforts on the courts, for the story of the Athenian *dikasteria* is that of an institution steadily gaining power. Both Aristotle's observations in the *Politics* and the narration in the Aristotelian *Constitution of Athens* indicated that the demos had first gained its influence through the courts.[11] Solon's reform instituting the right of appeal for all citizens was, according to the *Constitution of Athens*, "the feature which is said to have contributed most to the strength of the democracy . . . for when the people have the right to vote in the courts they control the constitution." This seed of democracy flourished when popular leaders augmented the courts' authority and weakened their institutional competitors. Aristides enlarged the jury to as many as six thousand people, and Ephialtes launched an attack on the Areopagus, the smaller and more deliberative council composed of citizens who had held the archonship, the highest office in Athens. Then Pericles, seeking to counter the influence of the oligarch Cimon by strengthening the democratic element of the city, introduced pay for citizens serving on juries. The final part of the *Constitution of Athens* offered detailed explanation of the *dikasteria*, noting its superiority to the deliberative council *(boule)*, explaining the power of the *dikasteria* to investigate and vet office holders, and investigating the way it tabulated votes. The careful treatment of the *dikasteria* in the *Constitution of Athens* reinforces the impression that these institutions had become a fundamental locus of political power in Athens. In describing the "present" state of affairs, the author of the *Constitution of Athens* remarked upon "the ever-increasing power being assumed by the people. They have made themselves supreme in all fields; they run everything by decrees of the *Ekklesia* and by decisions of the *dikasteria* in which the people are supreme."[12] Thus, when sophists focused their attention on the courts, they were teaching their students how to dominate an institution that itself had become dominant in Athenian politics.

Aristotle criticized both aspects of this development, warning about the growing power of the *dikasteria* and opposing the sophists, who taught rhetoric as a skill of litigation. He portrayed the courts as a forum in which popular leaders would stir up the people, arousing their envy and ill will against the oligarchs and persuading them to confiscate property and power. Aristotle voiced his concern in an unusually explicit recommendation to politicians of his time: "The popular leaders of the present, seeking to win the favor of the people, undertake many confiscations through the courts. Those who cherish the regime should take action against this." The problem was that the popular leaders active in the courts tended to bring about one of three outcomes: sometimes they went too far and provoked the oligarchs into revolution; sometimes they became tyrants themselves; and sometimes, knowing that giving power to the people was a way of giving power to those who could persuade the people, they encouraged the citizens to rule by decree. Aristotle drew a close parallel between democracy by decree and tyranny, noting that both failed to provide the rule of law that dictated the arrangement of offices in a regime and that therefore neither could be called a "regime" in the strict sense of the word.[13]

Most interesting for our purposes is the similarity that Aristotle found between the political discourse of citizens living under tyranny and that of citizens living under democracy by decree. He argued that just as concentrating power in the hands of a tyrant gave rise to sycophants and flatterers, so too did concentrating power in the hands of the people.[14] The sycophants of the people were the demagogues, popular leaders who catered to the people's wishes in an effort to gain their trust. Aristotle agreed with a critic who had linked this development to the courts; it was the strength of the courts that had given rise to leaders who "tried to gratify the people as if it were a tyrant."[15] Aristotle associated the courts with a style of politics in which political rhetoric was a form of flattery. On this point he agreed with the charges that Socrates leveled against the rhetoric of the day in Plato's *Gorgias*.[16]

Why Jurors Did Not Judge Well

If we turn to the *Rhetoric* with this political background in mind, we should not be surprised to find Aristotle beginning with an attack on the rhetoric of the courts. But in criticizing judicial rhetoric, he placed more emphasis than

Plato did on how the audience allowed itself to be manipulated. After all, the popular leaders had the support of the people; the rhetoric of the courts would have disappeared had it not been effective. Despite the common metaphors equating rhetoric with force, orators really did nothing more than put words in the air.[17] Their efforts would have been for naught had citizens not taken these words in and allowed themselves to be persuaded. Aristotle blamed the problems of judicial rhetoric on the fact that jurors "strictly speaking, [did] not fulfill the character of judges."[18]

Aristotle argued that when citizens sat as jurors, they listened with an ear for gratification *(pros charin)* and let their own feelings of pleasure or pain *(to idion hedu e luperon)* distort their judgment.[19] He accused jurors of wanting to be charmed by charismatic speakers. Aristotle's formulations here echoed a key phrase used in the *Gorgias* by the character Polus, who claims that rhetoric aims to produce pleasure and pain *(charis kai hedone)*. This is precisely the phrase that allows Socrates to introduce the famous analogy between rhetoric and cooking, since chefs also aim at *charis kai hedone*. And it is the link with cooking that allows Socrates to call rhetoric a form of flattery.[20] Socrates suggests that because rhetors are guided only by the pleasure of their audience, they are not equipped to give a reasoned account of their practice. In making pleasure their guide, they allow the body to judge and so corrupt judgment. If one followed their method, one would hardly be able to judge at all, for "all matters would be mixed up together in the same place."[21] Thus when Aristotle argued in the *Rhetoric* that jurors listened with an orientation *pros charin* and therefore failed to fulfill their function as judges, he was echoing Socrates' view that pleasure could corrupt judgment. In the *Constitution of Athens*, the same phrase, *pros charin*, was directly linked to the political actors who took advantage of this failure of judgment, "the wicked mischief-makers who flattered the people to their disadvantage."[22]

Many readers have interpreted these early passages in the *Rhetoric* as Aristotle's effort to scold orators for appealing to emotions.[23] But the concern about jurors listening *pros charin* need not be read as an effort to rule emotions out of rhetoric. The mere presence of emotions in judges should not be a problem from Aristotle's perspective. As a number of interpreters have shown, Aristotle thought emotions were integral to and partly constitutive of judgment and deliberation.[24] In book 2 of the *Rhetoric* he claimed that emotions were relevant to rhetoric because they helped determine how people judged; he defined emotions as types of judgment.[25]

The problem in judicial pleadings must therefore be cast more precisely. The difficulty was not simply that judicial orators aroused emotions but that they aroused the wrong emotions, at the wrong times, and in the wrong way. They appealed to emotions that drew upon irrelevant facts. When Aristotle accused most rhetoricians of having nothing to say about deliberative rhetoric, he explained that "it is less serviceable to speak things outside the subject matter in deliberative situations," implying that the techniques the rhetoricians taught led orators in the courts to stray into territory unrelated to the cases at hand.[26] When he approvingly cited regulations that prevented inappropriate speeches, he described them as rules that "forbid speaking outside the subject."[27] Aristotle thus located the problem with these appeals to emotion in their straying "outside the subject." He did not argue that all emotions were outside the subject but simply that some could be. The problem lay not in the appeal to emotion per se but in the selection of emotion.[28] Because orators and listeners aimed at *charis*, they did not appropriately judge the relevance of the emotions they invoked and felt; they allowed themselves to be diverted from the matter at hand.[29] The emotional rhetoric of the courts that Aristotle opposed was the rhetoric of distraction.

It is true that Aristotle argued in this chapter of the *Rhetoric* that judicial orators were wrong to try to warp jurors by making them angry, envious, or pitying. His metaphor here was that if we were intending to consult a straightedge, we would not first make it crooked. Though often read as implying that any appeal to emotions involved a warping of judgment, the metaphor actually implied only that one should not warp whatever guide one intended to use when judging. If emotions were a part of one's guidance, as they surely were in Aristotle's view, the analogue to making a straightedge crooked would be stirring up emotions inappropriate to the situation. The primary requirement of an accurate ruler was that it be appropriate to what it was measuring. Thus in the *Ethics* Aristotle famously invoked the image of a flexible straightedge, used by the architects of Lesbos to accurately measure curved stones.[30] The image was a reminder that there were some matters about which laws, with their impartiality and generality, did not guide us well. The two straightedge metaphors are consistent if we see that they both concern the importance of using measures appropriate to what is being measured.

Aristotle suggested that elaborate and specific laws regulating judicial speech could help avoid irrelevant emotional appeals. But he did not regard these laws as ones that would make judicial settings good for addressing general topics. The laws enforcing relevant speech, even if effective, were not meant to create a realm of impartial reasoning about matters of legislative justice. They merely limited the jurisdiction of the courts to the sorts of appeals that would help in determining matters of fact. Judicial rhetoric tamed by law was not his model for rhetoric as a whole. In deliberative situations, he noticed, no laws about relevance were necessary, for listeners did not allow themselves to be lured so easily away from the subject matter. "In deliberative assembles," he wrote, "the judges themselves adequately guard against this."[31]

Aristotle's adaptation of the argument against rhetoric in the *Gorgias*—his view that an audience and speaker united in an orientation *pros charin* failed to judge and therefore sank into flattering demagoguery—was aimed explicitly at judicial rhetoric. His *Rhetoric* attests to how he could imagine the possibility of an artful public discourse different from what he saw taking place in the courts. He could imagine such an alternative because while he might have agreed with Plato's Socrates that being oriented toward *charis* corrupted judgment, he did not accept Socrates's view of what would be necessary to draw out good judgment. Whereas Socrates suggested that people could judge well only when they grounded their judgments in a general philosophic account of the good, Aristotle seems to have thought that they could judge well enough when situated in a view of what was good for themselves. A judge in a deliberative assembly "guards against" irrelevant rhetoric because he "judges about matters that affect himself."[32] He finds that his capacity for practical judgment is best utilized when he is engaged in the activity of deliberation.

Situated Judgment

Just as he articulated the importance of prudence and equity in the *Ethics*, Aristotle also acknowledged a role for particularistic judgment in the *Politics*. In book 3 he suggested the need to supplement law with kingly discretion or even, he tacitly admitted, democratic decree.[33] The unavoidable fact in politics as well as ethics was that law was general while human life was comprised of particulars.

At the most abstract level of analysis, this fact was the cause lying behind the growing influence of the courts. According to the *Constitution of Athens*, Solon had purposefully made his laws vague so as to create more disputes for the *dikasteria* to resolve, insuring that the people would in this way gather power for itself. The *Constitution of Athens* defended Solon against the accusation by saying that he had not intended for the laws to be especially vague. Rather, it was in the nature of law to be silent about particulars and therefore to require supplementation by individuals in a position to judge. "Hence," it concluded, perhaps with exaggeration, "the courts have to decide everything, public and private."[34]

This pronouncement might be seen as the challenge that Aristotle faced. He held that the most necessary thing in a regime was "judgment concerning the advantageous things and the just things."[35] Yet he opposed giving too much authority to the courts and its juries because, as we have seen, the judges in the courts "strictly speaking, do not fulfill the character of judges." In describing the courts in the *Politics*, he carefully divided them into different sorts, each with strictly limited areas of competence, as if to insure that no one court would gain final authority over the regime. When Aristotle described the functions of a regime, he almost always linked judgment with deliberation, rarely letting judgment appear on its own; it was the deliberative part of the city that he called "authoritative."[36] Through making deliberation authoritative, he aimed to accommodate the need for particularistic political judgment without allowing the courts to consolidate political power. He seemed to trust judgment most when it was part of an activity of deliberation.

But why was judgment better when it was a part of deliberation? It may help to quote more fully the passage from the *Rhetoric* that we have already mentioned in which Aristotle criticized the rhetoricians who specialized in judicial orations:

> [They] have nothing to say about [deliberative speaking], and all try to describe the art of speaking in a lawcourt, because it is less serviceable to speak things outside the subject in deliberative situations; for there the judge judges about matters that affect himself, so that nothing is needed except to show that circumstances are as the speaker says . . . Thus, as we said earlier, in many places the law prohibits speaking outside the subject [in court cases]; in deliberative assemblies the judges themselves adequately guard against this.[37]

What seems to have led a deliberator to guard against succumbing to irrelevant appeals in this account was that he was considering matters that affected his own interests. Having his own good at stake exerted an influence on the direction of his thought, perhaps acting as an anchor pulling him back to the matter at hand, as a standard against which he could easily measure the worth of various arguments and feelings, and as a motivation to pay attention. Because he was an interested party, a deliberator applied his interest as a criterion in making his judgments, basing his judgments on his determination of what was good for him.

In the *Ethics* Aristotle described deliberation as a process through which we could discover how to achieve a set goal: "We deliberate not about ends, but about what promotes ends; a doctor, e.g., does not deliberate about whether he will cure, or an orator about whether he will persuade, or a politician about whether he will produce good order, or any other about the end."[38] Thus the judgment employed in deliberation referred to a relatively clear and definite standard—the end or goal. That goal might itself be the result of deliberations that had occurred previously, and it might be subject also to renewed deliberative evaluation in the future. But at the moment an end was being used as a standard, it was not being evaluated. A doctor could not deliberate about how best to cure someone while simultaneously deliberating about whether to cure him. Judging the best means to cure presumed the end of curing.[39] It is true that the doctor might revise his understanding of what a cure consisted of while deliberating about a particular patient's situation, but that revision would itself be based upon some further criterion. Deliberation occurred when one was anchored, for a moment, to some criterion of judgment. The true complexity of Aristotelian deliberation reveals itself only when we realize that in the next moment we could be called upon to reconsider or revise our understanding of the very commitment or goal that had functioned as a criterion in earlier deliberations and that this reconsidering could in turn send us back to revisit the earlier decision. Judgment enmeshed in deliberation required a more or less continuous activity of both constructing and dismantling standards, holding one commitment provisionally steady while evaluating others in light of it.

From where did one draw the goals or ends that acted as criteria in one's deliberations? In the *Ethics* Aristotle noted that the subject of deliberation was what was good for oneself.[40] But he assumed that deliberative individuals would not confine themselves to thinking about their private affairs. In consulting what was good for themselves, citizens found that they needed to ask about their households and about their polities. For this reason, Aristotle did not seem to regard as a great threat the possibility that individuals would deliberate only about private matters. He seems to have assumed, perhaps due to the character of the polis, that someone deliberating about his own good would necessarily be drawn to consider the ways in which public affairs influenced that good. Thus Aristotle asserted that the practical wisdom involved in good ethical deliberation was, in a sense, the same as political wisdom.[41] Nevertheless, citizens with the sort of practical wisdom evident in good deliberations began by ordering their own desires, arranging them as necessary to accomplish those goals that seemed most important.

The sort of judgment employed in this everyday sort of deliberation was the judgment gained from experience. This type of judgment was in turn the kind that Aristotle accused the sophists of lacking. Because they underestimated the importance of experience, Aristotle explained, the sophists mistook rhetoric for political science:

> Those of the sophists who advertise appear to be a long way from teaching; for they are altogether ignorant about the sort of thing political science is, and the sorts of things it is about. For if they had known what it is, they would not have taken it to be the same as rhetoric, or something inferior to it, or thought it an easy task to assemble the laws with good reputations and then legislate. For they think they can select the best laws, as though the selection itself did not require comprehension [*suneseos*], and as though correct judgment [*krinai orthos*] were not the most important thing, as it is in music.
>
> It is those with experience in each area who judge [*krinousin*] the products correctly and who comprehend [*suniasin*] the method or way of completing them, and what fits with what.[42]

The interesting allusion to music in the passage was fleshed out near the end of the *Politics*, where Aristotle argued that children should be educated in music not simply by listening but by participating, since "it is an impossible or a difficult thing for them to become excellent judges without participating in the works."[43] The general point is that the sophists overestimated their expertise or competence because they discounted the importance of practical experience and in particular because they lacked the special capacities of comprehension *(sunesis)* and judgment *(krisis)* that a person tended to learn through practice.

The two qualities that Aristotle accused the sophists of lacking, *sunesis* and *krisis*, were the same ones that appeared when he described the deliberating part of the regime in the *Politics*.[44] The distinguishing or differentiating activity of *krisis* and the synthesizing or grasping of *sunesis* together seem to comprise the activity of deliberation. When evaluating beliefs and desires in light of a goal, deliberators both distinguished and combined the various possibilities they were considering. They distinguished the possibilities by evaluating their different propensities to contribute to the achievement of the end, and they joined the possibilities together by referring them all to one standard.[45] Judgment or *krisis* was best when it was tied to the synthesizing capacity of *sunesis*. Since Aristotle routinely associated *sunesis* with the sort of judgment found in deliberative settings, it makes sense that he would have thought that the rhetoricians taught by the sophists, who lacked *sunesis,* had "nothing to say" about deliberative rhetoric.[46]

The main point about the superiority of judgment situated in deliberation is that people tended to judge better when they considered matters related to their own ends than when they strived to take on a perspective detached from those concerns.[47] The problem with the judgment in the courts was not simply that the people were in control there—Aristotle was not anti-demos in such a simple way. The problem lay in the fact that the judicial setting asked people to judge without reference to the only sort of criteria that they had experience using: the complex, differentiated and ordered set of goals and standards that they had developed throughout their lives as deliberative actors. Only experience could create the intricate structures of belief and emotion that gave rise to mature judgments, and only deliberation that somehow involved one's own good would spur one to draw upon those structures and produce such judgments.

It is true that Aristotle also noticed that individuals tended to be bad judges in their own cases. When discussing the various political claims made about equality in the *Politics,* Aristotle showed that each party tended to identify its own strength as the relevant measure of desert. And when discussing the arrangement of lands in an ideal city, Aristotle suggested that citizens should not have all their interests tied up in lands close to the border, since their self-interest would then lead them to be too skittish of war.[48] This same example, however, also demonstrated the way in which partiality could help deliberation—citizens with a stake in the border lands would not go to war rashly.[49] In general, Aristotle acknowledged citizens' partiality, and he did not condemn them for it, nor did he ask them to leave their perspectives wholly behind. Rather than dismissing the worth of their partial claims about justice, he suggested that those claims provided starting points for political deliberation. Though Aristotle did not recommend ending deliberations with the partial claims of partisans, he suggested that we should not hesitate to begin with them. In deriving political deliberation from the deliberations that individuals practiced with regard to their own good, he linked political judgment to the ethical realm in which judgment showed its best face.

We might call the sort of judgment at work in deliberation "situated judgment." When we engage in situated judgment, we make decisions using criteria drawn from our own perspectives—from our experiences, our emotions, and even our prejudices. Insofar as Aristotelian deliberation involved thinking through our intentions in relation to an end of our own, it incorporated and encouraged situated judgment. As we shall see next, Aristotle aimed to turn rhetoric into a skill of engaging this sort of judgment; he aimed to turn rhetoric into a technique of deliberation.

A Technical Art

If rhetoric was to draw out the best of practical judgment and if the best of practical judgment was found in the activity of deliberation, then Aristotle had to show that rhetoric could become a means of facilitating and encouraging deliberation. To see how he restricted rhetoric to this function, we must attend to the careful way in which he showed that only certain rhetorical appeals were susceptible to the sort of technical analysis that comprised an art *(techne)*. In joining the usual translation of *techne* as "art" to the English words "technical" and "technique," I do not mean to suggest that the study of rhetoric was, for Aristotle, reducible to a set of rules. It was not, for he thought the practice of rhetoric itself required the activity of judgment that we have been exploring. Still, it was a crucial part of his argument that the subject matter of rhetoric could be studied and organized in a more stable way than Plato had allowed, and the internal organization that he aimed to impart to that subject matter may not come across given contemporary connotations of our word "art"—so let us say that Aristotle aimed to show that rhetoric could be made a "technical art."

The question of whether rhetoric could be made a *techne* may seem a rather academic issue, but another glance at Plato's *Gorgias* suggests that the politics of demagoguery were not far beneath the surface even on this point. In that dialogue Socrates joins two accusations in one speech. He links his assertion that rhetoricians do not have a subject susceptible to technical analysis with the claim that they flatter their audiences. With no technical-artistic standards to guide them, Socrates suggests, rhetoricians have nothing to aim at except their listeners' pleasure and gratification. For this reason, he calls rhetoric the counterpart *(antistrophe)* of cookery.[50] Aristotle, in contrast, opened the *Rhetoric* by asserting that rhetoric was the *antistrophe* to dialectic and could therefore be subjected to more rigorous analysis. Implicit in his approach was the view that rhetoricians could practice rhetoric with regard to standards other than the gratification of their audiences.[51]

But what standards were these? Experts in a *techne* were usually judged on their success in producing the product of their craft. What did rhetoric produce? One answer would be that it produced persuasion in the audience. This is the definition that Gorgias accepts in Plato's dialogue.[52] Aristotle offered a different definition. He claimed that the goal of rhetoric was not to persuade but rather to observe the available means of persuasion in any particular case.[53] Even before introducing this definition, he had argued at the beginning of the work that the function of a *techne* was to observe the causes of success in a practice.[54] Medicine, for example, was properly described as the ability to see the available means of making someone healthy. In making observation central to the definition of a *techne*, Aristotle provided people practicing the arts with a certain type of standard to use when evaluating their success. That standard, in turn, made success in a *techne* less dependent on external factors and more dependent on the practitioners and their activity. In the case of medicine, again, Aristotle argued that "it is nevertheless possible to treat well those who cannot recover health."[55] One could be a good doctor even if one's patient died. By analogy, a technical art of rhetoric that was focused on observing the available means of persuasion would allow one to say that an orator who did not manage to persuade a particular audience might nevertheless have practiced his craft well if he had surveyed the various possible means of persuasion and observed which means were appropriate to the particular situation at hand.[56] In giving students of rhetoric this intellectual ambition, Aristotle offered them a goal outside the gratification of their audiences and internal to the practice of rhetoric itself. He suggested that rhetoric could be mastered as a *techne* only insofar as it had such a goal.

This is why Aristotle's defense of rhetoric must be described so carefully. He did not defend rhetoric as he saw it theorized and practiced in his day. He did not claim that all parts of rhetorical practice were susceptible to technical analysis. To the contrary, he criticized earlier rhetoricians for focusing their efforts on the parts of oratorical practice that were not susceptible to such treatment, such as the forensic efforts to arouse irrelevant emotions that we have already discussed.[57] Actors and poets knew a whole variety of ways to arouse feelings and moods, but few of these could be analyzed in the way a *techne* demanded. What was susceptible to technical treatment, according to Aristotle, were the ways in which orators could make listeners come to believe something, the "proofs" or *pisteis*. Generally speaking, Aristotle noticed that listeners would come to believe something because they followed and accepted an argument *(logos)*, because they trusted the judgment and goodwill of the speaker *(ethos)*, or because they felt moved by an emotion *(pathos)*. His major claim was that all three ways of affecting belief could be influenced by spoken arguments. Just as dialectic offered an account of logical arguments, rhetoric could offer an account of these rhetorical arguments *(enthymemes)*.[58]

In constructing their arguments, rhetoricians could draw propositions from the large collections that Aristotle provided. But to take full advantage of Aristotle's analysis, they would have to pay attention not only to the propositions listed but also to the way in which Aristotle had ordered them. For Aristotle did not simply offer the materials for enthymemes in an undifferentiated heap. He ordered them into hierarchies meant to reflect the various structures that might be found in an audience's set of beliefs. In this way he asked rhetoricians to study the patterns found in public opinion. Their task was, in a sense, to map out the landscape of thoughts and desires in their audience and thereby to see what pathways might exist from one belief to another. These pathways were the same ones that an individual audience member might have found himself following as he deliberated himself, as his thought process naturally transmitted his desire from a goal to the various steps required to reach it.[59] We might call these steps "deliberative pathways." Someone who practiced the Aristotelian art of rhetoric well would be able to observe potential pathways in the structure of an audience's opinions and would know how to make use of them. At the most abstract level rhetoricians studied the *topoi*, or most general patterns of reasoning.[60] Aristotle catalogued general relations of greater and smaller quantity, possibility and impossibility, degree of magnitude, and the like. These *topoi* are awkward to state in the abstract, but it is precisely their abstraction that makes them applicable to so many different fields. They are patterns of reasoning that most people use unconsciously whenever they deliberate. In making them explicit, Aristotle was articulating the structure of ordinary deliberative reasoning.

In directing the attention of rhetoricians to this structure and to the deliberative pathways he found there, Aristotle made certain assumptions about their audiences. Just as he stipulated that dialectic aimed at people interested in logical argument, and so drew premises from what seemed plausible to such people, he stipulated that rhetoric was concerned with deliberation and used arguments that would appeal to people accustomed to deliberating.[61] These were people accustomed to debating about matters that did not fall under any distinct area of expertise and that could be resolved in more than one way. They were not people interested in engaging in long and detailed examination. They would respond to brief arguments, they could draw upon probable truths, and they could supply the second half of an obvious argument themselves.[62] The assumption that the audience members were competent at and interested in deliberation suggested that they could exercise their judgment when addressed by a speaker, that they could evaluate arguments according to criteria, and that they were willing to allow their desires and emotions to be affected by new considerations. Competence in deliberation might also suggest a degree of humility, for in the *Ethics* Aristotle noticed that people enlisted partners in deliberation when they distrusted their own ability to judge well.[63] Aristotle did not assume an audience to be thoroughly rational; they were not engaging in dialectic. Nor did he require them to focus only on logical arguments; good deliberators also followed their emotions, which is why a good deliberator had to have been brought up well. Finally, though he did not require them to be willing to make Spartan sacrifices for the polis, Aristotle did assume that they would consider their own good to be somehow linked to matters of public concern.

The fact that the audience was presumed capable of deliberation was what allowed Aristotle to systematize and sort the various possible arguments and appeals under different headings, for the headings were the principles or starting points *(archai)* that deliberative listeners would bring to bear on what they heard. Aristotle began by laying out a schema that included the roles that audience members were most likely to play when listening. They might be acting as observers or they might be acting as judges. If they were judges, they might be judging matters that had occurred in the past or wondering which course of action to take in the future. That is, listeners could be spectators, jurors, or deliberators in an assembly. Thus the three types of rhetoric—epideictic, judicial, and deliberative—arose from sorting listeners by their functions. This approach presumed that listeners would allow their function or purpose to influence the way that they judged the arguments they heard.

Once the function of the particular speech situation had been identified, the rhetorician would know the criterion on which it was most appropriate to base his appeals. When accusing or defending in court, the appropriate criterion to refer to was justice, while in exhorting or dissuading it would be more appropriate to refer to interest or advantage. Even at this very general level of abstraction, the sorting could help speakers avoid mistakes. For example, a speaker defending someone but forgetting that the standard was justice might focus too much on persuading the jury that the defendant had benefited the city in many ways. This approach would leave the jury free to agree and yet decide that the particular action under review, while it brought the city advantages, was nevertheless unlawful or unjust. Similarly, a speaker trying to dissuade the people from adopting a certain course of action but forgetting that the appropriate standard was advantage might err by focusing too much on showing that the action was unjust, leaving an audience free to agree but to conclude that the action had nevertheless been necessary. Aristotle's organization did not show that the criterion that tended to dominate one type of speech situation would never come into play in others; in fact he advised speakers giving advice about the future to consider what it was they would have praised in the past, and vice versa.[64] But in his analysis, different standards were most likely to carry the day in different situations, and part of the art of rhetoric was learning to recognize and make use of the appropriate standards. For this reason, the most important thing about the long lists of propositions found in the first book of the *Rhetoric* is not so much the propositions themselves as their organization. If one were to make a chart out of Aristotle's lists of propositions, the headings and subheadings would provide increasingly specific criteria of appropriateness to guide a rhetorician looking for the appropriate means of persuasion in any particular situation.

Of course a heading or standard such as "advantage" was too abstract to be very useful, so Aristotle offered more specific examples of what sorts of things people generally took to be advantageous. He started with broad categories—happiness and goodness—and then offered lists under each. He placed wealth, reputation, and beauty in the category of happiness, and virtue, easiness, and pleasure in the category of goodness. He also pointed out that people would only be persuaded to act if they felt it was within their power, and therefore he offered for consideration propositions about the various means a people had of effecting change—they could use laws, soldiers, or money, for example. But even all of these specifications remained fairly general, and they offered no way of choosing among different accounts of happiness.

To specify more accurately which considerations would be most persuasive in any particular case, Aristotle noticed, we would have to know more about the audience's character. In Plato's *Phaedrus* Socrates suggests that a speaker cannot persuade an individual without knowing in some depth the composition of that person's particular soul.[65] Aristotle suggested that for public deliberations it would often be sufficient to understand what political regime an audience came from:

> The greatest and most important of all things in an ability to persuade and give good advice is to grasp an understanding of all forms of constitutions [*politeia*] and to distinguish the customs and legal usages and advantages of each; for all people are persuaded by what is advantageous, and preserving the constitution is advantageous . . . A deliberative speaker should not forget the "end" of each constitution; for choices are based on the "end." The "end" of democracy is freedom, of oligarchy wealth, of aristocracy things related to education and the traditions of law, of tyranny self-preservation.[66]

Knowing about political regimes allowed speakers to be more specific in observing which means of persuasion were appropriate in each case.[67] Without the specification offered by the regime, it is not clear that propositions could have been organized in as detailed a way as was necessary to make rhetoric a practical art. Rhetoric was susceptible to technical treatment at a useful level of specificity because it occurred within a regime that helped to structure citizens' opinions. In this way, too, Aristotle's conception of rhetoric followed his conception of deliberation. In the *Ethics* he noticed that deliberation was usually limited to a particular political context: "We do not deliberate about all human affairs; no Spartan, e.g., deliberates about how the Scythians might have the best political system. Rather, each group of human beings deliberates about the actions *they* can do."[68] The situation was a bit more complicated in judicial rhetoric. Insofar as the written laws of the polity were the criteria of justice, arguments were similarly relative to the regime. But there were also unwritten laws and a concept of fairness or equity that allowed speakers to question the accepted standard of justice in any particular city. This feature of judicial rhetoric made it more independent of the regime than deliberative rhetoric, and helps to explain why Aristotle focused on deliberative rhetoric when trying to tame the art.

Thus far we have concentrated on the arrangement of propositions for rhetorical arguments, or *logos*. But Aristotle believed that studying political regimes helped to specify the means of advancing the other types of proof, or *pisteis*, too. After the passage quoted above he continued, "Now, since *pisteis* not only come from logical demonstration but from speech that reveals character [*ethos*] . . . we should be acquainted with the kinds of character distinctive of each form of constitution; for the character distinctive of each is necessarily most persuasive to each. What these [kinds of character] are will be grasped from what has been said above; for characters become clear by deliberate choice, and deliberate choice is directed to an 'end.'"[69] Thus it is clear that the strategy of building a technical art of rhetoric around the study of citizens' deliberative capacity remained intact when Aristotle turned to *ethos*, for in describing how one might learn the various sorts of characters, he presumed that characters were formed by deliberative choice in light of an end. And as was the case with *logos*, he presumed that rhetoricians would be able to study their audience with sufficient specificity by studying the ends supplied by the political regime in which it lived.

To put all this together, we can say that Aristotle marked out as susceptible to technical-artistic analysis the following practice—that of observing which considerations were most appropriate to advance when trying to persuade people accustomed to deliberating, whose desires and goals were characterized by some degree of organization, an organization provided in part by their political context. Rhetoric could be a technical art of deliberation insofar as it studied the internal structure of public opinion, looking for deliberative pathways between various beliefs and emotions. One key question that arises from this perspective, however, is whether the third resource for orators, emotion, or *pathos*, was well structured enough to be equally susceptible to such analysis.[70]

Deliberative Partiality

The passions could not be integrated into the art of rhetoric that Aristotle was describing unless they too had a structure that was susceptible to technical analysis, a structure through which their involvement in the practice of deliberation could be studied. But insofar as passions seem closely related to pleasure and pain, they seem to be more slippery than propositions or characters, less easily differentiated and organized. As we saw in the discussion of why Aristotle did not think that jurors listening for the sake of pleasure judged well, pleasure seems to interfere with standards of judgment rather than to help articulate them.

Part of Aristotle's achievement in the *Rhetoric* was to surmount this challenge and show how pleasure could be brought into a technical art of deliberative rhetoric. He noticed that pleasures and pains were not always as simple and as disorderly as Plato's *Gorgias* suggested they were.[71] They were usually woven together with beliefs, so that a change in opinion could have an effect on them. People experienced these links between thought and pleasure or pain as emotions. The important fact about emotions from the perspective of rhetoric was that they integrated pleasures and pains into the structure of our opinions and imparted to them some of that structure. Recognizing emotions as coherent and relatively steady complexes helped make pleasure and pain susceptible to technical study and ultimately to the influence of artful persuasion.[72] In outlining this approach to the passions, Aristotle also noticed the special role that emotions of a distinctly political kind could play in linking pleasures and pains to deliberative judgment. It was the very partiality of these political emotions that linked them to deliberation.

Aristotle did not include all appeals to the passions in rhetoric's realm of competence, as is made clear from the difference between his treatment of the passions in the first and second books of the *Rhetoric*. In the first book, when examining the motivations that an orator could plausibly cite in court to explain why defendants had acted as they had, Aristotle looked at a certain set of emotions.[73] There he included among the motivating emotions the irrational, passionate desires *(epithumia)* such as hunger, thirst, lust, and more generally the desires for bodily pleasure. Since an audience would find it plausible that a defendant had been motivated by such passions, Aristotle included a great number of propositions about them in this part of the text. The forensic rhetorician had to know about these passions so that he could use them as parts of a spoken argument about someone on trial. But there was no suggestion that the orator himself should try to arouse the *epithumia* in trying to motivate the jurors. In the second book of the *Rhetoric*, when surveying the emotions that the rhetorician might stir up in an audience, Aristotle noticeably left *epithumia* and the direct pursuit of pleasure out of his analysis. He defined the emotions in relation to judgments and relegated pleasure and pain to an auxiliary role: "The emotions [*pathe*] are those things through which, by undergoing change, people come to differ in their judgments and which are accompanied by pain and pleasure, for example, anger, pity, fear, and other such things and their opposites."[74] The subordinate status of pleasure and pain was evident in the fact that when distinguishing the various emotions from one another, he did not refer to the quality of pleasure or pain that each involved. Instead, he claimed that the emotions could be analyzed and distinguished by attention to cognitive factors such as the reasons behind the emotions, the people at whom they were aimed, and the state of mind they reflected. To know how to wield a particular emotion as a means of persuasion, the orator had to know how to recreate its cognitive components; he could not aim directly at the pleasure or pain itself.[75] Thus, when treating emotions as components of deliberation, Aristotle left to one side those that were tied most closely to pleasure and pain, those least susceptible to the influence of arguments. The *epithumia* did more to obscure deliberative judgment than to engage it; they were resistant to argument. Aristotle carefully distinguished these emotions from those with more cognitive content, which were more amenable to argument.

In his selection of emotions in the second book of the *Rhetoric*, Aristotle indicated that orators should be particularly interested in political emotions. The emotions that he described in detail were ones that arose from social contexts and relations, passions directed at other people rather than at food or drink. The cognitive elements of these emotions concerned the listeners' sense of how they appeared to others or what they deserved in terms of public honor. The emotions sprang from judgments about what was good, just, and noble for them and for their friends. A person would become angry, for example, when someone leveled a public and unjustified slight against him or his friend.[76] Aristotle did notice that people tended to become angry at those who stood in the way of their satisfying an appetite, such as quenching a thirst, but he interpreted even this instance of anger through a political lens. He explained that the anger in such a case resulted not from the frustrated thirst alone but from the fact that the person who stood in the way of its satisfaction seemed thereby to belittle the one who was thirsty, to insult him by slighting the importance of his appetite.[77] Aristotle's account of the emotions in the second book of the *Rhetoric* thus deemphasized *epithumia* and emphasized the spirited and judgmental passions of *thymos*. It is no accident that Aristotle discussed anger first among the emotions.[78]

Aristotle's accounts of anger, shame, hatred, and friendship all presumed that citizens would harbor marked preferences for their friends and fellow citizens and that they cared a great deal about their honor. Far from impartial, the emotions Aristotle described were rooted in a deep prejudice in favor of one's own. It was this partiality that made these emotions especially susceptible to the sort of rhetoric that aimed to engage deliberative judgment. The concern with honor gave citizens a measure of independence from their bodily concerns, a freedom from the narrow sort of self-interest driven by pleasure. This sort of detachment from one's desires was necessary for deliberating and judging well. At the same time, the attachment to one's self and one's polis evident in the political emotions offered a locus around which opinions and desires were organized. In this way the partiality helped provide a foundation for the ordered lattice of commitments that deliberation required. The political emotions of anger, honor, and their relatives helped give citizens the mixture of "sympathy and detachment" that made for good practical judgment.[79] Here Aristotle's account again offers a perspective radically different from that we saw in Hobbes, who blamed such passions as honor and pride for making democratic debates inherently unruly, prone to factionalism and likely to devolve into conflict that was in no way deliberative.

When Aristotle discussed in the *Politics* the sort of character required in a "political" citizenry—a citizenry that could engage in the deliberative sort of rule found in a polity—he remarked upon the crucial role that spiritedness *(thymos)* played. Citizens capable of ruling themselves would have to have not only thoughtfulness *(dianoia)* but also spiritedness. The affection that arose among fellow citizens (and presumably the same affection necessary for effective rhetoric) arose from partiality, he argued, and he referred explicitly to the guardians of Plato's *Republic*.[80] In the *Republic* Socrates argues that the partiality of the guardian's *thymos* gave them not only courage and affection for their fellows but also prudence *(phronesis)*.[81] By allowing their partiality for the city to order their commitments, the guardians were able to resist the "wizardry" of persuasive speakers who might try to interfere with their opinions. When *thymos* helped them to resist being "charmed by pleasure or terrified by some fear," it did so not only by sparking physical courage but also by providing intellectual steadiness.[82] As we have seen, Hobbes, Rousseau, and Kant would in different ways argue that citizens needed to chain themselves to a shared and sovereign standard of judgment outside their private opinions to resist rhetorical manipulation. Aristotle, in contrast, suggested that a spirited love of one's own might help citizens maintain their independence of judgment.

The emotions described in the second book of the *Rhetoric* as susceptible to technical analysis by a rhetorician were those that had cognitive components that could be influenced by argument and that were closely tied to the sort of judgments and distinctions that citizens naturally made in the ordinary course of political life—most obviously, the distinctions between just and unjust and between friend and enemy. In drawing the attention of rhetoricians to these emotions, Aristotle did not recant on his promise early in the first book to oppose the irrelevant emotional appeals of the forensic specialists. His treatment of the emotions differed from theirs in that he showed that appealing to certain emotions could be a way of engaging judgment rather than obscuring it.

Rhetoric and Reform

The initial question of this chapter was how the Aristotelian capacity of practical judgment could be made available to democratic polities without permitting the lawlessness and independence of that capacity to undermine the rule of law. I have suggested that Aristotle saw the danger of overly independent judgment most clearly in the people's courts in Athens. His opposition to judicial rhetoric arose from the fact that it presented jurors with decisions that they could not make by deliberating within the hierarchies of goods that they knew best, the structures of value within which they deliberated about their own ends. Aristotle's faith in practical judgment was a confidence in our ability to evaluate our intentions in the light of criteria drawn from within our own concerns. Practical judgment was best, he thought, when it engaged in deliberative reflection on how to achieve one's own goals, however broadly understood. This view meant that rhetoric could be a technique that helped facilitate good political judgment insofar as it addressed itself to observing the cognitive and emotional structures within which citizens deliberated about their own good. Because these structures were powerfully shaped by the laws and customs of the city, practical judgment came into its own when exercised within the context provided by a particular city.

A crucial question that might arise for us when considering the view I have attributed to Aristotle is whether this sort of situated judgment traps us and the orators who address us in our situations, leaving us unable to question the structures of opinion and value in which we have been raised. Does Aristotle's account go too far in taming judgment? Does it fear too much the independence of judgment and therefore tie citizens too closely to their existing contexts and opinions? Today when we think of exemplary rhetoric, we often think of great moral or political crusades, the speeches of abolitionists or civil rights activists, or humanitarians. These speeches seem impressive, in part, precisely because of the independence they display in bringing to bear a moral point of view that has thus far been left out of public deliberations. How would such speeches fit, if at all, within the art that Aristotle described? Does an Aristotelian understanding of rhetoric allow for the rhetoric of criticism or reform?

In trying to answer this question, two remarks seem in order. On the one hand, it seems true that Aristotelian rhetoric was not meant to justify revolutions or radical reform. In a sense, the point of our inquiry was to show precisely that judgment and rhetoric could be made integral to the political life of a city without always threatening to upend that life. The rhetoric of reform shades quickly into that of revolution, and when tinged with moral indignation, it can slide quickly into speech claiming the perspective of superior virtue, the perspective of the person who cannot be integrated into the city and who is "like a god among human beings." Like the Puritan rhetoric of conscience that concerned Hobbes, such speech is not easily integrated into ordinary deliberative politics. If there is room for such truly revolutionary judgment in Aristotle's thought, it probably lies in his account of philosophy rather than his treatment of rhetoric, and the challenges that a truly independent reformer faces are probably closer to those that face a philosopher wanting to influence politics than those facing an orator practicing the art that Aristotle described in the *Rhetoric*. That art is one meant for everyday politics within the city rather than for extraordinary reform. Still, if this approach seems to leave out a type of rhetoric that we value today, it should also remind us of a quieter but perhaps more pervasive practice of persuasion, an activity of citizenship that democratic citizens will have a hard time living without.

On the other hand, one should not go too far in portraying Aristotelian rhetoric as a rhetoric of quietism. Against the conventional interpretation of Aristotle's thought, I would assert that it is wrong to think that the structures of value presumed by Aristotle's account of the polis are monolithic pyramids in which every argument is already mapped out, every opinion put in its place beneath one dominant Good. There is in fact a great deal of diversity, difference, and conflict presumed in his accounts of even the best city.[83] The view of Aristotelian rhetoric that I have described requires only that our opinions and emotions have enough structure to make them susceptible to deliberative engagement. They can retain a significant degree of indeterminacy and plurality. If we compare, for instance, Aristotle's account of what happiness is in the *Ethics* with his survey of opinions about it in the *Rhetoric*, we find that he left many more options open in the *Rhetoric*.[84] He noticed that people might seek money, power, or honor, and he did not settle which of these was in fact best. To achieve his goals in the *Rhetoric* he only needed to show how each criterion imparted some order onto citizens' opinions, giving them the structure necessary for making rhetoric a technical art. If such variation could exist in small city-states with relatively homogenous populations, it seems fair to suppose that at least as much plurality and indeterminacy exist to some degree in the political opinions of most societies. In this indeterminacy we can, if we are looking, find room for freedom and innovation in the art of rhetoric that Aristotle described. The orator who studies the structure of opinion and emotion can do so with an eye for finding new patterns in common opinion, for capitalizing on old ambiguities, or for introducing wholly new interpretations of old images. Orators practicing the sort of political rhetoric described by Aristotle, studying ways to influence situated judgment, do not find themselves without means of innovation. Aristotle's approach simply requires that they study the structure of people's opinions, characters and emotions as they actually exist, looking for deliberative pathways, and that they begin their arguments inside the framework these pathways provide. When they look for new arguments, they look for possibilities within citizens' opinions rather than outside them. In practicing the politics of persuasion in this way they engage in the difficult work of combining deliberation with democracy.

CHAPTER 5

Conviction and Controversy: Cicero

Considering the great difference between the expert and the un-
schooled in terms of performance, it is remarkable how little they
differ when it comes to making a judgment.

—Cicero, *De oratore* 3.197

When citizens commit themselves to a politics of persuasion,
do they thereby commit themselves to any particular principles? The art of
rhetoric—most familiar to us today as the lawyer's art—is associated more
often with pragmatism than with principle. People who are skilled at making
both sides of a controversy seem persuasive display an argumentative dex-
terity that can seem incompatible with strong moral and political convictions. In fact, many theorists defend rhetoric precisely because it promises
to undermine the dogmatism implicit in principled political opinion. As we
saw in Hobbes, citizens who hold their views with the unwavering certainty
of divine inspiration or conscience are poor candidates for a deliberative
politics. We might be tempted to conclude that the advantage of a rhetorical
politics is that it encourages citizens to abstain from staunch political commitments altogether and to adopt a pragmatic, even skeptical view about
the ultimate truth of any side in a political controversy.

But while it is true that the politics of persuasion requires citizens to remain somewhat open to argument and willing to occasionally change their
minds, it would be a mistake to think that it leaves them free to avoid firm
political commitments altogether. In fact, certain commitments are implicit
in the concept of persuasion itself. If persuasion is understood as the practice of appealing to judgment, then any effort to persuade which under-
mines the audience's capacity for judgment is ultimately self-defeating.

Therefore anyone with an interest in using speech to wield power over a sustained period of time will find that this interest alone suggests certain limits on how rhetorical power should be used. If orators were all-powerful, as rhetoricians such as Gorgias claimed, they could practice their craft without worrying about the backround conditions under which persuasion was possible. But orators depend on their audience's capacity to be influenced by speech, and in this dependence they encounter the bounds of their power and the limits of their freedom. The politics of persuasion requires speakers with at least one firm commitment—they must be committed to protecting the possibility of persuasion.

This requirement might seem modest, even tautological, but its implications are broader than one might think. In this chapter I argue that Cicero's political thought provides an example of how the simple commitment to protecting a role for persuasion in politics can ground a substantial set of firm moral and political convictions. Cicero's convictions were the Stoic principles of natural law and duty that he elaborated in the *Republic* and the *Laws*, and in his long letter to his son, *On Duties*. These convictions offered him a source of guidance distinct from the immediate approval of his listeners and therefore provided a check on the orator's natural tendency to pander. Cicero was keenly aware of his audience's fickle nature. Hailed as a hero of the republic at one moment and exiled the next, he was profoundly frustrated with his listeners, whom he thought had been seduced by Caesar's populism. Forced by personal and political circumstances to reflect on the conditions under which persuasion could succeed, he found himself firmly defending a set of Stoic principles that were unpopular with the audience to whom one might expect him to have pandered.

Since Cicero presented himself as a philosophical skeptic, the grounding of his commitment to these Stoic principles has always presented a puzzle to observers. Was he merely inconsistent? Did he adopt these positions for opportunistic reasons of political expediency or convenience?

The explanation put forth in this chapter is that Cicero's convictions reflected his understanding of what was necessary to protect the influence and sustainability of the practice of persuasion, a practice whose centrality to the republic was closely tied to his own success and indeed to his survival. If orators were going to play a central and sustainable role in politics, Cicero suggested, they would have to consider the background conditions under which their practice proceeded. Implicit in his writings was the view that the practice of persuasion could find a function and flourish only among people with a certain capacity for moral and political judgment and that this judgment would best be exercised in certain institutional contexts and by citizens with a certain moral grounding. It was above all from his position as orator, with all of its precariousness and vulnerability, that Cicero reflected on the demands of rhetorical politics, and it was from that position that he derived his firmest moral and political principles.

The firmness with which Cicero held these convictions points to the way in which his understanding of the politics of persuasion differed from that of rhetoricians who were closer in spirit to the ancient sophists. Like Cicero, the sophists took pride in being able to argue on every side of any controversy, but unlike Cicero they did not regard this exercise as a means of coming closer to truths nor did they reflect, in the works that we know of, on the conditions of its political effectiveness. Instead they tended to boast of their freedom from the constraints that political principle or conviction might impose on their arguments. They overestimated the power of speech and so underestimated the need to protect themselves and their practice of persuasion.

It is important to recognize the differences between Cicero's view of rhetorical politics and the sophistic view because today some of the strongest calls for seeing the virtues of rhetoric have come from theorists who admire the sophists. One influential theorist, Stanley Fish, argues, for example, that adopting a rhetorical view of politics would involve accepting an "antifoundational" understanding of political principle in general. Citing the sophists as models, he draws favorable attention to their flexibility and their reluctance to make firm claims about truth: "To the accusation that rhetoric deals only with the realms of the probable and contingent and forsakes truth, the sophists and their successors respond that truth itself is a contingent affair . . ." Calling this argument "the strongest of the defenses of rhetoric," he suggests that only once we embrace an antifoundationalist view of political principle can the art of rhetoric move "from the disreputable periphery to the necessary center."[1] In *The Trouble with Principle,* Fish explains the antifoundationalist view: "There is nothing that undergirds our beliefs, nothing to which our beliefs might be referred for either confirmation or correction." The language of principle, he argues, can best be understood as "facilitating the efforts of partisan agents to attach an honorific vocabulary to their agendas."[2]

Though Cicero was a skeptic in some sense, he would not have endorsed this sort of antifoundationalism about his moral and political positions. Indeed, when writing on those topics, he insisted on "the particular point that Justice springs from Nature" and argued against Carneades' articulation of the contrary view.[3] Cicero thought that the belief in natural law was necessary both to ground one's commitment to republican institutions and to motivate one's interest in the controversies that took place within them. Since orators aimed to persuade and since people were persuaded when they evaluated their current beliefs against some standard, orators had an interest in opposing any deep and widespread sophistic skepticism about the existence of such standards. Cicero would have viewed antifoundationalism not as a necessary presumption of rhetorical politics but rather as a threat to it. In contrast to the ancient sophists and their recent champions, he not only practiced and praised persuasion but also tried to describe the sort of regime in which persuasive speech could play an important and sustained role. His defense of that regime required firm conviction and displayed how such conviction fit best into—and indeed was necessary to—a politics of persuasion.

This chapter begins by presenting the puzzle that Cicero's endorsement of Stoic natural law poses in light of his skepticism. Cicero's own explanation of his position was that he held his beliefs to be "probable" in the sense that Academic skepticism allowed. But this explanation can be misleading, since one interpretation of "probable beliefs" would leave Cicero advocating something very close to the sophist's position. I therefore devote some space to showing why he should not be understood in this way and how his understanding of probable beliefs differed from the sophistic one. Implicit in the difference between these two understandings of probable beliefs was a deep difference beween Cicero and the sophists about the epistemic value of opinion, with Cicero asserting a link between opinion and knowledge that the sophists would not have conceded. Cicero's position led him, I suggest, to a political approach that respected the partial truths buried in the partisan political opinions on each side of a controversy. Interestingly, this view of partisan opinion points toward a view of representation very different from the one we saw in Hobbes. In Cicero's view, good representation was exemplified not by impartial judges but by the practice of lawyers or advocates who identified closely with the one-sided positions of their clients.

Cicero's position on the link between opinion and knowledge also made possible his famous effort to end the old antagonism between philosophy and rhetoric by uniting them in the figure of the ideal orator. As we will see, however, this project was complicated by the fact that orators in Rome faced an audience deeply suspicious of philosophy; Romans regarded philosophy as an effeminate Greek luxury unsuited for the manly realm of politics. The care with which Cicero portrayed the orators in his dialogue *De oratore* responding to this suspicion reveals his appreciation for the vulnerability of their position in the republic. From firsthand experience Cicero knew that orators were deeply dependant on the changeable will of their audiences. This vulnerability pointed, in turn, to orators' interest in protecting the institutional settings where audiences best responded to oratory—the forum and the senate. But because such institutions could not guarantee that citizens would not be lured to follow popular demagogues, Cicero was also concerned with instilling in his listeners a certain moral compass, an ability to hold their own convictions steady enough to resist demagogues and ground responsible judgment. It was in a certain adaptation of Stoic principles of natural law that Cicero found not only the basis for his defense of the senate but also the source of such steady moral convictions.

The Convictions of a Skeptic

By suggesting a link between Cicero's views on rhetoric and his commitment to Stoic principles, I mean to introduce a new solution to an old puzzle in his philosophy. Cicero considered himself a philosophical skeptic and called into doubt the veracity of his perceptions and opinions, even dwelling on optical illusions of the sort that Hobbes would emphasize. But Cicero also argued that political regimes and ethical duties should be based on firm principles of natural law, which he showed no signs of doubting. These two aspects of his thought were drawn from two different schools of Hellenistic philosophy; the skepticism came from the New Academy and the conviction from the Stoics. Usually the two schools were seen as competitors. The Stoics claimed to be able to distinguish true perceptions from false ones, while the Academic skeptics claimed that no mark of truth could be discerned. The Stoics claimed access to a natural ordering of things, while the skeptics denied such knowledge to humans. Cicero offered one of the most thorough defenses of Academic skepticism in ancient literature, and he clearly viewed that philosophy as the source of his intellectual independence.[4] Thus his readers are justified in asking how he could have endorsed the principles of Stoic natural law that he made central to his moral and political writings. Were his convictions consistent with his skepticism?

If we are tempted to explain Cicero's convictions by relating them to his practical orientation in the world of action, as many readers have been, the question about the consistency of his position appears to be a particular version of the dilemma that confronted all ancient skeptics: how could they go about their day-to-day lives in the world of action without believing in the truth of at least some of their beliefs?[5] How, for example, could they avoid walking off a cliff if they did not believe that the cliff they saw was in fact present and dangerous? The founder of the later school of skepticism, Pyrrho, is said to always have been surrounded by disciples guiding him away from dangers in his path.[6] Whether apocryphal or not, the story illustrates a dilemma for skeptics both Academic and Pyrrhonist: could they survive in the real world without being escorted by less-skeptical friends? The dilemma only intensified if skeptics wanted to do more in the world of action than merely stay alive. For while the skeptic prided himself on the indefinite openness of his inquiries, the man of action did not so much inquire as deliberate, the distinction being that deliberation leads to decision and so must end.

Cicero found himself caught in different versions of this dilemma throughout his career as an orator. As he admitted in his own writings, his critics did not shy away from pointing out his apparent inconsistency. Consider the situation he faced at the greatest moment of his consulship, when he discovered the conspiracy of Catiline. Having learned of the plot earlier than other senators, he tried to warn them. Far from being skeptical, he opened himself to ridicule by insisting with all the force of his rhetoric that he knew of Catiline's guilt.[7] His words, however, fell on deaf ears, and he was dismissed as a paranoid.[8] In fact it was his opponents in the senate who were skeptical. In the First Catilinarian speech, Cicero claimed that those senators who had refused to heed his earlier warnings had "built up Catiline's hopes with their mildness, strengthened his plot as it grew by their skepticism."[9]

Cicero called attention to the larger significance of this incident in *Academica*, his dialogue defending skepticism. There he raised the crucial question about his own action: how could an avowed skeptic have been so certain of Catiline's guilt?[10] Two characters in the dialogue, Lucullus and then Catulus, confront him with this question, the latter teasing him by saying that a tribune might "cross-examine you in a public assembly as to your consistency in both denying the possibility of finding anything certain and asserting that you had discovered some certainty."[11] Cicero responds in that dialogue with nothing more satisfying than a claim of modesty. He was not wise enough, he replies, to have refrained from holding an opinion as a truly wise man would have. But elsewhere Cicero always insisted that his action against Catiline had been the greatest of his career. With this weak reply to his accusers in the dialogue he declined to answer the question of whether a more thoroughly skeptical person could have been as effective in politics when action was required.

Cicero's certainty about Catiline might be seen as exposing a tension between theory and practice. But that tension closely paralleled one within his theory itself—the tension between his Academic skepticism and the Stoic principles on which he based his politics. In both the *Republic* and the *Laws* he relied heavily on Stoic arguments, especially "the particular point that Justice springs from Nature." He followed the Stoics by beginning with "a certain social spirit which nature has implanted in man." He characterized his argument as a response to the skeptic Carneades, who had put forth the idea that "everything is just which is found in the customs or laws of nations." Against Carneades, Cicero claimed that there was a "supreme Law which had its origins before any written law existed or any State had been established" and that this was "a standard by which the things we are seeking may be tested." His strategy was "to seek the root of Justice in Nature," and he deemed the finding of that root to be the most important product of philosophizing: "out of all the material of the philosopher's discussions, surely there comes nothing more valuable than the full realization that we are born for Justice, and that right is based, not upon men's opinions, but upon Nature." He went on to say that he expected to find adherents to his approach in all the major Hellenistic schools except for the Epicureans and the New Academy, echoing his claim that all the others shared essentially Stoic beginnings because they all admitted the natural impulse toward justice. Finally, he based his account of natural law on a rationalistic theology that was Stoic in origin.[12] In the *Laws* he explicitly acknowledged that his fellow skeptics would not appreciate his debt to the Stoics, and he begged for their indulgence:

> And let us implore the Academy—the new one, formed by Arcesilaus and Carneades—to be silent, since it contributes nothing but confusion to all these problems; for if it should attack what we think we have constructed and arranged so beautifully, it would play too great havoc with it.[13]

Here Cicero again sidestepped the philosophical issue of what allowed him as a skeptic to appropriate the Stoic view, declining to offer a theoretical justification for his departure from skepticism.

A number of explanations for Cicero's position have been offered by commentators. Some have suggested that he changed his mind and gave up his skeptical outlook during certain times in his life.[14] But this interpretation cannot explain why his endorsement of Stoicism coincided so neatly with his various moral and political writings. We cannot ignore the fact that Cicero never wrote dogmatically about perception and always wrote firmly about politics. The Stoicism coincided with a topic rather than with a stage in his career and thus should be explained by consideration of that topic.

Other readers view the Stoic elements of Cicero's thought as attempts to preserve not the preconditions of effective oratory but instead other conditions. C. Wirszubski suggests that the Stoic principles were designed to preserve the public conditions necessary to dignified privacy *(cum dignitate otium)*.[15] Malcolm Schofield suggests that the references to Stoic natural right in Cicero's thought aimed to preserve political liberty and rights *(res publica)*.[16] Both insights are related to the argument presented here, insofar as liberty and privacy may both be seen as bulwarks protecting a sphere in which individuals can judge opinions for themselves and thus preserve the independence of mind necessary to a healthy politics of persuasion.

Finally, many readers have proposed that Cicero simply abandoned his professed Academic philosophy for the sake of political expediency.[17] The least sympathetic version of this view asserts that Cicero endorsed Stoic ideas, not out of any reflective political insight, but instead because those ideas helped him defend the privileged status of his class. The influential historian M. I. Finley, for instance, accuses Cicero of opportunism. In Cicero's writings on politics,

> there is only rhetoric, in which I include the Stoic notions of "natural law" and "natural reason" that have loomed so large in western writing from the Church Fathers to our own day. Whatever genuinely philosophical meaning those terms may have had for the Stoics themselves, Cicero turned them into mere rhetoric, terms of "approval for whatever idea (one) wanted to recommend at any particular time," in his case the Roman constitution of the good old days.[18]

Finley writes this in a book on ideology in ancient politics, and he suggests that Cicero's political convictions should be dismissed as ideological preferences. In Cicero's hands, he argues, Stoicism was the language of the landed interests, a rhetorical tool used to justify the rule of oligarchs.

There is no denying that Cicero's political commitments, though not as conservative as those of Cato and his allies, did tend to fall in with the Optimates and against the Populares. But it is also true that Cicero displayed in his own actions moments of undeniable independence, such as his refusal to join Crassus, Caesar, and Pompey in the alliance that would come to be known as the First Triumvirate. After studying Cicero's letters to his friend Atticus and even the poetry that Cicero wrote at the time, Elizabeth Rawson has concluded "that it was from shame and principle alone that he stood out of the alliance." She has also noted that Cicero was reading at this time works of Greek philosophy and "perhaps already beginning to think a little more deeply about the subject."[19] So while it is true that Cicero often took up positions close to that of the oligarchs, it is also true that he seems sometimes to have acted on principle informed by reflection. While he certainly had the instincts of a politician, I suggest that we allow the possibility of his convictions being at least in part the product of reflection rather than solely a manifestation of class interest.

In any case, the class with which Cicero would have consciously identified himself was not so much the class of the oligarchs or "the urban patriciate" as that of the well-spoken, the orators.[20] As an orator who feared that Caesarism endangered the practice of rhetoric, Cicero had particular reason to reflect on the interests and needs of the practice in general. His interests were tied to those of oratory itself. As a "new man" without a strong family history in Roman politics, Cicero had won and maintained his status in the republic primarily through his success at the bar. As he found the arenas of public speaking marginalized by Caesar, he was led to reflect on the conditions under which orators such as himself could maintain their influence. If orators as a class had an interest, it lay in protecting these conditions. Orators who recognized that interest were less free in their politics than their willingness to argue both sides might suggest; they were tied more closely to certain forms of government and to the parties within government most devoted to those forms. Cicero's Stoic defense of republican institutions arose out of his reflections on the interests of orators and oratory.[21]

Does this interpretation make his Stoicism more consistent with his skepticism? If Cicero were primarily interested in the philosophical aspect of the Academy, perhaps it would not. But his fundamental interest in the Academy itself seems to have arisen from the way in which it taught him to practice the orator's art of arguing both sides of any question, identifying the most probable claims on each side of a controversial issue, and elaborating on them. His identity as an Academic allowed him broad freedom to try different positions in philosophical and political debates and to draw from each sect or party whatever premises seemed most suitable for the argument at hand.[22] Once we grant that his primary commitment was to the practice of oratory, rather than to any philosophical school, the tension within his position seems to recede in significance. He took from both the Stoics and the Academics what he thought would best help him protect the practice of persuasion.

We should notice that while this interpretation shows Cicero choosing arguments for their utility in some sense, it does not reduce him to an opportunist. It does not assert that he merely appropriated whichever principles seemed most likely to help him win the case he was pleading at the moment. While this interpretation gives priority to his activity as an orator, it does not put his convictions in the service of any particular piece of oratory so much as in the service of the practice of oratory itself. In this way the interpretation distinguishes between his eclectic appropriation of political principles and the sort that a more sophistic view of rhetoric would defend. The distinction between Cicero's view and that of the sophists can be seen more clearly if we examine his most philosophical effort to defend his turn to Stoic principles—his claim that as a skeptic he was free to adopt whichever beliefs seemed most probable.

Two Kinds of Probable Beliefs

In *On Duties* Cicero raised the accusation that his critics had brought against his consistency: "Although our school [the New Academy] maintains that nothing can be known for certain, yet, they [his critics] urge, I make a habit of presenting my opinions on all sorts of subjects and at this very moment am trying to formulate rules of duty." Cicero responded that those critics misunderstood his skepticism, which was best seen as a mental habit of avoiding the "presumption of dogmatism" and "the recklessness of assertion" but which did not hinder him from "accepting what seems to be probable, while rejecting what seems to be improbable." He explained,

> We Academicians are not men whose minds wander in uncertainty and never know what sort of principles to adopt. For what sort of mental habit, or rather what sort of life would that be which should dispense with all rules for reasoning or even for living? Not so with us; but, as other schools maintain that some things are certain, others uncertain, we, differing with them, say that some things are probable, others improbable.

Later in *On Duties* and also in the *Tusculan Disputations*, Cicero returned to the notion of probable beliefs when justifying apparent departures from skepticism.[23]

In characterizing his convictions as "probable," Cicero was adopting a strategy that Academic skeptics had developed long before in response to the questions about how they could live without assenting to any certain beliefs. The idea was simply that one could orient one's actions according to perceptions, judgments, and opinions without thereby assenting to their truth. A wise man could live without fear of walking off a cliff and without need of a circle of disciples to protect him from obstacles by regarding his perceptions of these dangers as probable enough to warrant his attention. He did not think his perceptions were true, but he used them as a provisional basis for action.[24] This strategy did not fully resolve the issue, of course, for questions remained about the status of the probable beliefs. On what basis did skeptics give credence to certain *probabilia* and not others? Did the investigation of the grounds of these provisional beliefs not involve skeptics in just the difficulties that had led them to withdraw from the pursuit of truth?[25]

One answer to these questions was to claim that skeptics could find sufficient grounds for argument and action by drawing *probabilia* from the everyday beliefs of those around them. By allowing common opinion to judge for them, skeptics could maintain their calm and remain withdrawn from controversies about whether the beliefs they lived by were in any deep sense true. The strategy of drawing probable beliefs from common opinion was closely related to the teachings of certain rhetoricians about how best to persuade an audience. The task of convincing, *probare*, was one of the three traditional functions of oratory.[26] Orators therefore called *probabile* whatever views an audience would find persuasive. Although we might think that orators tried to change their audiences' minds, they had often been taught that the best way to "persuade" people was to make the case seem to rest on beliefs they already held.[27] Therefore when rhetoricians spoke of *probabilia*, they usually were referring to common opinions already present in the minds of their listeners. The art of rhetoric consisted, they argued, in studying these common views. One can find this view of rhetoric described as the usual one in Plato's *Phaedrus*, where the title character and Socrates discuss the teaching of sophists such as Tisias:

Socrates: For all in all, they say . . . that he who is going to be competently rhetorical has no need to have a share of truth about just or good deeds,

or about human beings who are such by nature or by rearing. For altogether, no one has any care for truth about these things in law courts, but
for what is persuasive; and this is the probable . . . [I]n all the ways one
speaks, one must pursue the probable, bidding many a farewell to the
true . . . Well then, let Tisias tell us this too: whether he says the probable
is anything else than what conforms to the opinion of the multitude.
Phaedrus: Indeed, what else?[28]

The sophists' understanding of the "probable" referred to here—beliefs
drawn from conventional opinion, selected for their persuasiveness rather
than for their truth—was one familiar to rhetoricians of Cicero's day as well.
In *De oratore,* a dialogue full of allusions to the *Phaedrus,* Cicero had the
character Antonius put forward on the first day of conversation a view of
rhetoric in which the orator's expertise lies in his familiarity with public
opinion and does not require knowledge of philosophy. Objecting to the
character Crassus's broad definition of the ideal orator as someone with true
expertise in philosophy and law, Antonius argues for a more modest conception of the orator. "I rather regard him as someone who, in cases such as
commonly arise in the forum, is able to employ language pleasant to the
ear, and thoughts suited to persuade," he argues, continuing,

We need someone of sharp intellect, with a resourcefulness that comes
from talent and experience, who with keen scent can track down the
thoughts, the feelings, the opinions, and the hopes of his fellow citizens
and of those people whom he wants to persuade with his oratory. He must
have his finger on the pulse of every class, every age group, every social
rank, and get a taste of the feelings and thoughts of those before whom he
is now, or in the future, going to plead some issue. As to the writings of the
philosophers, let him reserve those for times of rest and relaxation such as
we are now enjoying at this Tusculan villa.[29]

Antonius immediately concludes from this that orators should be wary of
introducing into their public arguments philosophical points that are not
easily accepted by the crowd. His first example is Plato's *Republic,* which is
"completely at odds with everyday life," and among his next examples are
tenets from the Stoics, such as the idea that a virtuous man can never be
harmed by being unjustly convicted in a court, or that most men are slaves
to their bodily desires.

It is significant that Antonius points to Stoic ideas as the ones least suited
for public display. The fact that Stoic principles do not fit easily into conven-

tional opinion is emphasized again later in the dialogue, where Crassus, the character who advocates the union of philosophy and rhetoric, repeatedly warns orators not to begin from Stoic principles precisely because they stray so far from what most people would find acceptable:

> [S]omething in [the Stoics'] views is quite at odds with the orator that we are trying to equip . . . It would be rather absurd to entrust a public meeting, a Senate meeting, or any gathering of people to someone who thinks that none of those present is sane, none a citizen, none a free man . . . [G]ood and bad do not mean to Stoics what they mean to the rest of the citizens, or rather, to the rest of the nations on earth, and they also have different conceptions of honor and disgrace, and of reward and punishment. Whether these are true or not is irrelevant for our present purpose, but if we follow their ideas, we would never be able to make anything understood through speech.[30]

Given these warnings, when Cicero defended his Stoic principles as beliefs that seemed to him most "probable," he could not have been thinking of *probabilia* in the way that the sophistic view of rhetoric suggests. He could not have been viewing his Stoic convictions as beliefs drawn from common opinion and selected for their persuasiveness. In fact, when Cicero invoked Stoic ideas, he was acting against the usual rhetorical advice and against the sophistical strain of skepticism. He was grounding his notion of probability in his best estimate of the truth rather than in conventional opinion. In spite of labeling them "probable," he intended his Stoic ideas to be firm commitments and convictions, in that they were meant to stand above political opinion as a guide for it. In *De finibus* Cicero suggested that he was searching for doctrines to "amend our lives, purposes and wills."[31] In *Academica,* in one of his more extended treatments of probability, Cicero used the word *probabilia* almost interchangeably with a phrase for "resembling the truth," *similia veri.* This language offers no trace of skepticism; to the contrary, it suggests Cicero's deep affinity for Plato.[32] At the very least, it seems fair to say that Cicero's view of probability did not give up on the possibility of improving his knowledge. He thought that he might come nearer to the truth. "The sole object of our discussions," he wrote in *Academica,* "is by arguing on both sides to draw out and give shape to some result that may be either true or the nearest possible approximation to the truth [*aut verum sit aut ad id quam proxime accedat*]."[33]

Understood as concessions to conventional opinion, probable beliefs could enable a skeptic to act without becoming embroiled in the search for truth and an orator to speak as his audience wished. If Cicero had viewed Stoic principles in this way, we might dismiss his convictions as opportunistic concessions to the demands of his rhetorical situation. But Cicero did not regard his Stoic convictions as probable beliefs in this way. As he used it, the notion of probable beliefs did more to moderate skepticism than to accommodate to it and more to distance him from his audience than to please it. That he granted to these results of his investigations only the status of probability did not suggest an antifoundational view about the grounding of his opinions. In fact, he justified arguing both sides of any question not with the sophistic insight that there is no standard by which to judge better and worse opinions, but with the almost opposite view that one could only make political judgments by looking for what truth there was on each side of the arguments about each issue. The opinions or convictions that he justified as most probable, including the tenets of Stoic natural law that he endorsed so firmly, were products of this reflection rather than concessions to popular belief. Though they might have arisen from the realm of opinion, they were meant in the end to stand above opinion as a refinement of it and as a guide to it.

Controversy and Advocacy

The difference between the sophistic understanding of probable beliefs and Cicero's own view of them reveals a deep disagreement about the epistemic value of opinion and therefore about the value of political controversy. Cicero's view tied opinion to knowledge, linked rhetoric to philosophy, and suggested that the successful practice of political controversy required some study of the more general truths implicit in ordinary opinion. This view can be contrasted to the one that he had Antonius put forth early in *De oratore:*

> [T]he whole activity of the orator is based not on knowledge but on opinions. We speak before audiences that are ignorant and we also say things about which we are ignorant ourselves. Accordingly, on the same issue they have now one view and judgment, then another, while we ourselves often plead opposite cases. I mean the latter not only in the sense that Crassus sometimes argues against me or I against him—and in that case, either of us must necessarily be saying something that is not true—but also in the sense that, on the same issue, each of us supports now one opinion, then another—whereas

not more than one can be true. Knowing, then, that this is a subject that relies on falsehood, that seldom reaches the level of real knowledge, that is out
to take advantage of people's opinions and often their delusions, I shall speak
about it—if you think you have a reason for listening.[34]

One way to see how thoroughly Cicero's dialogue as a whole ultimately rejected this view of rhetoric is to notice that Cotta, one of the orators who
begin the dialogue by asking for advice about how to become powerful
speakers, declares himself at the end convinced that he needs to study philosophy.[35] Somehow he has been persuaded that the "real knowledge" dismissed by Antonius is necessary for eloquence.

Readers sometimes misunderstand Cicero's campaign to combine eloquence and philosophy as an attempt to mitigate the amoralism of rhetorical technique. They assume that the philosophy was meant to provide the
orator with a set of firm ethical beliefs and so to guide him in using his skills
only for moral ends.[36] Though it is true that Cicero seemed to believe his
ideal orators would not use their skills in malicious ways, there is little evidence that he regarded their training in philosophy as an effort to supply
them with certain ethical views. When Crassus objects to traditional rhetorical training because it leaves out philosophy, he does not base his complaint on the danger that orators might act unjustly. Instead he emphasizes
different ways in which an unphilosophic orator will fail to be persuasive.
The danger is not that he will use his powers of persuasion for the wrong
purposes, but simply that he may not have much power to persuade at all.[37]

Indeed, Cicero maintained that one feature of many of the rhetorical
handbooks of his time that prevented orators from realizing their full potential was the lack of instruction on how to argue about general philosophic theses. Conventional handbooks made a division between two types
of issues: those that arose from particular occasions and disputes, such as
the question of whether to return Carthaginian prisoners of war at a particular moment, and those that were more general in nature, such as the
proper position about returning prisoners of war in general. The handbooks
of rhetoric confined themselves to the first type of question *(hypotheses)* and
ceded the second type *(theses)* to philosophers, Cicero complained: "We [or-
ators] have been ousted from our estate and are left with a paltry piece of
land (and even that contested), and though we are defenders of others, we
have not managed to preserve and protect what is our own."[38] Whereas the
practice of arguing both sides of all questions had once been the province of

orators as well as philosophers, Cicero wrote, orators had recently allowed themselves to be confined to the narrower questions, to the role of menial laborers in the courts, and had thus given up their rightful claim to political leadership on the broadest questions of statesmanship.[39] Cicero suggested that the power of orators in the state, their ability to work for themselves rather than others, to lead rather than follow, depended on their study of general or philosophic questions. In *De oratore,* Crassus asserts that even when interlocutors simply want advice about technique or style, they will need philosophic knowledge.[40] Crassus's chief contention is that general expertise in one's subject is crucial not simply to using oratorical power well but to having it in the first place.

Antonius's view was that persuasion requires only a familiarity with public opinion. Against this view Crassus sometimes suggests the simple point that audiences would not trust or be impressed by speakers who did not demonstrate mastery of their subjects. Elsewhere he makes the argument that orators could not manipulate emotions unless they understood psychology in some depth. He also tells several amusing stories of orators who lost important cases in the courts because they were ignorant about fine points of the law.[41] These considerations, however, do not reach the most fundamental assumption of Cicero's view and do not explain why orators might need a general or philosophic education simply to be persuasive.

For more on this point we might turn again to Plato's *Phaedrus.* Cicero's dialogue was an explicit attempt to continue the conversation of that work. The heart of the conversation about oratory begins in answer to this suggestion: "Say, Crassus, why don't we follow the example of Socrates as he appears in Plato's *Phaedrus?*"[42] In the *Phaedrus,* as in *De oratore,* we find a criticism of traditional handbooks of rhetoric that focus only on technique, and we also find an argument that orators will not be persuasive without philosophic knowledge. Socrates argues that persuasion works through manipulating "likenesses." Even if an orator aims to deceive people, Socrates points out, he will need to understand the truth about what is similar to what, for deception works by redescribing one thing as something else that is similar to it: "He who is going to deceive another, and not be deceived himself, must therefore precisely distinguish the likeness and unlikeness of beings."[43]

If we object that an orator need know only what people will think of as similar, that he need know only common opinion or the sophistic rhetorician's sort of *probabilia,* Socrates' answer seems to be the fundamental and absolutely crucial belief that "in fact this probability happens to spring up in the many through likeness with the truth."[44] He thus asserts that common opinion contains within it implicit reference to truths, or partial truths. Studying philosophy helped an orator to understand the structure of these truths and the relations between them. That in turn helped the orator to grasp the structure of common opinion and to understand where it might be led and how. The philosophic faculty of judgment through which one could distinguish "the likeness and unlikeness of beings" was, in the Platonic view, closely related to the faculty of judgment by which a successful orator discerned the similarities and differences necessary to build persuasive arguments.

Cicero did not make the argument about likenesses explicitly; he was not enthusiastic about Plato's doctrine of the forms and so would not have spoken of distinguishing "the likeness and unlikeness of beings." However, we can find something like this argument in the case that he made against the traditional handbooks' distinction between general categories *(theses)* and particular disputes *(hypotheses)*. Calling the restriction of orators to the latter "the greatest mistake of the teachers to whom we send our children," Cicero claimed that "all disputes can be related to one about the essential nature of a general category" and that "there is no case in which the issue to be decided is examined in terms of the actual persons of the litigants, and not as a question on a general level, about the categories as such."[45]

The example Cicero gave here is revealing: it is the case of Opimius, the consul who had put Graccus to death. Opimius had been successfully defended in court with the argument that he had been authorized by the senate to do anything necessary to save the republic. Cicero contended that the question at issue in that case was really the general philosophical one about whether someone who acted as Opimius had—killing a citizen against the letter of the law but under broad senatorial authority when the state was in mortal danger—should be punished. Of course, if the action is described at that level of generality, it perfectly describes Cicero's own actions against the Catilinian conspirators, for which he was eventually forced into exile. It is perhaps no accident that taking the more general or philosophic point of view, seeing the likenesses between these cases as described in the abstract, would make one more apt to liken Cicero to Opimius and therefore more likely to acquit Cicero.

Leaving aside that detail, though, the fundamental point concerns Cicero's campaign to end the long history of division between oratory and philosophy, a history that Cicero retold in the dialogue and of which the technical division of labor between *theses* and *hypotheses* was only one product.[46] The entire thrust of the dialogue *De oratore*, its dramatic structure as well as its arguments, aimed to move the reader, like the young interlocutor Cotta, toward accepting the vision of the ideal orator as one who could combine eloquence and wisdom. The dialogue thus sought to end the division between the tongue and the brain that the dispute between Socrates and the sophists had introduced. But the union of rhetoric and philosophy could only be brought about if expertise in public opinion was somehow related to philosophic knowledge.

Cicero's project thus seems to depend upon the idea that opinions contain the seeds of knowledge and therefore that having philosophic knowledge about subjects may help one to grasp the structure of ordinary opinion about them, and vice versa. This idea was in fact more familiar in ancient thought than it is in modern philosophy, and it helps to explain why the ancients were more open to the possibilities of rhetoric. One can see a similar presumption, for instance, in Aristotle's contention in the *Rhetoric* that if true and false positions were argued with equal skill, the true one would seem more persuasive.[47] Today we may not find this point convincing, perhaps because we are steeped in the mistrust of ordinary opinion that characterizes modern thought. And Cicero never laid out the position with any clarity, though that may be because he did not confront the modern alternative. Nevertheless, it seems difficult to make sense of his view that studying philosophy makes one more persuasive without attributing to him the view that ordinary opinion contains implicit philosophic knowledge and that the best way to make an argument persuasive is to articulate the element of truth in it.

The link between opinion and truth in turn suggests a view of political controversy particularly well suited to the ancient ideal of mixed government that Cicero endorsed in the *Republic*. In mixed government, the competing claims of the various parts of the city were each acknowledged and taken into account. Cicero's spokesman in the *Republic*, Scipio, resists the entreaties of his interlocutors to choose one form of government as best from among the standard varieties—kingship, aristocracy, or democracy. Instead, he gives the arguments for each form, admitting when pressed that kingship may be best if one has to choose but insisting that in practice a mixture of the forms is to be preferred.[48] His approach echoes Aristotle's treatment of partisan claims in the *Politics*. Aristotle assumed that each party's claim was based in a partial truth about justice and that the parties could be balanced against one another by doing justice to the element of truth in each claim. Oligarchs and aristocrats were correct in asserting that they contributed more to the city with their wealth and virtue and so deserved a greater say in its laws, but democrats were correct too in saying that all citizens deserved to take part in ruling. Mixed government, in Aristotle's view, aimed to do justice to both claims by incorporating practices such as lot and election.[49] Cicero's position suggested that orators who understood how to be persuasive would participate in this mixing. Rather than simply ceding to majority opinion, Ciceronian orators would search for the best arguments on a particular side of a controversy. In so doing, they would find themselves articulating the partial truth present in each of the various partisan claims they presented.

This understanding of the orator's role in politics suggests in turn a view of political representation at odds with some elements of our contemporary intuitions about representation. It may seem strange to speak of representation in the ancient world; Rousseau, the Federalists, Benjamin Constant, and others argued that representation was a medieval or modern innovation unknown to classical thinkers. But the ancient Roman republic was, unlike the Greek city-states, a mass democracy of a sort in which a great deal of political business was taken care of by officials selected to represent the citizens in some sense. Whereas Athenians spoke on their own behalf when accused in court, for instance, Romans were represented by lawyers or advocates such as Cicero. Insofar as there was an understanding of "representation" implicit in Roman advocacy, however, it was different from modern notions of political representation, and for our purposes it is especially important to see how it differed from the sort of representation that Hobbes introduced. In *Leviathan* the theoretical vocabulary of representation was introduced in a chapter devoted to explaining the metaphor of "personation," according to which citizens could agree to be personated by the sovereign and thus take his judgments and actions as their own. We have already seen in chapter 2 that Hobbes's language of personation came from the theater, where a "persona" was a mask worn by actors on the stage. But as Hobbes admits, the author who had appropriated this language into the realm of political representation was Cicero, and the passage that Hobbes quoted when explaining the notion of personation was in fact from *De oratore*. In describing the orator's activity of invention, the process by which he discovers which arguments to use in any particular case, Cicero had the character Antonius describe how he first speaks with his client—he makes his client respond to the opponent's case. Then once the client leaves, Antonius remarks, "I, just by myself, play three roles [*personas*] with complete calmness: my own, that of my adversary, and that of a juror."[50]

Hobbes quoted this passage in *Leviathan* and used the notion of role-playing it articulated to construct a sovereign independent from all partisan claims, asking citizens of all factions to have their personas played by one person or assembly. But Cicero envisioned the role-playing quite differently. Role-playing helped the orator to imagine the point of view of each party to the dispute. In doing so, the orator sought not to transcend those points of view so much as to sharpen his sense of the best arguments for his own side. It is true that in playing the role of juror as well as the disputing parties, the orator cultivated a degree of detachment from his client's claims, but the ultimate purpose of even that detachment was to judge which arguments would be most likely to persuade jurors of his own client's view of the case. Antonius reveals how deeply he identifies with his clients later in the dialogue, when discussing the need for an orator to himself feel the emotions that he wants the jury to feel. It is easy to become agitated on behalf of one's client, Antonius argues, because when one enters into the practice of pleading his case, seeing it from his perspective and voicing his position, one identifies with that position and feels the corresponding emotions. Indeed, Antonius remarks that "we cannot, even if we are defending total strangers, keep on regarding them as strangers."[51] He then turns immediately to the example of actors and poets, who cannot step into or write their roles without adopting the point of view of the people they impersonate. Whereas Hobbes would emphasize the distinction between actor and role, Cicero's Antonius says that he has always been struck by how the actor's own eyes "seem to blaze forth from his mask," demonstrating that the passion was the actor's own.[52]

The understanding of representation at work in Cicero's thought was thus one in which the representer closely sympathized with his client, adopting his partial point of view. It was a notion of representation close to our notion of advocacy, a lawyer's duty to represent his client. In contrast to Hobbes's appropriation of his example, Cicero's lawyerly view of advocacy or representation was one that fit into a politics of controversy and persuasion rather than trying to transcend it. The politics of controversy, in turn, was implicitly justified by the view that the practice of arguing both sides of a question helped to reveal the most probable arguments, those that most closely approximated the truth. The partisan arguments found in the forum and in the senate, driven as they were by advocates trying to advance partisan or partial causes, nevertheless contributed to a process of deliberation. Of course, we should not be naïve about this. Political argument is not philosophic dialogue, and Cicero was always clear about the distinction between these two activities.[53] The point is simply that he did not subscribe to the stark separation between opinion and knowledge that had divided the sophists from Socrates and that later thinkers, including Hobbes, would invoke in their condemnations of rhetoric. Cicero's view of rhetoric required orators to concede their dependence on philosophical knowledge. We shall now see that this dependence was something that orators in Rome were reluctant to admit. Their reluctance arose from their precarious political position in the city.

The Vulnerability of Oratory

If orators who studied philosophy were more persuasive than others, they also faced greater practical difficulties in Rome. For though they had to study to be powerful, they also had to avoid trespassing against the Roman prejudice against studying. All the handbooks of rhetoric agreed that orators could be effective only if they remained within the popularly accepted norms of behavior and language.[54] In Roman society, ordinary opinion tended toward a deep distrust of philosophers, especially Greeks. In 161 B.C. the senate had excluded all philosophers and teachers of rhetoric from the city.[55] Though the legal restrictions had eased by Cicero's time, the prejudices remained. An orator who exuded philosophical pretensions would immediately distance himself from his audience. In *De finibus* Cicero mentioned that Cato "braved the idle censure of the mob by reading in the senate-house itself, while waiting for the senate to assemble."[56] To avoid Cato's mistake and yet still reap the benefits of reading, orators would have to keep their studies to themselves.

One of the wonderful things about *De oratore* is the way in which it reveals this lesson through the action of the dialogue. As we have seen, the two principal speakers do not at first agree that successful oratory requires study of philosophy. In fact, on the first day of the fictional conversation much of Antonius's speech bows to and plays upon the popular point of view. He portrays philosophers as both useless and ridiculous, imitating Cicero's famous mockery of Cato in *Pro Murena*. He claims that the busy politicians of the forum have no time to study as widely as Crassus urges and furthermore that they have no need. Antonius mocks theoretical quibbles as irrelevant to rhetorical practice.

Even Crassus rejects the idea that he might enjoy Greek-style theorizing for its own sake. Though Crassus argues that orators need theoretical knowledge, he at first displays little patience with the philosophizing Greeks' approach. When Sulpicius asks Crassus whether there is an art of speaking, Crassus reacts in anger and objects that he is not a Greek, like Gorgias, who is willing to answer any question as if performing.[57] The question that Sulpicius asks is the one raised in Plato's *Gorgias,* and thus it exemplifies the Greek philosophical approach to rhetoric.[58] In rejecting the question, Crassus displays not only contempt for the showman Gorgias but also impatience with the Greek weakness for theory. Crassus has already dismissed philosophers who study "in their secluded corners, just to pass their leisure time."[59] His impatience with purely theoretical questions emerges again later, when he says explicitly that speaking about speaking is foolish, since speaking is always foolish except when necessary.[60] There are numerous other examples of the interlocutors indulging the Roman prejudice against theory. For example, Catulus tells of the time that Hannibal, the eminently successful military leader, was lectured on the art of generalship by the Greek philosopher Phormio, who had never seen battle. According to Catulus, Hannibal said that "he had often seen many raving old men, but none who raved more madly than Phormio."[61]

As we read further in the dialogue, however, we learn that much of what Antonius says against theory in the first book, on the first day of the fictional conversation, is not sincere. At the close of the first day's conversation, Crassus says that he suspects Antonius of speaking insincerely, and on the second day Antonius admits that much of what he said on the previous day did not reflect his true beliefs. It turns out that Antonius, who had ridiculed the Greek philosophers so adamantly the day before, in fact reads their works himself when he is at leisure in his country house. Thus he knows Greek and is far more learned than he has admitted earlier. He now insists that most teachers of rhetoric make the mistake of ignoring general and abstract considerations because they do not see that "all disputes can be related to one about the essential nature of a general category." Catulus says in surprise that he had never suspected Antonius of having such theoretical knowledge.[62]

Antonius explains that he has deliberately hidden his knowledge of Greek, the art that went into his oratory, and his philosophic learning; he reveals them on this day only because of a change in audience. When Catulus asks why Antonius declares war on philosophy, Antonius replies, crucially, with a rhetorical consideration: "I do think that a reputation for such pursuits, or any trace of the use of technical knowledge, works against the orator with those who are to judge his cases." It turns out that Crassus also obscures his philosophic expertise, and for a similar rhetorical reason. Whereas Antonius wants to seem unlearned, Crassus wants to seem as though he holds learning in contempt, as though he always admired the practical Romans over the theoretical Greeks; neither Crassus nor Antonius will risk seeming philosophic, for that would undermine their credibility in the forum. The second book of the dialogue therefore confirms a suspicion that had arisen in the first—that Cicero's combination of rhetoric and philosophy raises not one but two questions: The first is whether an orator can be successful without philosophy. Though that question is answered affirmatively by Antonius on the first day, neither he nor Crassus affirms the independence of rhetoric in the second book, during the sincere conversation. By the second day, the emphasis has moved to a different question: to what extent should philosophy be admitted to the forum? The primary problem for the orators is not whether they rely on theoretical inquiry but whether they can admit their dependence on it. The best orators, Cicero suggests in *De oratore*, must be knowledgeable enough to realize that they should hide their knowledge.[63]

The requirement to hide their knowledge gave rise to a class division between orators and their audiences. But such a division might have been necessary even if the Romans had not harbored a special distaste for theoreticians. The divide was necessary not only to protect the orators' reputation in the peculiar climate of Rome but more generally to secure psychological space in which they could form their own judgments. For a professional hazard came with the orator's constant need to bow to his audience's assumptions. The danger was that deference would become a habit of mind, that his listeners' norms would seep into his own outlook, especially since handbooks of rhetoric often counseled that the only way to win an audience was for orators actually to feel themselves the sentiment they wished their audiences to feel.[64] The rhetorical pressure on orators to avoid offending common sensibilities could, in the end, undermine the independence they needed to avoid pandering.

Cicero suggested that his philosophic orators could protect themselves against this danger by guarding carefully the conditions in which they could gain and maintain private beliefs different from the ones they had to propound in public. Every exemplary orator in the dialogue—Crassus, Antonius, and Cicero himself—voices approval for an *otium*, a period of retirement away from politics during which one can study. In the *Laws* Cicero claimed that statesmen needed leisure to discuss the laws and history.[65] A similar requirement for leisure explains why he took care to set his dialogues about rhetoric in locations far from the demands of political life. An *otium*, symbolized in *De oratore* by its setting in Crassus's Tusculan villa, functioned as a barrier protecting orators against the rhetorical pressure to conform to common beliefs. The key point about such settings is perhaps captured best in an offhand remark about the setting in Cicero's *Brutus*, another work on oratory: "here we are at liberty to say what we think."[66]

This liberty was linked to the intellectual independence that Cicero claimed to find in his identity as an Academic skeptic: "I live from day to day; I say anything that strikes my mind as probable; and so I alone am free."[67] But Cicero made this boast when speaking in private about his philosophical eclecticism. In the political realm he was in a somewhat different situation, for he was subject to his audience. In taking care to show that even Crassus and Antonius feel such pressure from their audiences, Cicero again demonstrated that his defense of rhetoric was different from that of the sophists. He did not make the mistake of overestimating the power of the orators, of ignoring the way in which they were constrained by the opinions of their listeners. And how could he? This fact about orators could not have been dramatized better than by his own political predicament.

Each book of *De oratore* began with a prologue in Cicero's own voice. These prologues served a number of functions, one of which was to highlight the political situation that Cicero and the other orators in the dialogue faced. The prologue to book 1 brought up Cicero's own situation. It alluded to the political turmoil that had engulfed Rome and threatened the republic and to the personal misfortunes that had made him the object of sustained attack by enemies. Cicero had been honored as a hero for a time but then was forced to go into exile. He had been brought back to Rome in a triumphant march but then was forced out into the countryside again. He had witnessed the murder of Julius Caesar and was saluted by the murderers as a hero of the republic, but in the end he would be found by Marc Antony's men and killed as an enemy of the state. The prologue reminds us that Cicero was a man profoundly aware of and disappointed by the fickle and inconstant nature of public opinion, which had drawn him up to greatness only to turn away from his leadership and toward that of the popular autocrats of the triumvirate, of Julius Caesar, and eventually of Octavian as emperor.

In Plato's *Gorgias* the title character worried that rhetoricians would be hated and expelled from the city. Cicero actually lived the life described by that anxiety and could never have forgotten the reliance of an orator on the opinions of his audience. Nor was Cicero's fate unique to him. The more general point he made was that politics was a realm of force as well as speech, that generals commanded more power than orators, and that the influence of speech always presumed the acquiescence of those with arms. Thus orators were reliant on the goodwill not only of their audiences but also of armies. Cicero's prologue to book 3 made clear that this was a feature of life for any orator. The prologue revealed the fates of the other great figures depicted in the dialogue: Antonius was killed when the general Marius returned to Rome and sought vengeance against his enemies, and Sulpicius was killed by a sword.[68]

In revealing that the fall of the republic had brought all of the key orators in the dialogue to ruin, Cicero indicated that the fate of oratory was linked closely to that of the republican institutions in which the orators had worked. Crassus was the ideal orator in Cicero's account, and his fate dramatized this link: he became sick and died after an exhausting effort to defend the senate as an institution against those who had slandered it and threatened to circumvent it. Crassus's firm political convictions—the ones for which he died—provide insight into Cicero's own. As orators reflecting on their own interests and hence on the interests of oratory itself, Crassus and Cicero were deeply suspicious of the sort of plebiscitary politics that might enhance the power of one powerful speaker for a time but that would ultimately eliminate the republican institutions of controversy in which the practice of persuasion could be sustained.

Institutions of Controversy

Cicero did not provide details about Crassus's defense of the senate, but he defended it himself in his more political works, the *Republic* and the *Laws*, and it was in these defenses that he most explicitly relied on Stoic arguments to bolster his political positions. We have already reviewed some of the Stoic elements of his account. What remains to be shown is how these elements define a legitimate regime as one that preserved a place for some sort of deliberative oratory, an institutional space in which orators could practice the politics of persuasion.[69]

Cicero argued in the *Republic* that the natural impulse for justice which the Stoics recognized enabled citizens not merely to associate with one another but to create "an assemblage of people in large numbers associated in an agreement with respect to justice and a partnership for the common good." He referred to this sort of assemblage as "a people" and went on to define a commonwealth *(res publica)* as the "property of a people" *(res populi).* With this definition as a criterion, he could declare that Syracuse, famous for its beautiful harbors and buildings, "could not be a commonwealth in spite of all these things while Dionysius was its ruler, for nothing belonged to the people, and the people itself was the property of one man. Therefore, wherever a tyrant rules, we ought not to say that we have a bad form of commonwealth, as I said yesterday, but, as logic demonstrates, that we really have no commonwealth at all." He argued that the same had been true of Athens under the Thirty and Rome under the decemvirs. As Malcolm Schofield explains, Cicero's definition of commonwealth as "property of the people" acted as a criterion of legitimacy.[70]

In a broad sense this criterion was democratic, since it required commonwealths to consider themselves as belonging somehow to their citizens. Cicero seems to have meant that governments must respect the actual things of the people—their property—and perhaps also the rights that justify ownership. But this did not mean that all democracies were legitimate commonwealths. Just as important as the "property" part of the definition was the "people" part. Cicero took a "people" to be not just any group of individuals but only a group "associated in agreement with respect to justice and a partnership for the common good." This definition of "people" meant that democracies could fail to be commonwealths. In the *Republic,* just after criticizing Athens and Rome for falling under the sway of tyrants, Scipio asks,

> For when everything is said to be administered by the people, and to be in the people's power; when the multitude inflicts punishment on whomsoever it will, when it seizes, plunders, retains, and wastes whatever it will, can you deny, Laelius, that we have a commonwealth then, when everything belongs to the people, and we have defined a commonwealth as the "property of the people"?[71]

Laelius responds that such an assembly is not "a people" in the sense already defined, "a partnership in justice," and therefore that the government described is not a commonwealth. Unfortunately, sections of the manuscript are lost at this point, but we can gather that the conversation went on

to establish that kingships, aristocracies, and democracies could all be legitimate commonwealths; nothing inherent to any type of regime would either
insure or preclude its being "the property of the people."

The only specific example Cicero offered of a legitimate democracy, however, was Rhodes, where "the senate possessed as much power as the multitude." The importance of senates was not incidental to Cicero's idea of
legitimacy. While he admitted that a people could in theory choose any
form of government so long as their original partnership in justice lasted, he
thought that they would best maintain that partnership if they elected an
aristocratic deliberative body: "every commonwealth, which, as I said, is
'the property of a people,' must be governed by some deliberative body if it
is to be permanent." Again, in theory the deliberative body could be comprised of the entire citizen population. Crowds, however, tended to lose the
characteristics of "a people." Instead, they acted as did the Athenians, whose
manner had "changed into the fury and license of a mob." In Cicero's view,
a mob magnified popular sentiment and radicalized popular demands rather
than evaluating them in light of more fundamental interests. Lacking deliberation, it was often unwilling to grant authority to the best citizens and
more likely to splinter into parties led by popular demagogues.[72]

Cicero required that a commonwealth be administered through deliberative advice *(consilium)* and thus introduced a check on the people's immediate wishes. This requirement for deliberation also introduced a link with
oratory, for rhetoricians taught that deliberative rhetoric aimed at giving
consilium and that the great orator was someone who could, in old age, take
satisfaction from the fact "that he is the one from whom, if not 'peoples and
kings,' then at any rate all his fellow citizens seek counsel [*consilium*] for
themselves."[73] Usually *consilium* of the sort described in the *Republic* emerged
not from a lone orator but from some public deliberation in which orators
played a role. "The people" in Cicero's special sense had two features con-
ducive to such deliberation. First, in being a "partnership," a people would
have the spirit of trust and fellow feeling that rhetoricians since Aristotle
had declared necessary for effective persuasion. Second, bodies which
maintained this spirit, such as the senate, would also preserve independent
judgment. Cicero asserted that senators were more likely to think freely,
since "a senator is not the kind of person to form his opinion on the basis of
another's authority."[74] Cicero clearly also thought that citizens who felt a
partnership in justice would to some extent be united about what justice required. Still, he emphasized not this substantive agreement so much as the

trust and independence of mind that would make deliberation about the specifics of justice possible.

The independence of mind that Cicero wanted to find in senators was an echo, faint but recognizable, of the liberty of thought that orators would enjoy when they found space away from their audiences, space where they could say, as Cicero did in *Brutus*, "here we are at liberty to say what we think." While Cicero did not think deliberative oratory should aspire to the model of philosophic conversation to be found in *otium*, he also did not agree with those who viewed oratory as nothing more than emotional manipulation and pandering demagoguery. The process of deliberation in which orators were engaged was meant to be a shadow of the Academy's philosophical investigations, adapted for practical life, just as political opinions were shadows of philosophical arguments. If philosophical conversation required a certain setting, so too did the practice of Cicero's oratory. Oratory did not need a villa in the countryside far from the pull of political opinion, but it did need some distance from the immense pressure of unrefined public opinion. The function of deliberative bodies was to preserve the spirit of justice among a people, and this in turn required distance from the narrower interests and temporary enthusiasms of public opinion.

Thus the political institutions that Cicero judged most legitimate were those most likely to preserve the possibility of some form of deliberation, most able to facilitate controversy in the way that the practice of oratory does at its best. As we have seen, Cicero did not think that deliberative controversy required orators to become impartial once they entered the senate chamber. Cicero never condemned senators for arguing strongly for their partisan position. He displayed great admiration for those, like Cato, who had firm convictions. The view of political representation that can be drawn out of Cicero's thought was, I have suggested, closer to advocacy than impartiality. But this sort of partisan argument among advocates required certain institutional protection against the plebiscitary politics of Caesarism. In adopting Stoic ideas of natural law as his own firm convictions and deploying them to ground a conception of what makes a commonwealth legitimate, Cicero used those ideas to protect the practice of persuasion.

Whether his audiences would be open to that practice, however, depended not only on the institutions of controversy remaining central to Roman politics but also on certain features of the citizens' characters. The final use of Stoicism that we shall briefly examine was to bolster these ethical preconditions of a politics of persuasion.

The Conscience of Republicanism

In *On Duties,* an open letter to his son about ethics and politics, Cicero offered Stoic ideas as a bulwark against the sophistic impulse to let convention or public opinion guide one's views on practical matters. Among the
most noticeable passages in Cicero's account of duties are those in which he
pleaded with his readers to judge for themselves what was right rather than
to follow popular opinion. In allowing themselves to be flattered by Caesar,
Cicero thought, the Romans had abdicated their responsibility to make political judgments from a standpoint outside of their short-term interests and
desires. Worse still, they had failed to preserve the moral and institutional
conditions under which their judgments could in the future be refined and
enlarged through public deliberation. Their weakness would diminish the
possibility that rhetoric could ever actually persuade and confine rhetoric to
the demagogic sort of flattery that Plato's Socrates had attacked in the *Gorgias.* While not as comfortable as a villa in Tusculum, nor as prestigious as
the walls of the senate, the Stoic moral ideals were designed to serve a similar function to a lesser degree—to help citizens preserve some measure of
intellectual independence, some perspective on currents of public opinion,
and some psychological space in which to evaluate their impulses.

Cicero blamed the fall of the republic on politicians who sought fame.[75]
They pursued reputation and took the short way to glory, in the process
corrupting the people. As a cure for this corruption, Cicero offered a new
understanding of glory, according to which "true glory" was not simply
public recognition but public recognition of what ought to be recognized.[76]
He anchored the normative element of this understanding of glory in the
Stoic concept of *honestum,* or moral goodness. While in some Roman writing
honestum may have slipped into meaning "what is honored," Cicero explained early in the first book of *On Duties* that he would not use the word
this way. He defined *honestum* as "something that, even though it be not
generally ennobled, is still worthy of all honour; and by its own nature, we
correctly maintain, it merits praise, even though it be praised by none."[77] He
redefined the virtue of courage in the same way, adopting a Stoic definition—"that virtue which champions the cause of right"—and immediately
drawing the implication that "no one has attained to true glory who has
gained a reputation for courage by treachery and cunning."[78] If glory were
conferred merely by the fact of public recognition, it would not be bound by
normative constraints such as these, and virtues such as courage would be

whatever the public said they were. But Cicero explicitly argued against letting common opinion or "fame" decide the issue:

> So then, not those who do injury but those who prevent it are to be considered brave and courageous. Moreover, true and philosophic greatness of spirit regards the moral goodness to which Nature most aspires as consisting in deeds, not in fame, and prefers to be first in reality rather than in name. And we must approve this view; for he who depends upon the caprice of the ignorant rabble cannot be numbered among the great.[79]

Thus Cicero tried to ground virtues such as courage outside common opinion. In bringing the Stoic notion of *honestum* to the center of his account of courage, he revived the attempts of Plato and Aristotle to build into the virtue a requirement to reflect carefully on the merits of one's cause.[80] He was vague about the specific content of *honestum*, though he did sometimes discuss the ill consequences that would follow a man's ignoring his nature.[81] He was certain, however, that *honestum* led one to consult "the standard of truth" rather than "the standard of public opinion," and he always stressed the implication that one should act well even when doing so would not bring public approval.[82] Often he seems to have been more interested in the way in which Stoicism gave citizens grounds for resisting popular opinion than in the more substantive content of Stoic beliefs themselves.

As an orator, Cicero could not disregard the people's opinions and impulses altogether. He had argued himself that the final judge of any orator was his audience. While Cicero might have been frustrated with the Romans for allowing themselves to be so easily flattered, he was nevertheless sometimes still optimistic about the capacity of public opinion to judge well what was just and what deserved glory. He argued that injustice would be unmasked and discredited in the long term and that glory would eventually come to those who deserved it. He seemed to think that the public would eventually come to appreciate actions that had advanced the common good and that were worthy of glory. In this sense he had, as all orators must, a democratic faith. He would have endorsed the view that pursuing the long-term approval of one's fellow citizens was a reasonable way of pursuing the republic's true interests. But it is important to see that the modifiers *long-term* and *true* placed a strong filter on public opinion as it was found at any one time. When public opinion could be relied upon to grant glory only to those who deserved it, the pursuit of glory was not dangerous. It could only be relied upon, however, when citizens could exercise good judgment for themselves.

The moral conditions under which they would exercise such judgment were precisely what Cicero feared his audience had lost. The difference between his view of rhetoric and the sophistic one can be seen as linked to his wish to protect Romans from an unreflective capitulation to short-sighted populism. When he asked his fellow citizens to acknowledge "the particular point that justice springs from nature," he was most interested in preserving their sense that their opinions could be refined and enlarged with reference to a standard outside themselves—he was interested in preserving a standard of judgment and hence the possibility of persuasion. In the *Republic* Cicero used the word *consilium*, the same word used to indicate the deliberative counsel which made a state legitimate, to refer to the capacity for judgment that prevented passions from gaining control within an individual's mind.[83] In the *Laws* he linked the defense of the tribunate to a Stoic position on moral goodness by having the same character articulate both.[84] And in the famous dream of Scipio at the conclusion of the *Republic,* Cicero associated a strong moral center of gravity with devotion to the republic. In all of these instances the description of an internal moral compass offered grounds for both criticizing unreflective public opinion and for defending republican institutions, two projects closely linked in Cicero's mind. Only if citizens maintained a moral perspective independent and firm enough to ground judgment could republican government, with its reliance on orators and on persuasion, sustain itself.

Many readers have seen in Cicero's internal Stoic source of moral conviction an anticipation of the Christian notion of conscience. This might lead us to ask why we should view Cicero's firm convictions about natural law as more compatible with the politics of persuasion than the Puritan rhetoric of conscience, and more so than the "public conscience" constructed by Hobbes and Rousseau. The difference lies in the political motivations behind these various sorts of "conscience." If Cicero did articulate a notion of conscience, it was a notion devised with politics in mind; it was the conscience of republicanism. Cicero's convictions arose from a wish to continue the practice of persuasion and the controversy that it implied rather than from an effort to provide a final resolution of that controversy; his convictions arose from within the practice of controversial rhetoric rather than as an attempt to end it.

It was the early moderns who abandoned the mode of politics full of persuasion and controversy. Like the sophistic orators who conceded to the common views of their audiences, early modern philosophers granted a great deal of credence to skepticism and concluded that a wise man should give way to the customs of his time and place, at least in the sphere of politics. Montaigne and Descartes both suggested that a skeptical attitude led them to live by whatever popular opinions were at hand. Montaigne advised the wise man to think as independently as he wished, but in politics to "follow the fashions and forme customarily received."[85] Descartes, when he resolved to doubt all his opinions, formulated a provisional code of morals, the first maxim of which was "to obey the laws and the customs of [his] country."[86] The connection between political quiescence and skepticism in these thinkers was precisely the idea that seems to have influenced Hobbes, who encouraged citizens to alienate their judgment to a sovereign for the sake of peace. In letting go of their judgments and consenting to be represented by one sovereign, Hobbes thought, citizens would unleash a strong dose of skepticism and so retreat from the war produced by their conflicting claims about natural law.[87] Whereas Cicero had tried to persuade skeptics not to "wreak havoc" by undermining Stoic principles of natural law, Hobbes tried to undermine the foundational claims put forth by the latter-day Stoics, the warring sects of Christianity.[88] In Hobbes's day, natural law, transformed into salvationist creed, had shown itself to be a more immediate political danger than skepticism.

In Cicero's time, however, Stoicism had barely begun to enter politics and had not yet been harnessed to a monotheistic religion; it had not yet revealed its capacity to encourage oppression or violence. Thus Cicero saw it not as a threat but rather as a source of much-needed political courage, a foundation for political conviction, and a means of protecting judgment. Cicero's Stoic ideas may seem to be dogmatic convictions in one sense, but they were grounded in the desire to preserve the conditions in which a people could moderate and rethink their opinions. In trying to clear space for deliberation, Cicero did not imply a certainty about the products of that activity. He instead demonstrated his belief that political controversy could be tamed and made more deliberative under certain conditions. The practice of persuasive oratory was, he thought, the best hope for taming political controversy, and his commitment to this task produced the sort of firm convictions that a politics of persuasion not only permits but requires.

CHAPTER 6

Persuasion and Deliberation

The parties must by their own accord, set up for right Reason, the Reason of some Arbitrator, or Judge, to whose sentence they will both stand, or their controversie must either come to blowes, or be undecided.

—Hobbes, *Leviathan*, chapter 5

The parties are, and must be, themselves the judges.

—Madison, *Federalist* #10

Sometimes people make a case for the importance of rhetoric by pointing to the way in which inspiring speeches can spark us to noble action. They admire the motivational power of Martin Luther King Jr.'s words to the crowds on the Mall in Washington, D.C. or Churchill's words to the Royal Air Force during the Second World War. This motivational defense of rhetoric is compelling. We do need people who know how to energize citizens and move them to action, especially in modern mass societies that encourage political apathy. But the motivational defense of rhetoric is also limited. In restricting rhetoric to the function of motivating us to act, such a defense leaves rhetoric out of the process of deciding how to act. In this final chapter I want to suggest a more ambitious defense of persuasive rhetoric, one that shows it to be not only a spur to action but also a constitutive part of deliberation. Building upon the historical work in the previous chapters, in this final chapter I will present more directly several arguments that have already been suggested through textual analysis and draw from them further implications about how we might think about the role of rhetoric.

Speech that aims to persuade can engage our capacity for practical judgment. As we have seen, this capacity is what allows us to integrate the various opinions, desires, and emotions that we have gained throughout our lives as active beings and to bring them to bear on a particular case in a way that yields a decision. In a time when we find our lives increasingly governed by the standardized rules of large bureaucracies and corporations and by the technocratic decisions of policy-making experts, it is important not to lose track of our natural human capacity to make sense of complex situations for ourselves. As humans we have a way of deciding what to do in particular situations that cannot be expressed in a set of rules. Citizens who can use speech to draw one another into exercising this capacity for judgment will find themselves more attentive to one another's points of view, more engaged in the process of deliberation, and more attached to its outcome. That, at least, is the ideal of rhetorical deliberation to which I would like to attract attention. While the ideal has problems of its own, to be discussed below, it deserves more attention than it has received in recent scholarly discussions of democratic deliberation.

In the first section of this chapter I argue that efforts to leave the politics of persuasion behind often ask citizens to alienate their judgment in a way that leaves them stranded from both the activity of public discourse and its outcomes. Efforts to avoid rhetorical controversy tend to produce new and potentially more dogmatic forms of rhetoric. Returning to themes raised at the end of each chapter in Part One, I identify and briefly consider three forms of rhetoric that can arise as a part of the attack on persuasion: the rhetoric of representation, the rhetoric of prophetic nationalism, and the rhetoric of public reason. Each aims to silence the politics of persuasion and end the controversies that it brings, and each attempts to obscure the alienation of judgment involved in this silencing. All three forms of rhetoric against rhetoric tend to produce resentment and frustration among citizens who are subject to them.

In light of the difficulties involved in silencing rhetoric it would often be better, I argue in the second section of this chapter, to engage citizens' judgments by trying to persuade them. This position is motivated by an impulse not so different from the one that has led political theorists to focus attention on the theme of deliberation during the past twenty years or so. Dissatisfied with the assumptions of traditional social contract theories, especially assumptions about the implicit requirement of unanimity, many theorists of deliberative democracy aim to do justice to the persistence of disagreement in democratic societies. In their own way, theories of deliberative democracy chafe at the restraints imposed by the tradition we have traced from Hobbes to Kant. But many of these theories also remain trapped within the confines of that tradition by an unnecessarily narrow view of the relation between deliberation and democratic legitimacy. In the second section of this chapter, I briefly examine the reasons for this confinement and suggest the ways in which rhetorical deliberation would be different from the sort of deliberation that these theories describe. I cannot outline a full "theory" of rhetorical deliberation here, but I will try to sketch out certain features that such a theory would have and call attention to what would make it distinctive. Drawing on the discussion of Aristotle as well as recent literature about the importance of partiality and emotions in practical reasoning, a theory of rhetorical deliberation would not emphasize impartiality, publicity, and respect for autonomy. Instead it would value deliberative partiality, privacy, and respect for judgment and opinion.

It is not possible to open the door to persuasive rhetoric without also opening the door to its perversions, however. Thus the third section of this chapter returns to the problem of demagogy. Is there a way of dealing with that danger that does not ultimately reproduce the alienation of judgment found in Hobbes and his successors? The fundamental political problem for Hobbes arose from the dispersal of judgment among disagreeing individuals. Can one address this problem without resorting to the fundamentally Hobbesian strategy of constructing a more unified and sovereign source of judgment? It turns out, I suggest, that we can find one attempt to meet this challenge relatively close to home—modern representative or constitutional government can offer an alternative to the Hobbesian strategy. The task that James Madison set himself when designing the Constitution of the United States was, I argue, precisely that of minimizing the effects of demagogy while resisting the impulse to construct a unitary sovereign. In his view a constitution was meant neither to execute a sovereign popular will nor to embody sovereign public reason. Instead, a constitutional system was meant to protect and facilitate sustained dispute, drawing it toward less demagogic and more deliberative forms of controversy. Madison's thought may seem a surprising place to look for an approach to the problems we have raised; it may seem too close to home, too comfortable and somehow too American. But seen from the perspective provided by earlier chapters of this book, his view of constitutionalism (which is not the dominant view of legal scholars today) becomes surprisingly fresh and relevant. Though it does not solve the problems of persuasion, it does point toward a distinctive and attractive approach to them, an approach that holds out hope that judgment can be tamed without being alienated.

Alienating Judgment

One way of describing Part One of this book is as an alternative history of public reason, the concept so important to contemporary theories of democratic discourse and deliberation. In place of Jürgen Habermas's story that links public reason to a bottom-up development originating in eighteenth-century coffeehouses and then broadening into a "public sphere," I have suggested an intellectual top-down story, in which the notion of public reason is invented by political philosophers seeking to quell religious political controversy by subjecting debate to an authoritative standard.[1] In the context of contemporary political theory, any argument that tries to draw favorable attention to rhetoric will likely be seen as an attack on public reason. In the chapters on Hobbes, Rousseau, and Kant, I have tried to show that this diagnosis in some sense inverts the historical truth of the matter, which is that the concept of public reason was the attacker and the classical-humanist tradition of rhetoric was, from the beginning, its target. The history of the concept of public reason must begin not, as commonly assumed, with Kant's notion of enlightenment but earlier, with Hobbes's attack on rhetoric.

We have seen that when Hobbes devised his understanding of representation, he was asking citizens to disregard not only their own judgments and dictates of conscience but also, and perhaps more importantly, those judgments supplied to them by preachers and prophesiers. He asked citizens to protect themselves from the influence of these orators by chaining their ears to the lips of the sovereign, whose words he called the "public conscience" and, in chapter 37 of *Leviathan,* the "publique reason." For the sake of peace, he argued, "the Private Reason must submit to the Publique."[2] Public reason was thus created as a means of avoiding controversy by providing an external source of unified judgment. It sought to avoid the political tumult that resulted when each citizen was left to judge for himself and thus made prey to the influence of orators.

Against Hobbes's monarchism, Rousseau reclaimed public reason for the people, removing it from the hands of the external sovereign and depositing it deep within the reconstructed conscience of each citizen. No less than Hobbes, however, he viewed rhetorical deliberations as a danger to the people's capacity to recognize and heed the public conscience or reason. Citizens were prone to being "seduced by special interests, which certain shrewd people, by means of influence and eloquence manage to substitute for the general will."³ Rousseau sought to immunize citizens against such appeals and achieve the harmony of opinion produced by Hobbesian sovereignty without turning to an external authority. He therefore tried to internalize and naturalize sovereignty, producing citizens who judged freely and yet from a shared, unitary, and public point of view. He followed Hobbes in his theoretical aspiration for unanimity among the citizens on matters of public decision; he departed from Hobbes in his estimation of what could produce such unanimity and how it could be made consistent with freedom. The "public reason" he wrote of in *Political Economy* was, no less than Hobbes's notion, meant to describe what would count as a reason to someone inhabiting a shared authoritative, public point of view and thus to render impotent whatever other arguments "shrewd people" representing special interests might wrap in their eloquence.

With this line of argument in mind, the usually cited sources of public reason in Kant's thought appear in a different light. When Kant argued for the free "public use of reason," he understood reason itself to be a sovereign tribunal whose judgments offered a resolution to controversies that arose on the plane of opinion. In the realm of metaphysical disputes, critical reason thus played the role of Hobbes's sovereign, as we saw Kant to have pointed out himself in the *Critique of Pure Reason.* Enlightenment was the process of accustoming individuals to making their judgments from this authoritative critical perspective, through which even long-standing controversies could quickly be resolved. The disputes to be resolved by consulting enlightened reason included not only metaphysical questions but also political ones, such as whether revolutions were justified. It is true that in politics Kant did not advocate the direct rule of reason—he criticized Plato's philosopher-kings—but he did hope for its indirect rule. As we saw in chapter 3, Kant thought that actual sovereigns should, when making decisions such as those about war and peace, heed the arguments made public by philosophers and scholars. Insofar as those arguments were made from the perspective of critical reason, they were made from a standpoint specifically constructed to stand outside and above that of ordinary opinion and judgment, outside the perspective within which rhetorical argument operated.

In viewing these familiar thinkers through the lens of their stance on rhetoric, we find that the common thread linking Hobbes's "publique reason" to Kant's "public use of reason" was the imperative to construct an authoritative or sovereign source of shared judgment. That shared perspective functioned as Hobbes's external sovereign had, as a source of public judgment to which we chained ourselves to avoid being deceived or carried away by people appealing to our private judgments. Thus, if we today sometimes have the sense that the practice of arguing within the bounds set by public reason is a chain on us, that it ties us to one sovereign perspective designed to prevent real controversies from erupting, that it restrains us from drawing upon our own particular judgments, sentiments, and consciences when debating public affairs, or that it rests on fragile assumptions about what we unanimously accept—if we sometimes have these frustrations, one thing we can find in the study of Hobbes and his successors is an explanation. These sources of frustration are not incidental or accidental by-products of the discourse of public reason. They are the intentional results of a well-thought-out early modern program of political thought, a program that explicitly aimed to quell controversy by having us alienate our capacity for private judgment.

While that project sought to minimize the role of rhetoric, it could not avoid what we might call the rhetorical moment in politics: the moment in which individuals are persuaded to accept the judgments of the authorities, the moment in which they are ruled. In a politics of persuasion this rhetorical moment is a feature of politics generally, and the work of influence and rule that it represents is diffused throughout many small acts of persuasion about many particular issues. When, however, we envision politics as a whole being conducted from a unanimously shared perspective, such as that provided by public reason, the rhetorical moment must be condensed to one moment of founding or construction in which individual perspectives give way to the public one. The decision to alienate one's judgment to such an authoritative perspective is itself a judgment that must be instigated by rhetoric. This rhetorical moment in the construction of sovereign public reason is the moment in which Hobbes's rhetoric against rhetoric and Rousseau's persuading without convincing perform their function. Because they must accomplish all the work of ruling in one moment, these forms of rhetoric can be more insidious and more dogmatic than the sorts of persuasion they aim to displace.

The three chapters of Part One each highlighted a different version of this rhetoric against rhetoric: the rhetoric of representation in Hobbes, the rhetoric of prophetic nationalism in Rousseau, and the rhetoric of public reason in Kant. The rhetoric of representation asks citizens to identify with the judgments and actions of their rulers. It asks them to regard the laws and decisions to which they are subject as products of their own wills and as examples of self-rule. The understanding of self-rule at work in the rhetoric of representation can be distinguished from the classical view which distinguished between the activities of ruling and being ruled and asked the same citizens to perform those activities at different times. In that classical view citizens took turns ruling and being ruled, and the element of time allowed them to learn from one activity and apply what they learned when performing the other. The rhetoric of representation eliminates the element of time and suggests that the two activities can be combined into one, thus neutralizing one another. The implication is that citizens can avoid being ruled (by identifying as their own the rules they are made to follow) and also avoid the trouble involved in ruling (by allowing the work to be done by their representative). But since in practice the identification between ruled and rulers is never complete, the rhetoric of representation often finds itself making a difficult case, forced to insist to those who are not benefiting from the rulers' actions that they are nevertheless the authors of them. In Hobbes's thought the strain involved in making this case appeared when he insisted, for instance, that people who made conscientious objections to the king's laws were in fact disobeying their own consciences, since they had agreed to take his judgment and law ("the public conscience") as their own. In the vehemence of his readers' angry responses we find an illustration of the sort of reaction that the rhetoric of representation can provoke. In our politics we see this phenomenon in the protests of long-marginalized minorities. When their claims have repeatedly and over long periods of time been met with arguments about their supposed consent but never with a chance to actually influence policy, they sense the artificiality of representation and insist with renewed and often intensified vigor on more radicalized versions of their positions. When the rhetoric of representation fails to persuade, which it frequently does, it seems to make citizens less likely to submit their private views to public deliberation and compromise than they might otherwise have been.

The two modes of rhetoric highlighted at the ends of the chapters on Rousseau and Kant—the rhetoric of prophetic nationalism and that of public reason—can be seen as further developments of the rhetoric of representation. Leaders make use of the rhetoric of prophetic nationalism when they aim to create or draw out a nonrational and deeply felt sentiment of sympathetic identification among citizens. Such leaders aim to instill in citizens a love of one another not only as political equals but as

essentially similar beings, each of whose identity is constituted by his identification with his fellow nationals. That identification or love is ultimately
itself based not on a shared commitment to any government or culture or
even to any piece of land. Instead the fellow feeling that the rhetoric of
prophetic nationalism aims to inculcate is based simply on the perceived
fact of similarity itself. As Arthur Melzer has argued, the "seed of nationalism" lies in this basic relation of identity or unity, which in turn lies at the
heart of Hobbesian sovereignty.[4] Rousseau himself might have deplored actual manifestations of prophetic nationalist rhetoric, but the structure of
his political thought seems to call it forth, for the same reasons that it calls
forth a legislator who can "persuade without convincing." The rhetoric of
prophetic nationalism arises from the desire to find a way to internalize the
unitary, sovereign, public standpoint that Hobbes had created and thus to
eliminate or hide its artificiality.

Such rhetoric is "prophetic" insofar as it claims to speak from the perspective of the divine or, more often today, in the language of providence or des-
tiny. Forms of prophetic nationalism can be found that use the language of all
three major monotheistic religions. Leaders wielding such rhetoric are often
described as "charismatic," and that word, ultimately from the Greek *charis*
for "grace," carries with it the suggestion that these leaders have somehow
been touched by a divine hand, that they speak not as politicians aiming to
rule in their own name but as prophets carrying out a calling they have received from some higher source of truth and rightness. Thus the rhetoric of
prophetic nationalism obscures the fact of human rule just as the rhetoric of
representation does and perhaps more passionately and insistently, since it
claims not only that such rule represents all citizens but also (and somehow
simultaneously) that the source of its authority lies above and outside
human willfulness.

The final sort of rhetoric that can arise from the attack on rhetoric is the
rhetoric of public reason. Can this reasonable language really be tied in any
way to the nonrational, passionate mode of speech just described, nationalist in scope and religious in grounding? My claim is not that the language
of public reason is ultimately just as irrational as prophetic nationalism, nor
that it has no greater claim to legitimacy, nor even that it relies ultimately
on unacknowledged sources of social unity that lie in sentiments of identity.
I intend only to point out that the rhetoric of public reason arises in the
same theoretical space as other forms of anti-rhetorical rhetoric and in response to the same fundamental theoretical dilemmas. Those dilemmas in

turn arise from basic facts about the structure of political theories that give pride of place to a sovereign, public source of judgment. When viewed from the perspective provided by questions of persuasion and judgment, the language of public reason does in fact have certain similarities to prophetic nationalism: it aims to find a basis of social cooperation upon which all citizens can unite and that all can potentially endorse as their own even when they do not share more particular private opinions or judgments; it disdains the politics of self-interest or bargaining as insufficiently ethical and therefore regards the overlapping or sharing of interests as an insufficient basis for political society; and it dismisses or ignores the mode of politics that would incorporate deeply divergent partisan opinions in a piecemeal way rather than seeking one shared basis of social cooperation upon which to resolve all fundamental controversies. Like the rhetoric of representation and the rhetoric of prophetic nationalism, the rhetoric of public reason aims to reconstitute individuals in such a way that they can be said to inhabit one shared perspective on public questions, making the unanimity that would eliminate the need for rule possible in principle if not in practice.

Why seek to displace the natural dispersal of judgment among parties and individuals with an authoritative source of public judgment? All three sorts of rhetoric just described seem to be motivated by a suspicion of private judgment and opinion, or at least by deep doubts about the role that they can be expected to play in public deliberations. Individuals' judgments are implicitly understood not as harboring partial truths and insights from experience that might be drawn into such deliberations but instead as cloaks for self-interest, instruments of pride, or vestiges of prejudice; private opinion is viewed as too subjective and dogmatic to offer material for deliberation. Private judgments are thus seen as analogous to the Puritan claims of conscience that Hobbes thought had turned controversy into intractable conflict. The alienation of judgment that produces the sovereignty of public reason seems necessary only insofar as one agrees that private opinion has something of the character of those claims of conscience.

Though the fact is not often emphasized, John Rawls's approach to public reason began from just such a view about the stubborn character of opinion and the intractable nature of political conflict.[5] He stated the problem that political liberalism aimed to confront in this way: "How is a just and free society possible under conditions of deep doctrinal conflict with no prospect of resolution?"[6] In his last full statement on "the idea of public reason" he remarked that his theory set itself in opposition to citizens who harbored "a zeal to embody the whole truth in politics."[7] He explained in *Political Liberalism* that he believed the danger posed by uncompromising beliefs to be the distinguishing characteristic of modern democratic politics:

> This is not the problem of justice as it arose in the ancient world. What the ancient world did not know was the clash between Salvationist, creedal, and expansionist religions. That is a phenomenon new to historical experience, a possibility realized by the Reformation . . . What is new about this clash is that it introduces into people's conceptions of their good a transcendent element not admitting of compromise. This element forces either mortal conflict moderated only by circumstance and exhaustion, or equal liberty of conscience and freedom of thought . . . Political liberalism starts by taking to heart the absolute depth of that irreconcilable latent conflict.[8]

Rawls denied that his emphasis on the Reformation as the central political problem was outdated, arguing that the threat posed by zealous comprehensive doctrines remained the key danger in liberal-democratic politics even when those politics were dominated not by questions of salvation but by issues of race, gender, and ethnicity. In fact, Rawls seemed to interpret nearly all major threats to liberal constitutionalism as various forms of religious zealotry. In a striking passage near the beginning of *The Law of Peoples*, he suggested that we should understand even Adolf Hitler's fascist rhetoric as essentially religious in nature.[9]

Is this the best way of understanding the most dangerous sources of modern political stridency? While Hitler may have used religious language in some of his speeches, the fascist ideology that he represented was at heart a very different phenomenon from traditional religious fanaticism. We might even say that it arose as a response to, and a reaction against, the liberal society and discourse that had grown out of the early modern efforts to quell religious fanaticism. The religious language in Hitler's speeches obscured this source of his stridency, which was fueled not only by longstanding Christian anti-Semitism but also, more fundamentally, by the frustration and alienation of a modern secular people. Not experiencing the material rewards of liberalism, his listeners felt especially acutely what had been sacrificed for it—a certain sort of direct and deep ethical engagement among citizens in the political realm. Ethical disengagement had been the intended consequence of the early modern attack on religious rhetoric, and the sense of alienation that it produced should be seen as a sign of the alienation of judgment involved in that attack. The fact that demagogues exploiting this alienation have often used traditional or fundamentalist religious language should not be allowed to obscure the particularly modern source of frustration they tap into. This modern source of frustration—let us call it liberal alienation—was at least as important to the appeal of fascism as the sort of religious zeal that characterized post-Reformation politics.

We do not need to turn to the extreme example of twentieth-century fascism to find the phenomenon of liberal alienation, however. Less intense manifestations of it can be found throughout our politics. As a number of commentators have noticed, frustration, disaffection and a move toward fanaticism are common responses to liberal efforts to disengage from substantive conflicts over seemingly intractable matters, especially those involving moral or religious issues. In looking at the rise of the Christian Coalition during the 1990s, for example, Stephen Carter argues that efforts to avoid a politics of persuasion or direct engagement made religious citizens more susceptible to demagogy. When they found their fears of secular society dismissed as forms of intolerance rather than taken seriously, those citizens responded by becoming willing prey to any pandering politician who seemed to sympathize with their fears; "they rush[ed] into the waiting arms of the next demagogue."[10] Michael Sandel writes in a similar vein, "A politics that brackets morality and religion too completely soon generates its own disenchantment. Where political discourse lacks moral resonance, the yearning for a public life of larger meaning finds undesirable expression . . . Fundamentalists rush in where liberals fear to tread."[11] More recently, Jeffrey Stout has reached similar conclusions when considering the reason for the new dominance of "radical orthodoxy" and "new traditionalists" in universities and divinity schools, concluding that "secular liberalism has unwittingly fostered the decline of the religious Left by persuading religious intellectuals that liberal society is intent on excluding the expression of their most strongly felt convictions."[12] Similarly, in commenting on the politics of abortion that have followed *Roe v. Wade*, Bonnie Honig notices that political solutions usually involve "remainders," aspects of a problem left unaddressed and parties left dissatisfied and frustrated, and she remarks that "if those remainders are not engaged, they may return to haunt and destabilize the very closures that deny their existence."[13] Nor is this dynamic one that arises only in the context of religious questions. Looking primarily at issues of slavery and race, Robert Burt has argued that efforts to make the courts sovereign sources of authority whose judgments can resolve otherwise intractable disputes has produced, at various points in U.S. history, intensified conflict over precisely the issues that the courts were aiming to resolve.[14] These very different arguments all converge on one point—that liberal strategies of political and moral disengagement, strategies that ask in one way or another for citizens to allow their private judgments to be replaced by judgments made from a separate public perspective, tend to produce forms of opinion more dogmatic and less prone to deliberative engagement than those they initially sought to displace. The call for unanimity that we have seen to be implicit in the creation of an authoritative public source of judgment chafes and constrains; it is from that implied unanimity that dissenters feel alienated; and it is against the asserted sovereignty of that unanimity that they rebel. Whether one is considering the rise of the Christian Right in the United States or the rise of fundamentalist Islamic politics in Europe and elsewhere, it seems important to acknowledge the role that these sentiments of liberal alienation can play.

The way that we perceive the twin dangers of religious zeal and liberal alienation is crucial to determining our stance on the desirability of a politics of persuasion and the possibility of rhetorical deliberation. If we think that our primary worry now is at heart similar to the one that Hobbes faced, then perhaps adhering strictly to a narrow language of public reason is the best solution.[15] But if we are equally concerned about those who feel the principles of secular liberalism as chains, restraining them from acting on their consciences and judgments and demanding that they make what seems an unacceptable sacrifice in engagement with one another in the political realm, then part of our solution should involve an effort to engage more directly with them and their views. We may not be especially optimistic about our ability to actually persuade them. We might be driven to a politics of persuasion in large part because there are no good alternatives, because efforts to avoid it tend to produce increasingly dogmatic forms of rhetoric and increasingly intransigent forms of conflict.

Engaging Judgment

There are signs that Rawls himself, in his later writings, looked more closely at the need to attend to "unreasonable" opinions. To the account of public reason that he had given in the original version of *Political Liberalism* he soon added two complexities that pointed in the direction of engaging religious believers in deliberative discourse even when they did not accept public reason as an authoritative standard. The first new feature was a *proviso* that allowed citizens to introduce their comprehensive doctrines into political argument, provided that they eventually introduced public reasons to make the same point.[16] Rawls explained the need for this proviso by noting, first, that citizens' allegiances naturally attached them to their comprehensive doctrines rather than to public reasoning and, second, that the mutual understanding of different comprehensive doctrines bred a sort of civility different from that which arose from simply agreeing not to discuss one another's deepest beliefs.[17] He noticed that in cases of deep polarization—he cited the example of public funding for church schools—it might be more productive for the parties to directly address one anothers' comprehensive views than to try to speak in a more neutral language of public reason. He also cited the speeches of abolitionists and civil-rights leaders, who routinely made religious imagery and arguments a vital part of their discourse. The proviso was Rawls's attempt to incorporate this rhetoric into his idea of public reason.

The second way in which Rawls relaxed the requirements of public reason was the *argument from conjecture:* "we argue from what we believe, or conjecture, are other people's basic doctrines, religious or secular, and try to show them that, despite what they might think, they can still endorse a reasonable political conception that can provide a basis for public opinion."[18] This formulation sounds strikingly like a sympathetic portrayal of rhetorical argument, in that it recommends beginning with a particular audience's opinions and trying to use those opinions as a basis of persuasion. As an example of reasoning from conjecture, Rawls offered a case in which arguments could be made to show how liberty of conscience and toleration might be required by religious law. He cited such an analysis of Islam, remarking that "an Islamic justification and support for constitutionalism is important and relevant for Muslims."[19] I cannot here investigate with enough care whether such concessions leave intact the rest of Rawls's argument about the need for public reason. For now, the main point is that in these exceptions Rawls indicated ways in which even religious opinion might be engaged by attending to its particular commitments. In modifying his original theory Rawls displayed hints of a new optimism about the possibility for rhetorical deliberation, a hopefulness that was missing in the rest of his work on political liberalism, which tended instead to view all controversy on the model of the wars of religion.

The possibility toward which these moments in Rawls's late work point—
that of attending to and engaging the particular opinions of a certain audience
in political discourse—is the possibility that we explored in the chapters on
Aristotle and Cicero. Both thinkers tried to show how orators might appeal to
citizens' capacity for judgment and to identify the moral and political preconditions of such appeals. In the rest of this section I first show how recent theories of deliberative democracy point toward the possibility of engaging
judgment but then fail to pursue it, and then draw from the discussions of
Aristotle and Cicero several ideas that we should consider when devising an
account of rhetorical deliberation that encourages such engagement.

Theories of deliberative democracy point toward the possibility of facilitating argumentative controversy because they challenge utilitarian and social
choice models of politics that reduce opinions to interests or preferences. In
turning their attention to deliberation, Jon Elster and Jürgen Habermas, for
example, object to the utilitarian focus on interests and question the view
that political compromise is best understood as a process of bargaining. Elster introduces a distinction between "the marketplace" and "the forum,"
and Habermas offers a distinction between "strategic" and "communicative"
action.[20] Both Elster and Habermas aim to clear a space for argumentation
by attacking the view that politics is only a matter of interests. Interests
make arguments superfluous, and in fact the concept of interest developed
out of the early modern effort to escape the uncertainties and controversies
involved in arguments, especially arguments about religion. A shared interest in avoiding religious war could persuade more effectively than any
orator could, especially insofar as individuals could be assumed to have
worldly interests that such a war prevented them from pursuing. Self-
preservation was a shared interest that made the pursuit of other interests
possible, and insofar as individuals were devoted to their private interests,
they could be presumed to share the common interest in mutual preservation or peace. The politically important point about interests is therefore
that they aim to diminish the role of argument in politics.[21] In challenging
the centrality of interests to our view of politics, the deliberative democrats
aim to usher argument back into the center of political theory.

Thus when Bernard Manin, to take one of the most interesting examples,
seeks to introduce deliberation to the heart of contemporary theory, he does
so by arguing, against Rawls's *A Theory of Justice* and much of the social con-

tract tradition, that individuals simply do not have a set of preexisting preferences or interests.[22] Therefore, he reasons, it is not helpful to say that governments are only legitimate if they represent or respond to citizens' interests. Manin suggests that we define democratic legitimacy differently: "[T]he source of legitimacy is not the predetermined will of individuals, but rather the process of its formation, that is, deliberation itself . . . We must affirm, at the risk of contradicting a long tradition, that legitimate law is the *result of general deliberation*, and not the *expression of the general will*."[23] For our purposes, the most interesting part of Manin's argument is the way in which he characterizes the activity of deliberation. He describes deliberating individuals learning new information, broadening their perspectives, and changing their preferences, but he also places great emphasis on the rhetorical character of their activity. Drawing from Perelman and Olbrechts-Tyteca's *The New Rhetoric*, Manin makes persuasion of the sort described in the rhetorical tradition central to his view of deliberative argument:

> But deliberation is not only a process of discovery; the parties are not satisfied with presenting various and conflicting theses; they also try to persuade each other. They argue . . . One starts by taking propositions one assumes are generally accepted by the audience being addressed . . . Argumentation is always relative to its audience. Someone who does not share these values will not be convinced by the arguments presented. Nor are the procedures of linking the propositions logically binding. One may use, for example, arguments by analogy and *a fortiori* arguments . . . The force of an argumentation is always relative.[24]

Along with this portrayal of rhetorical deliberation, however, Manin also invokes a different description of deliberation. The second description derives its content not so much from a view about what counts as deliberate argument as from considerations of what sort of procedure might confer legitimacy on the outcome. The process of deliberation can legitimate majority rule, he suggests, when it is a process "in which everyone [is] able to take part, choose among several solutions, and remain free to approve or refuse the conclusions developed from the argument."[25] Stated briefly and rather casually by Manin, these are the sort of conditions that other theorists transform into a much more elaborate theory of legitimacy-conferring deliberation. Joshua Cohen, for example, outlines an "ideal deliberative procedure," with requirements such as equal access for all, a shared commitment to allow nothing but "the force of the better argument" to influence opinions, and a shared motivation to find terms upon which all participants can reasonably be expected to agree.[26] This sort of theory, which now predominates among deliberative democrats, discards Manin's description of deliberation as rhetorical argumentation and emphasizes instead the importance of producing arguments that are deemed "legitimate" because they are, or could be, produced by procedures acceptable to all.

Cohen's theory of deliberative democracy, and others with the same structure, embrace moral disagreement about first-order principles but require acceptance of second-order maxims of fairness to regulate and define the process of deliberation itself. In endorsing such a two-layered approach, theories of deliberative legitimacy adopt the basic structure of social-contract theory. To return to a distinction introduced in chapter 1, they view deliberation as a discourse of justification rather than one of persuasion. In *A Theory of Justice* Rawls noticed that in the original position "each is convinced by the same arguments," a feature of his theory that might remind us of Rousseau's assertion that the general will reigns when there is harmony in the assemblies rather than long debates.[27] In theories of deliberative democracy strongly influenced by Rawls, Cohen or Habermas, the Rousseauian requirement of harmony—the need for unanimity—is displaced but not eliminated. Such theories suppose that each citizen can be convinced by the same arguments about what counts as deliberative argument. That supposition poses a problem for someone interested in persuasion. Since persuasion requires adjusting not only the substance but also the form of one's argument to one's audience, it seems to require more flexibility in choosing types of argumentation than these guidelines permit. In bringing a concern with deliberation to the center of political theory, deliberative democrats open the door to persuasion, but insofar as they view deliberation primarily as a process of finding arguments acceptable to all at once, they close it again. The constraints that the quest for unanimity imposes on political discourse can often rule out precisely the types of arguments that would be most persuasive to certain audiences. The most familiar and perhaps the most contentious examples are again those concerning religion. Do arguments based on sacred texts, for example, count as acceptable forms of deliberative argument? What about arguments from faith? As abolitionists, prohibitionists, civil-rights leaders and other activists have all shown, arguments that invoke biblical language and ideas will often be the most effective way of engaging the judgment of certain audiences and trying to persuade them.[28]

Our response to the question of how religious and other particularistic sorts of rhetoric fit into deliberation therefore depends on what we mean by "deliberation." If we mean a process of legitimizing one shared and authoritative perspective from which to judge all public controversies, perhaps we will be reluctant to include such rhetoric. But if we mean by deliberation a process of drawing upon citizens' capacity for judgment, we will be more likely to admit the value of such forms of speech. Not all theorists writing about deliberative democracy emphasize the first understanding of deliberation as much as Habermas, Rawls, and their students do. Joseph Bessette, one of the first to introduce the term "deliberative democracy," uses a more intuitive definition of deliberation: "reasoning on the merits of public policy," which he elaborates as a process of gaining information, arguing, and persuading.[29] James Fishkin and Bruce Ackerman also rely on a more familiar understanding of deliberation as "serious and balanced public discussion" oriented in large part toward "informing" public opinion.[30] Deliberation is, in Fishkin's balanced view, only one of several conditions of democratic legitimacy. (The other two he considers are political equality and non-tyranny.)[31] The advantage of following Fishkin's lead on this particular point is that one is relieved of the burden of building every democratic principle into the conception of deliberation itself, and thus made freer to explore tensions between deliberation and other democratic commitments, such as equality and participation.

The distinction between the two understandings of deliberation, one premised on universally acceptable procedures of argumentation and the other concerned with drawing out good judgment, will not hold, however, if one thinks that ultimately what it means for individuals' judgments to be good or valid is that they could emerge from a dialogue conducted according to universally acceptable procedures. This is essentially the view put forth by Habermas. In *Between Facts and Norms* he argues that his discourse theory is the only viable way to describe criteria of rationality and moral validity—and hence of good judgment—for modern individuals. He dismisses earlier understandings of practical reason as relics, invalidated by their old-fashioned claims about human nature or their nongeneralizable roots in particular cultural histories.[32] Thus he leaves no basis on which to ground judgments other than whether they could be defended in fair discourse. The democratic procedures that instantiate the conditions of fair dialogue therefore also—by definition—produce the most reasonable or deliberative judgments: "Democratic procedures are meant to institutionalize the forms of communication necessary for rational will-formation," Habermas writes.[33]

It is his deeply public definition of reason and judgment, which can be traced back to his understanding of "communicative rationality," that makes possible the tight and relatively unproblematic conjunction of deliberation and democracy in his political thought:

> The democratic procedure for the production of law evidently forms the only postmetaphysical source of legitimacy. But what provides this proce-dure with its legitimating force? Discourse theory answers this question with a simple, and at first unlikely, answer: democratic procedure makes it possible for issues and contributions, information and reasons to float freely; it secures a discursive character for political will-formation; and it thereby grounds the fallibilist assumption that results issuing from proper procedure are more or less reasonable.[34]

If we accept the idea that the quality of citizens' judgments can only be gauged by looking at the procedures guiding the public discourse from which they emerge, or could have emerged, the view that Habermas him-self characterizes as "unlikely" but endorses may seem plausible. That is, cri-teria of democratic inclusiveness, like the ones that Cohen identifies, will also serve as criteria of deliberativeness, and the challenge of making demo-cratic politics more deliberative will thus be reduced to one of making its procedures conform to a universally accepted democratic ideal.

But to adopt a Habermasian criterion of deliberativeness and reason-ability is to adopt another version of the deep suspicion of individuals' ordi-nary private judgments and opinions that we have noticed in Hobbes, Rousseau, and Kant. Discourse theory follows these philosophers in asking citizens to substitute for private judgments ones that emerge from one au-thoritative public point of view—a sovereign set of procedures. Theorists of deliberative democracy who follow Habermas on this point thus remain within the grip of the campaign against controversy and the art of contro-versy. In spite of their interest in disagreement, they often find themselves opposing rhetorical deliberation and the politics of persuasion.

An alternative approach would be to adopt a more intuitive or direct view of what makes decisions deliberative and then, in a separate stage of argu-ment, to work out the relation between deliberation and other democratic goods, such as legitimacy. Deliberation itself does not have to be viewed as a means of constructing an authoritative and unitary public standard of reasonableness. An intuitive view of deliberation suggests that we are deliberative when we make decisions deliberately—that is to say, when we purposefully consider as completely as possible within the time we have the factors relevant to our decision, bringing to bear upon our choice whatever different sorts of knowledge and information seem relevant, including perceptual, emotional, intuitive, experiential, theoretical, and scientific knowledge. Deliberate decisions need not be slow but they are by definition not "hasty" in the sense of ill-considered. Alexander Hamilton, for example, contrasted "the deliberate sense of the community" with "unqualified complaisance to every sudden breeze of passion, or to every transient impulse which the people may receive from the arts of men, who flatter their prejudices to betray their interests."[35] To speak of deliberation in the ordinary sense is to adopt Hamilton's distinction between one's impulsive responses to situations and arguments and one's more considered responses, as Fishkin and Bessette, for example, emphasize. The capacity that we use in coming up with the more considered response is the faculty of judgment.

If we adopt this sort of view about what deliberation requires, the ideas that we drew from Aristotle's consideration of deliberative rhetoric, the concepts of situated judgment and deliberative partiality, may help to show how persuasive speech can contribute to deliberation. These concepts together articulate how speech that invokes particular and personal forms of knowledge and emotion can draw citizens into exercising their capacity for judgment. We can only judge using criteria that we accept. The activity of judgment is therefore one in which we adjust certain commitments in light of others. Over time, such adjustments give to our beliefs and emotions a certain structure, producing hierarchies of criteria to which we turn, consciously or unconsciously, when evaluating new situations. We judge best when we are situated within these structures of value, able to draw on their complexity and able to feel, emotionally, the moral and practical relevance of different considerations in as subtle a way as experience has equipped us to do. And because the patterns of thought and emotion are not set in stone, because much of the art of rhetoric consists in drawing new pathways between hitherto weakly related parts of these structures, we need not view ourselves as trapped in our situation but simply grounded there.

If individuals have such a capacity for judgment, and if a deliberative democracy is one that encourages them to use it, then someone wanting to encourage deliberation should aim to put questions to citizens in ways that allow them to draw upon the knowledge they take from their situations and from their particular commitments. In Aristotle we saw an argument that the ancient Athenian courts often failed in this respect. They asked citizens to judge about matters unconnected with their own interests and concerns and thus elicited poor judgments. In a deliberative assembly Aristotle saw more hope, for there citizens found their own good more directly at stake. The point is not that deliberation is best when it begins in self-interest. In fact, most people's partial attachments include certain loyalties and commitments to principle, perhaps a sense of honor or dignity or justice or, most commonly, a sensitivity to injustice. These too are parts of the structure of belief and emotion that judgment draws upon, and anyone trying to persuade an audience will look to see what deliberative pathways link these commitments to the case he or she is trying to make. But often even this effort will require careful study of the particular characteristics of one's audience. Here is one description of such persuasion at work:

> During the election campaign of 1960, John Kennedy sent Lyndon Johnson into the South. Johnson was to meet the South's angry criticisms of the Democratic Party's platform of civil rights; and he did make one epic speech, in New Orleans—his equivalent, in addressing southerners, to Kennedy's speech to the Baptists in Houston. But it was not of this that the journalists talked for years afterward. From small town to small town across the South, he went, on a whistle-stop tour on a train called "The Yellow Rose of Texas," facing the sullen crowds of rednecks—"mah people," as he later put it to me. And head-on he spoke to them, as Stewart Alsop once characterized it, "with the tongues of angels." How would you feel, he demanded of them, if your child was sick, and you could not take him to the hospital in this town, but had to go twenty miles away? How would you feel if you were shopping and your child was thirsty, and you could not give him a cold soda at the counter in the drugstore? And again and again, he won the sullen audiences. The inspiration was partly in his conviction, partly in his courage, but also partly in his interaction with the audiences he had to win.[36]

Johnson spoke to his audiences about small points to which they could immediately relate, hoping to arouse in them emotions of indignation and to capitalize on the links between these emotions and a sense of injustice. He also spoke to them, as this telling of the story hints at but does not describe, in language close to their own. His accent, his stories and manner of speech, and even sometimes his characterizations of the races all conformed more closely to southern ways than those of the northern civil-rights activists who had come south to preach their cause. Not only did this give him credibility, but it also reflected his shared background and was a sign of his insight into the structure of his audience's beliefs and emotions. Thus he could find deliberative pathways within his listeners' commitments through which he could draw them out of their habitual mindset on the issue of race, provoking them to consider his view with a greater degree of reflection than they otherwise would have. Of course, even this modest summary of what he was doing risks overstating his effectiveness. Persuasion is, in the end, a weak force in politics, and Johnson may have produced more enemies than converts. But he also seems to have contributed to deliberation, in the ordinary sense of the word, insofar as he apparently did bring some people to think more deeply about the issues he raised. He did so by not giving in to the view that southern opinion was irredeemably prejudiced and dogmatic but instead indulging the hope that there could be found, even within opinions characterized by great fear and prejudice, deliberative pathways and a capacity for situated judgment. He maintained a fundamentally democratic faith in the possibility of persuasion.

In thinking through what this sort of persuasion or rhetorical deliberation requires, we may find ourselves arriving at guidelines quite different from those put forth by the theorists of deliberative democracy discussed earlier. Where they emphasize impartiality, we might focus on the need for partiality and passion; where they insist upon publicity, we might point out the usefulness of privacy and even secrecy; where they grant priority to respecting citizens' autonomy, we might focus instead on respecting their opinions and their capacity for judgment. It is worthwhile to briefly consider each of these points in turn.

Partiality and Passion

Since effective deliberation aims to take advantage of the tacit knowledge each citizen has within his or her experience, and since that knowledge is intricately intertwined with his emotional ties and attachments, deliberation should not aim to ground itself in a standpoint that denies the relevance of those attachments. A parent's fear for his or her son, for example, is a relevant consideration when deliberating about war; so too are the son's feelings of honor and indignation on behalf of his country. Deliberation need not disregard the judgments implicit in those emotions. This is not to say that deliberation never requires putting one's personal feelings aside but only that it does not necessarily require doing so. The relevance of one's emotions is itself a matter for judgment, and that judgment will in turn draw upon the knowledge implicit in other emotions. In spite of the oft-drawn distinction between passion and reason, there is no escaping the fact that considered judgments draw upon both.

We can find this insight in Aristotle, as I have indicated in describing the idea of "deliberative partiality," and we can also find it confirmed in recent research in neuroscience, economics, and political psychology.[37] At the level of theory, we can identify a number of specific ways in which emotions seem to play a role in deliberative judgment. First, as a number of philosophers have noticed, emotions seem necessary to direct us to the relevant features of a situation or argument. In the ordinary course of a day we are presented with an overwhelming amount of material, and deliberation requires focused attention. Emotions lead us to identify certain moments as presenting a choice and also to identify which material is relevant to making that choice. Many deliberations include a moral component, and emotions help to define which considerations seem morally relevant.

Second, as Hobbes noticed, passions seem necessary to direct us from one thought to another in a comprehensible, coherent way. In *Leviathan* he wrote of the incoherence that could result when one's thinking was not guided by a "passionate thought." There are, he remarked, two kinds of mental discourse:

> The first is *Unguided, without Designe,* and inconstant; Wherein there is no Passionate Thought, to govern and direct those that follow, to it self, as the end and scope of some desire, or other passion: In which case the thoughts are said to wander, and seem impertinent one to another, as in a Dream . . . [as] a wild ranging of the mind.
>
> The second is more constant; as being *regulated* by some desire, and designe. For the impression made by such things as wee desire, or feare, is strong and permanent, or (if it cease for a time,) of quick return: so strong it is sometimes, as to hinder and break our sleep. From Desire, ariseth the Thought of some means we have seen produce the like of that which we ayme at; and from the thought of that, the thought of means to that mean; and so continually, till we come to some beginning within our own power. And because the End, by the greatnesse of the impression, comes often to mind, in case our thoughts begin to wander, they are quickly again reduced into the way.[38]

Hobbes's phrase "passionate thought" neatly describes the way in which reasoning and feeling are intertwined with one another, not just in the sense that we must be motivated to act on our thoughts, but in the deeper sense that thinking itself must be motivated at each moment. Desires and emotions focus us on particular goals and thus exert a unifying force to our reasoning, giving it coherence.

A third function of the passions in deliberation can be seen in the role played by political emotions such as honor, pride, and indignation. These emotions are passionate and in some ways self-centered, but they also give us a stake in asserting and maintaining our mastery of ourselves, and such self-command fosters the exercise of deliberative judgment. Honor supports a sense of agency, and it ties us to principles and a sense of justice, as Sharon Krause notices; a love of honor is, she writes, "a particular desire to uphold a general obligation."[39] Along with indignation and other political emotions, concern for our honor can draw us out of smaller forms of self-concern and help provide the distance from the narrowest forms of self-interest that is necessary for reflection.

A fourth role that passion can play is to stimulate reflection or judgment by disrupting ordinary habits of response. As George Marcus has shown, voters who are made to feel anxiety tend to study much more carefully the positions of the candidates and to rely less on habitual partisan or ideological affiliation in making their choices.[40] Deliberation and judgment therefore seem to emerge not in sedate citizens who reason, as Rousseau once proposed, in "the silence of the passions" but instead in citizens who have been disturbed out of their calm and made attentive by sharp feelings of anxiety.[41] Partiality and passion together, in the form of anxiety, can prod reflection.

There are other ways, too, in which emotions contribute to deliberation, but the point is by now clear. If these passions play a constitutive role in the sort of practical reasoning that characterizes judgment, the sort of arguments and appeals that engage these passions would seem to be an important component in deliberation too. While passions can overwhelm and undermine deliberations, they do not necessarily do so.

Privacy and Secrecy

Insofar as persuasion requires the freedom to change one's mind, rhetorical deliberation may be hampered by the requirement of publicity. In Cicero's defense of the Roman senate and also more informally in his appreciation for the practice of *otium*, or temporary retirement away from political activity, we saw the importance of protecting institutional space in which immediate political imperatives do not overwhelm deliberations about long-term interests. Once again, we find this view confirmed in recent theory and practice. A number of writers and politicians have noticed, for example, the detrimental effect that the so-called "sunshine laws" of the 1970s had on policy-making in Congress. These laws, which opened many committee hearings to the public and instituted more recorded votes, sweeping away secrecy in the name of accountability, probably did help to eliminate some forms of backroom corruption. But they also made it much more difficult for representatives to engage in anything like true deliberation by making it nearly impossible for them to remain open to persuasion. Television cameras insure that there is more posturing and less discussion. The careful recording of every vote insures that lawmakers remain more closely tied to positions they have already declared or those they think necessary to shore up their electoral base. The presence of "interested citizens" (usually lobbyists paid for their interest) at committee meetings or markup sessions insures that legislators remain focused on the special or regional interests watching over their shoulders, rather than reflecting on how those interests balance against interests unable to afford lobbyists. Joseph Bessette points out that the pernicious effects of publicity were so clear in one case that sunshine legislation was actually repealed: tax legislation in the House of Representatives was drafted in open sessions for ten years, but in 1983 the chamber again began drafting it behind closed doors. While this may have allowed unjust loopholes to be slipped into the law, it also allowed the sort of deliberative balancing that publicity had made impossible. Bessette sums up: "[I]f lawmakers are properly to carry out their deliberative responsibilities for the citizenry, they must to some extent be protected against the intrusions of unreflective public opinion. The institutional environment in which they work must allow, and even encourage, legislators to proceed wherever reasoning on the merits leads, even if this is some distance from initial public sentiments."[42]

The same need for distance from immediate political considerations explains why fiscal policy at the Federal Reserve, military base closings, and trade agreements, for example, are still deliberated in private settings.[43] The point is not simply that these are technical matters that require expertise, but that immediate and local interests would otherwise overwhelm and corrupt good judgment. The same motivation explains why the framers of the Constitution met for so many months in secret before presenting their work to the country. Of course, these considerations do not touch upon the point that the outcome of deliberations should be made public to garner legitimacy, but they do remind us of the important role that privacy and even secrecy can play in securing space for deliberation itself, insofar as deliberation requires the opportunity to change one's mind.

Respect

If deliberation involves the sort of judgment that uses criteria found within our existing opinions, the persuasion involved in deliberation will involve deferring to certain opinions even as it aims to change others. In this sense persuasion, which may initially seem a more intrusive and coercive form of argument than public reasoning, actually affords more respect to the opinions of one's audience than the discourse of justification does. The presence of that respect can be seen in its perversions, in the slide to deference or to outright pandering. When real persuasion occurs, however, it does not collapse into pandering. Speakers treat their listeners' existing opinions with a certain deference, and yet they do not cater to them.[44] This respect for the actual opinions of one's audience serves to acknowledge the particular features of individuals—their histories, identities, commitments, and needs—in a way that respect for their autonomy does not. It is a respect for what Seyla Benhabib has called "the concrete other" rather than the "generalized other."[45] Because persuasion requires attentiveness to the concrete situation of the people one is trying to persuade, it avoids provoking the feelings of alienation that can be produced by a discourse of justification.

Partiality and passion, privacy and secrecy, and respect for opinion are not maxims of deliberation that must be unanimously accepted or always followed. They are simply characteristics of rhetorical deliberation; they help to describe what it means to try to engage the capacity of judgment in other people through persuasive speech. They also point to certain goods that rhetorical deliberation brings to politics. Chief among these goods is a certain attentiveness to others. To influence the judgment of another person, as rhetoric aims to do, one must pay close attention to his or her particular commitments, sentiments, and tastes. Arguments that aim primarily at being accepted by all reasonable people can seem to encourage an insensitivity to individuals' lives as they are actually lived. The universality of arguments deemed legitimate in many recent models of deliberation is meant to insure that those arguments are not coercive. Many people, however, seem to feel coerced by the implicit claim that their own judgments are not reasonable. They believe that their commitments and convictions deserve as much respect as their capacity to revise those commitments. They may find a discourse of justification less respectful than the rhetorical alternative in which their opinions and sentiments—and their capacity for judgment—are directly engaged.

Taming Judgment

In thinking about how persuasion can engage judgment, I have painted a rather rosy picture of the politics of persuasion. But as was noted in the Introduction, efforts at persuasion do not always, and perhaps do not often, strike the golden mean that lies between manipulation and pandering. This is the fault not only of those who try to persuade but also of those who listen and judge, or fail to judge. The truth is that there can be something exciting and gratifying in letting oneself, as a listener, be swept away in a momentary political passion or flattered into more stubbornly believing one's existing prejudices. Even if citizens were generally on guard against these tendencies, even if they exercised good judgment most of the time, the dispersal of judgment involved in the politics of persuasion would still generate heated moral and political controversy. As even proponents of deliberation admit, public debate often tends to exacerbate and radicalize the disagreements that divide us rather than mitigate them, creating enclaves of like-minded believers.[46] The politics of persuasion is a risky enterprise. That is why the early moderns sought to avoid it in the first place.

We should not underestimate the threats of demagogy and polarization. In trying to clear a space for persuasion and the controversy it generates, we cannot simply shrug our shoulders and hope for the best. While it may be liberating to unearth the influence of the Hobbesian legacy in contemporary liberal theory and to reveal what Sheldon Wolin calls the "homogenizing, oppressive character of public reason," a full and responsible treatment of the issue of rhetoric requires that we not lounge in the feeling of liberation that this unmasking provides.[47] To free ourselves from the grip of Hobbes's attack against rhetoric is to unleash the sources of instability and unfreedom that Hobbes aimed to eliminate. Even as we assert that Hobbesian sovereignty and its later manifestations unduly constrained political controversy, we should not presume that the disputes springing up in the absence of sovereignty will be benign. Demagogy is a recurring challenge for democratic citizens, and nowhere is it more in evidence than in the tumultuous moments of revolution that have been glorified as opportunities to "activate the demos."[48] To laud the restorative power of such controversial, revolutionary politics without also noticing the insecurity, unfreedom and misery that can come with such an "active" politics is to take the easy way out and to fail in our responsibility to think through the conditions of democratic liberty. It is a testament to the seriousness of Hannah Arendt's thought, for example, that she objected to such an attitude on the part of the French revolutionaries in spite of her own commitment to the restorative power of revolutions.[49] Hobbes's attack on rhetoric was an effort to address serious problems posed by persuasive speech. In rejecting his approach one does not solve the problems of controversy and demagoguery so much as decline a proposed solution to them. The problems remain to be addressed.

Insisting on the danger of demagogy raises the point that emerged in chapter 5, on Cicero, where we saw that a commitment to the politics of persuasion should not lead one to endorse the formless democratic politics of the sophists. Rhetorical deliberation may require resistance to Hobbesian sovereignty, but it does not require resistance to all settled institutions, codes, and constitutional formalities. On the contrary, we saw, in considering Cicero, how an interest in protecting the practice of persuasion led him to firm convictions about the importance of certain types of institutions and morals. The growing irrelevance of the senate threatened to eliminate the influence of persuasive argument and turn the work of governing over to demagogues like Julius Caesar and Marc Antony, whose use of the military demonstrated the close link between demagogy and force. Cicero's old-fashioned convictions about the importance of constitutional institutions and formalities arose not from a desire to contain or constrain the demos, but rather from an effort to sustain the politics of persuasion in which he himself had been so successful. Few are as sensitive to the threat posed by demagogues as those who compete with them and lose.

How then can demagogy be avoided? It cannot. Because persuasion is a central practice of democratic life, democracies will always be subject to its vices. Demagogues arise at the head of factions, and we might say of demagogy what James Madison said of faction in *Federalist* #10—that there are only two ways of eliminating it, "the one, by destroying the liberty which is essential to its existence; the other, by giving to every citizen the same opinions, the same passions, and the same interests."[50] We have seen in Hobbes, Rousseau, and Kant both of these strategies at work. There was a sacrifice of liberty involved in the alienation of private judgment, and there was an effort to produce unanimity in the construction of an authoritative sovereign judgment. Insofar as the creation of sovereignty in Hobbes and its internalization in Rousseau and Kant aimed to eliminate the danger of demagogy, these theoretical innovations represented the strategy of the "theoretic politicians" that Madison warned against.[51]

What I want to suggest in the final section of this chapter is that it is not only Madison's negative assessment of these efforts that should interest theorists who would like to protect the politics of persuasion. In fact, when we look at the writings of Madison through the lens provided by our current inquiry, what seems surprisingly relevant is his understanding of the problems of rhetoric as we have set them out and his effort to address them in a manner wholly distinct from what we found in the earlier authors. Madison viewed the problem of conflict from a perspective not so different from Hobbes's. He did not dispute the view that popular governments were prone to factionalism and demagogy and that the history of such republics was one of disorder, instability, and civil strife. Nor did he disagree with Hobbes about the political dynamics driving such disorders:

> A zeal for different opinions concerning religion, concerning government, and many other points, as well of speculation as of practice; an attachment to different leaders ambitiously contending for pre-eminence and power; or to persons of other descriptions whose fortunes have been interesting to the human passions, have, in turn, divided mankind into parties, inflamed them with mutual animosity, and rendered them much more disposed to vex and oppress each other than to co-operate for their common good. So strong is this propensity of mankind to fall into mutual animosities, that where no substantial occasion presents itself, the most frivolous and fanciful distinctions have been sufficient to kindle their unfriendly passions and excite their most violent conflicts.

The familiar elements of Hobbes's diagnosis are present in this analysis— most notably the zealotry of religion and the inflaming influence of orators. In *Federalist* #51 Madison even likened the condition of factionalism to "a state of nature." Though he emphasized the importance of property divisions more than Hobbes had, even his analysis of conflict between propertied classes and the poor acknowledged the role of demagogues.[52]

This may be because Madison had seen the way that local politicians had been manipulating economic issues in the states during the 1780s, inflaming opinion on the debt crisis after the Revolutionary War and demanding immediate solutions, such as the issuance of paper money. As Joseph Bessette shows, the problem of demagogy was not simply a theoretical one for Madison. He viewed it as a practical challenge that was severely afflicting the state legislatures in his time. In a 1787 document, "Vices of the Political System of the United States," he complained about the irresponsible way in which state legislatures had ignored the Articles of Confederation; trespassed on the rights of other states; generated too many laws, many of which treated creditors or other states unjustly; changed the laws too often in response to momentary passions stirred up by opportunistic politicians; and generally driven their states into economic ruin and civil disorder. The legislators of Rhode Island and other states had taken the shortsighted and economically self-defeating measure of issuing paper money to satisfy debtors who had been whipped into a frenzy by clamoring orators. Madison complained that a local representative often became "the dupe of a favorite leader, veiling his selfish views under the professions of public good, and varnishing his sophistical arguments with the glowing colours of popular eloquence." Just months prior to the Constitutional Convention, the debtors in Massachusetts had taken to armed insurrection under the leadership of Daniel Shays, but once that rebellion was put down, Madison was concerned not so much about violence as about the influence that popular leaders would have within the legislature itself. During the debates at the convention over how to elect members of the House of Representatives, he voiced his concern about "the danger of demagogues." In the *Federalist* he blamed "men of factious tempers, of local prejudices, or of sinister designs," worried about citizens being "misled by the artful misrepresentations of interested men," and sought ways to mitigate "the influence of factious leaders" who might "kindle a flame" such as "a rage for paper money, for an abolition of debts." Like Hobbes, Madison thought the demagogy of ambitious men was a major cause of disorder and civil strife in his own day.[53]

The crucial theoretical point, however, is that Madison also endorsed the basic Hobbesian view that the ultimate source of these vices of popular government lay in the dispersal of judgment. His analysis in *Federalist* #10 traced the origin of faction to the fact that individuals were allowed to be judges in their own causes.[54] What distinguished Madison from Hobbes,

Rousseau, Kant, and their followers, however, and what makes his thought most interesting from our perspective was his response to this fact. He regarded the dispersal of judgment as nonnegotiable; he did not advise parties to political disputes to alienate their judgment to an impartial arbiter: "The parties are, and must be, themselves the judges," he stipulated.[55] It was this fundamental commitment that led him to seek a wholly different approach to demagogy and faction than the one initiated by Hobbes.[56] Specifically, this commitment prevented him from turning, as the other theorists had in one way or another, to the solution of unified sovereignty.

In fact, Madison understood representative or republican government to be an alternative to unified sovereignty and a guard against it. He viewed representative government as a way of dealing with the problems of factionalism and demagoguery while resisting the temptation to locate authoritative judgment in one sovereign power. In "Vices of the Political System" he wrote of the need for a "modification of the Sovereignty" so as to avoid the dangers of both absolute rule and small republic demagoguery. The modifications Madison recommended were a limitation of sovereign authority and an extension of the territory of the republic, the second of which he thought would make unlikely a prolonged concentration of authority in any one faction. The fact that Madison could simultaneously support representative constitutional government and reject sovereignty suggests what is wrong with viewing constitutions as merely an insidious new manifestation of the Hobbesian impulse to suppress democratic political debate.[57] Madison, at least, thought that institutional design could help to control the effects of demagoguery and faction without stifling controversy in the way that a strong notion of sovereignty did.

The Hobbesian view—that it was necessary to turn to some external source of sovereign authority to settle controversy—can be found in several positions against which Madison found himself arguing. The most obvious and least influential example of it was the position that Alexander Hamilton took early on at the Constitutional Convention in favor of eliminating state governments and instituting an executive with a lifetime appointment on the model of the British monarch. After listing the defects of confederated governments, Hamilton said, "How then are all these evils to be avoided? only by such a compleat sovereignty in the general Government as will turn all the strong principles & passions above mentioned on its side." He noted that in all societies there would be a division between the few and the many, between debtors and creditors, and that the "amazing violence & turbulence of the democratic spirit," evident in the recent efforts of debtors to issue paper money, could never be constrained except by a permanent senate on the model of the House of Lords as part of a government with unquestioned sovereignty. Elsewhere Hamilton articulated the need for sovereignty in a response to an anti-federalist writer: "In every government, there must be a supreme absolute authority lodged somewhere . . . to which all the members of that society are subject; for otherwise there could be no supremacy, or subordination, that is, no government at all."[58] Strong sovereignty was necessary, Hamilton told the Convention, because "when a great object of Government is pursued, which seizes the popular passions, they spread like wild fire, and become irresistible."[59] Madison's famous argument in *Federalist* #10 should be understood as a direct response to Hamilton's point. Madison had recorded the speech in his notes; he alluded to the demagogic responses to the debt crisis by mentioning "the rage for paper money"; and he used Hamilton's fire metaphor. But Madison contended that in an extended republic "the influence of factious leaders may kindle a flame within their particular States but will be unable to spread a general conflagration through the other States." In replying to Hamilton in this way Madison was resisting the Hobbesian impulse to turn to a unified sovereign.[60]

Madison found himself resisting that impulse on the other side of the political spectrum too. The temptation to turn to an external sovereign source of authority also appeared in Thomas Jefferson's proposal for calling a constitutional convention whenever two of the three branches thought necessary. As Madison pointed out, Jefferson's proposal was premised on the idea of popular sovereignty. Since "the people are the only legitimate fountain of power," it seemed to make sense that "an appeal to the people themselves" would be the only way to settle disputes among the branches of government.[61] But while Jefferson located sovereignty in the people's constitutional convention rather than a king, his position no less than Hamilton's presumed the necessity of finding one source of sovereign judgment when controversy arose.

Madison's response to Jefferson went beyond his well-known remark that frequent appeals to the people on fundamental constitutional questions would erode the veneration necessary to maintaining a law-abiding citizenry. Madison also advanced two considerations that he deemed more important. First, he thought that such appeals would stir up deep partisan passions so that "the public decision . . . could never be expected to turn on the true merits of the question." He pointed out the problems that had arisen when the state of Pennsylvania had implemented something close to Jefferson's proposal by calling a Council of Censors in 1783–1784 to arbitrate disputes between the executive and legislative branches. Such conventions intensified the problems of demagoguery and factionalism rather than addressing them.[62]

Second, Madison argued that in practice Jefferson's proposal would usually have the effect of increasing the power of the legislature rather than preventing its encroachments on the other branches, since it was the members of that body who were closest to the people, most accustomed to influencing them, and most likely to be elected to the convention itself.[63] Madison's general point was that asserting the absolute sovereignty of the people in the way that Jefferson's proposal sought to do would in practice amount to asserting the sovereignty of whichever branch of government could most successfully claim to represent the popular will. In Hamilton's skillful hands, for example, popular sovereignty became an argument for allowing the courts to overrule laws passed by Congress. In *Federalist* #78 Hamilton made the case for judicial review by identifying the Constitution with the will of the people and concluding that when the court struck down a statute, it was simply asserting the priority of the people's sovereign will over the will of Congress: "the Constitution ought to be preferred to the statute, the intention of the people to the intention of their agents." He asserted, misleadingly, that judicial review did not imply the superiority of the courts to the legislature but only "that the power of the people is superior to both." Judges enforcing constitutionality, he argued, were merely exercising popular sovereignty.[64]

Madison objected to both Jefferson and Hamilton on these various points because he was convinced that unified sovereignty itself was a danger, whether located in the legislature, the people, or the courts. As Robert Burt points out,

> Madison . . . took the conventional precept that every government by definition must have a single locus of sovereign authority and turned this idea upside down to maintain that a well-designed government could and should divide and then subdivide all authority . . . and by this means, no single sovereign could be found.[65]

Madison's opposition to unified sovereignty was in turn tied to his refusal to countenance an alienation of judgment of the sort necessary to construct a unitary sovereign, to his insistence that "the parties [to a controversy] are, and must be, themselves the judges." He listed a number of divisive and lasting controversies, such as those between debtors and creditors and between manufacturers and landed interests, that seemed to require resolution from a just and impartial perspective that neither side could be expected to provide itself. His argument was that no such perspective could be relied upon. His famous remark that "enlightened statesmen will not always be at the helm" appeared in this context and was meant to show not simply that governments could not rely on virtue but more specifically that they could not expect to govern from a point of view wholly separate from the partisans' perspectives. No external source of impartial judgment could be relied upon to settle controversy once and for all.[66]

Therefore "pure" democracy would always be the site of civil strife that Hobbes had described. The "republican remedy" for this republican "disease" consisted in delegating government to representatives and extending the size of the republic. Neither part of this remedy should be understood as seeking to replace the partiality of partisan judgment with the impartiality of a sovereign tribunal. The system of representation that sought to "refine and enlarge the public views" did open the possibility of finding legislators who would take "the true interest" of the country as their own, but it equally opened the door to the "men of factious tempers, of local prejudices" who would betray that interest. Madison hoped the worst candidates would be excluded by the process of election, but in the end the representatives would be chosen by the people from their interested and partisan perspectives. The greatest innovation, which he introduced as his own, was the thought that the variety of interests in a large republic would make it difficult for "the influence of factious leaders" to spread very far or for very long and thus prevent the accumulation of power in any one faction or leader for any significant length of time. Madison returned to this argument in *Federalist* #51, alluding directly to the recent troubles in Rhode Island surrounding the paper-money fiasco. He noted that if the state were left to itself, the oppressions of the majority faction (presumably against creditors) would have grown so pernicious that "some power altogether independent of the people" would have been called in to resolve the situation. In an extended republic, where such a "rage for paper money" would be unlikely to gain majority support for very long, Madison noted that there "must be less pretext, also, to provide for the security of the former [the minority], by introducing into the government a will not dependent on the latter [the majority], or, in other words, a will independent of the society itself." Thus Madison's conscious intent was to eliminate the pretext for calling in an external sovereign by moderating the effects of demagogy from within. The danger of factional strife was to be met by accommodating and channeling controversy through the structure and extent of government rather than by settling controversy from the outside.[67]

The unacceptability of appealing to an external source of judgment to resolve disputes also explains why Madison turned, at the beginning of *Federalist* #51, from the "external provisions" or constitutional conventions that Jefferson had proposed to an effort to arrange "the interior structure of the government" so as to contain each part to its proper place. Madison's theory of "checks and balances," which Americans take for granted and which political theorists now regard as quaint, takes on new significance when seen in this light. It was designed to show that the vices of democratic government could be avoided without asking citizens to alienate their judgments to any sovereign authority—not even to one claiming to represent the majority.

How could the interior structure of government do the work of managing controversy and taming judgment? The reason that each man being judge in his own case posed a threat, according to Madison, was that "his interest would certainly bias his judgment." Madison's solution therefore specified that "the interest of the man must be connected with the constitutional rights of the place."[68] The offices of representative government were designed to influence the judgment of the individuals within them. Madison's insight extends beyond the familiar point that an officeholder's personal ambition should be tied to the prerogatives of the office and thus harnessed in the protection of those prerogatives. The larger point is that institutional offices shape the way in which officeholders deliberate, influencing the criteria that they bring to bear on their judgments, the sorts of considerations that they find persuasive, and the sorts of rhetoric they employ. After years of service, for example, a senator develops certain legislative habits of mind and ways of speaking, different from those he or she would have developed as an executive or an activist.

Offices produce these effects partly by arranging "incentives" or interests but not only in that way. Offices also set the terms on which politicians are judged and so help to define the office-holders' sense of pride, honor, and reputation, which is why Madison wrote not only of the "interests of the man" but also of his ambition. Offices affect the perspective from which the individuals who inhabit them judge. As was suggested in the discussion of Aristotle, people who view themselves as performing a particular role or function tend to organize their thoughts and emotions within structures appropriate to the function. Individuals' situations include their role, so their "situated judgment" is influenced by the office they hold. This influence occurs within each of the three branches of government but also outside of them. A system of representative government diffuses deliberation into a variety of offices and proto-offices, creating not only an executive, judiciary, and legislature but also by implication the activities and roles associated with them, such as that of candidates running for office, activists lobbying for new laws, and attorneys trying cases in court. These informal practices supplement the formal institutions and derive meaning from them.[69]

Because the internal structure of a government creates a range of different offices, each carrying with it different and particular conceptions of success, calling forth different qualities and offering different incentives, the influence of the internal structure upon judgment is not a pressure toward uniformity. In fact, insofar as the offices are designed to check and balance one another, the pressure they exert upon the judgments of the people within them will help to encourage, preserve, and channel controversy rather than resolve it. At the same time, the variety of different offices and the differences among them have the effect of dividing large controversies about broad issues into smaller ones about more narrowly specified matters. Thus the diversity of offices has an effect analogous to extending the size of the republic, creating a greater variety of perspectives, and making it less likely for one broad resolution of an issue to gain control for any length of time. One purpose of a constitution understood in this way is thus to provide the activity of governing with an internal structure that makes it resistant as a whole to any sustained settlement of the kind that either a demagogue or a sovereign authoritative point of view might try to impose.[70]

The various offices and institutions therefore seem to influence deliberations in two ways. First, they impose a certain structure to individuals' thoughts and emotions, a structure that persuasive speakers can make use of. Second, they do not merely give structure to deliberation; they also limit and direct it in a way that prevents deliberators from assuming the entirety of rule for themselves. Citizens who have never involved themselves in politics often take a global "if I were king" perspective in their political judgments, whereas those who inhabit particular offices find their deliberations shaped by a sense of what they can do from within that position. The latter, narrower perspective is more limited but also often more productive, responsible, and informed. It is a perspective situated within the scheme of government rather than outside it, and it produces better judgment for some of the same reasons that Aristotle thought citizens deliberating about matters related to their own concerns judged better than those sitting as jurors judging more distant matters. Madison's effort to connect "the interests of the man" with "the constitutional rights of the place" should not be understood simply as an effort to broaden the former, but also as a recognition of the good that can come from narrowing the latter. The perspective of an officeholder with a limited sphere of responsibility and interest is one that resists demagogy because it does not presume the possibility of wielding final or sovereign authority.

In this view of constitutional democracy there is in fact a sovereign but not one that exists outside the activity of self-government itself. What is sovereign is the people's will as it emerges from all the various activities of representative government. There is no sovereign general will prior to or separate from those activities, no popular will that can be discerned by careful attunement to public opinion as found in a public sphere or in opinion polls, nor one that can be derived by careful reasoning about the sense of the community, the history of its principles and values, or a hypothetical account of deliberation under ideal conditions. Implicit in much constitutional theory today is the view that a constitution exists to enact or execute such an independently existing sovereign popular will.[71] Such a view of constitutions invokes an external source of authoritative judgment and ultimately returns to the Hobbesian strategy of alienating private judgments to a unitary sovereign perspective. Madison's view, in contrast, tames judgment by drawing citizens into the various and differentiated activities of self-government.

Like the individuals depicted in the frontispiece to Hobbes's *Leviathan*, citizens and theorists today remain too often transfixed by the image of a sovereign to whose judgments we can gratefully yield whenever controversy appears. This book has argued that the visage of Hobbes's sovereign has loomed over our politics and our political theory for too long. Wearing different masks at different times, taking on distinct personas in a variety of theories, unified sovereignty in its various incarnations since Hobbes has insistently drawn to itself our eyes and chained to its mouth our ears. As a result we have continued to relate to one another and rule one another only indirectly, through an intermediary. This book has argued that we should tear our gaze away from the face of this interloper, that we should once again look directly at one another and speak directly to one another.

There exists no sovereign authority to settle our disputes, neither a king nor an enlightened statesman nor a shared conception of public reason nor even a common public conscience deep within our hearts. Only once we have acknowledged that fact will we find it necessary to engage in the work of trying to persuade one another. Only once we have acknowledged with Madison that "the parties are, and must be, themselves the judges," meaning we ourselves in our variously situated and partial perspectives, will we find ourselves ready to engage in the politics of persuasion. Ultimately politics is not analogous to a courtroom; there is no judge to offer a final verdict; we are always, in that sense, in the state of nature. Instead of resolving our fundamental disputes all at once we are left to struggle over them as they arise repeatedly in different forms in particular cases over a long period of time. Seeing this path ahead and seeing how efforts to cover it up tend to produce more insidious forms of discord is what may convince us that the difficult project of persuasion is worth our efforts.

What does that project require of us? Not that we become brothers or comrades, nor that we befriend those with whom we disagree, nor even that we join them in a contract. It requires instead that we pay attention to our fellow citizens and to their opinions.[72] The politics of persuasion asks that we look to understand the commitments, beliefs, and passions of the other side if only for the purpose of trying to bring them to our side—or, more often, for the purpose of trying to rebut their views in front of people who have no settled position of their own. The effort of attention that persuasion requires is thus often motivated by our partial and political passions, but it nevertheless draws us out of ourselves. Trying to persuade others requires us to step outside our particular perspectives without asking us to leave our particular commitments behind.

The politics of persuasion is a politics of disagreement and controversy. Although those who are trying to persuade in any instance seek to end the immediate dispute in their favor, ultimately they also have a stake in the continued availability of persuasion when the next disagreement arises. If controversy were to end altogether or if one side of a permanent cleavage were to gain a permanent advantage, the space for persuasion would diminish. Thus proponents of the politics of persuasion should hope that there is at least some truth in Madison's argument about the extended republic—they should hope that the winners of current contests can never be sure of finding themselves in a permanent majority. And they should seek not to settle controversies with grand philosophical resolutions but rather to facilitate the ongoing practice of controversy in smaller disputes, piecemeal, as they arise in particular situations and in smaller settings. Such an approach may produce uncertainty and temporary defeats, but that simply means that we may have to take turns ruling. Taking turns is the price of democratic citizenship and also one of its defining characteristics.

In a politics of persuasion victories are always provisional, and they depend on the judgments of others. The frustrations that go along with this dependence are unavoidable, as are the indignities to be endured by anyone who steps into the ring of democratic politics and tries to engage political adversaries in argument. Hobbes saved some of his most eloquent and personal prose for articulating such feelings. In response to those who asked what greater disadvantage there could be than not being able to participate in public debate, he wrote,

> What is a disadvantage, if this is not? I will tell you. To see the proposal of a man whom we despise preferred to our own; to see our wisdom ignored for empty glory; to hate and be hated because of differences of opinion (which cannot be avoided, whether we win or lose); to reveal our plans and wishes when there is no need to and to get nothing by it; to neglect our private affairs. These, I say, are disadvantages. But to lose the opportunity to pit your wits against debaters, is not such a disadvantage for them, unless we shall say that it is a disadvantage for brave men to be forbidden to fight, for the simple reason that they enjoy it.[73]

Hobbes's frustrations are understandable. The best ideas will not always carry the day in democratic debate, and even the most attentive and skillful efforts at persuasion often fail for reasons unconnected with the merits of the cause. But it would be a mistake to say, as Hobbes did, that the controversies found in democracies are nothing more than a chance "to pit your wits against debaters." Every virtue is flanked by vices. The posturing and pontificating we find in our messy public discourse are neighbors to a genuine democratic good—the practice of persuasion. In addressing our fellow citizens directly, we make an effort to influence them, not with force or threat or cries, but with articulated thoughts that appeal to their distinctly human capacity for judgment. In trying to persuade, we attend to their opinions without leaving behind our own, and so we try somehow to combine ruling and being ruled in the way that democratic politics requires. While neither as powerful nor as ubiquitous as rhetoricians themselves might claim, persuasion is nevertheless a real possibility in democratic life, and it is a possibility that we ought to protect.

NOTES

BIBLIOGRAPHY

INDEX

Notes

Introduction: Persuasion

1. Alexis de Tocqueville, *Democracy in America*, trans. Harvey C. Mansfield and Delba Winthrop (Chicago, Ill.: University of Chicago Press, 2000), 2.1.21.
2. Plato, *Gorgias*, trans. James. H. Nichols, Jr. (Ithaca, N.Y.: Cornell University Press, 1998), 452d.
3. Thomas Hobbes, *The Elements of Law, Natural and Politic*, ed. Ferdinand Tönnies (London: Frank Cass, 1969), 2.2.
4. See Robert E. Goodin, *Manipulatory Politics* (New Haven, Conn.: Yale University Press, 1980), chap. 4.
5. Plato, *Gorgias*, 517a.
6. Aristotle, *The Politics*, trans. Carnes Lord (Chicago, Ill.: University of Chicago Press, 1984), 1332a11–27; Michael Walzer, *Spheres of Justice: A Defense of Pluralism and Equality* (New York: Basic Books, 1983), 303–311.
7. See Jon Elster, "The Market and the Forum," in *The Foundations of Social Choice Theory*, ed. J. Elster and A. Aanund (Cambridge: Cambridge University Press, 1986), 103–132.
8. For a recent account of the group dynamics that lead public discourse toward conformity and enclaves, see Cass R. Sunstein, *Why Societies Need Dissent* (Cambridge, Mass.: Harvard University Press, 2003).
9. A collection of essays from this perspective has recently been published. See Benedetto Fontana, Cary J. Nederman, and Gary Remer, eds., *Talking Democracy: Historical Perspectives on Rhetoric and Democracy* (University Park, Penn.: Pennsylvania State University Press, 2004).
10. An enormous literature falls into the category of justificatory liberalism as it is broadly understood, including the influential work of John Rawls and Jürgen Habermas. Stephen Macedo offers a succinct characterization: "The moral core of this [liberal] order is a commitment to public justification: the application of power should be accompanied with reasons that all reasonable people should be able to accept." Stephen Macedo, *Liberal Virtues: Citizenship, Virtue, and Community in Liberal Constitutionalism* (Oxford: Clarendon Press, 1990), 40–41. See

215

also Gerald F. Gaus, *Justificatory Liberalism: An Essay on Epistemology and Political Theory* (New York: Oxford University Press, 1996); Charles Larmore, *The Morals of Modernity* (Cambridge: Cambridge University Press, 1996), 41; Jeremy Waldron, *Liberal Rights: Collected Papers, 1981–1991* (Cambridge: Cambridge University Press, 1993), 36–37, 50.

11. John Rawls, "The Idea of an Overlapping Consensus (1987)," in *Collected Papers*, ed. Samuel Freeman (Cambridge, Mass.: Harvard University Press, 1999), 426.

12. For an assessment of the place of the "agreement motive" in justificatory liberal theory, see Sharon Krause, "Partial Justice," *Political Theory* 29 (2001): 315–336.

13. Judith Shklar lists "persuasion" alongside physical might, the military, and the police as powers of the government that liberals ought to fear. See Judith Shklar, "The Liberalism of Fear," in *Liberalism and the Moral Life*, ed. Nancy Rosenblum (Cambridge, Mass.: Harvard University Press, 1989), 21, 27.

14. Immanuel Kant, *Critique of Judgment*, trans. J. H. Bernard (New York: Hafner Press, 1951), §53, 173.

15. Plato, *Gorgias*, 517a.

16. See Gorgias, *Encomium of Helen*, in Aristotle, *On Rhetoric: A Theory of Civic Discourse*, trans. George Kennedy (New York: Oxford University Press, 1991), 283–287.

17. Ronald Beiner, whose work helped to inspire this project, offers a good start in identifying the various sorts of judgment. See Ronald Beiner, *Political Judgment* (Chicago, Ill.: University of Chicago Press, 1983).

18. Aristotle, *Nicomachean Ethics*, trans. Terence Irwin (Indianapolis, Ind.: Hackett Publishing, 1985), 1112a20–3.

19. This account of practical judgment is drawn from Aristotle and is indebted also to accounts given recently by writers sympathetic to the Aristotelian view of practical reasoning: Ronald Beiner, *Political Judgment*, chap. 4; Anthony T. Kronman, *The Lost Lawyer: Failing Ideals of the Legal Profession* (Cambridge, Mass.: Belknap Press, 1993), 11–108; Jonathan Lear, *Aristotle: The Desire to Understand* (Cambridge: Cambridge University Press, 1988), 141–208; Martha C. Nussbaum, *The Fragility of Goodness: Luck and Ethics in Greek Tragedy and Philosophy* (New York: Cambridge University Press, 1986), chap. 10; Martha C. Nussbaum, *Love's Knowledge: Essays on Philosophy and Literature* (New York: Oxford University Press, 1990); and Stephen G. Salkever, *Finding the Mean: Theory and Practice in Aristotelian Political Philosophy* (Princeton, N.J.: Princeton University Press, 1990), chap. 3.

20. This is one theme of Philip K. Howard, *The Death of Common Sense: How Law Is Suffocating America* (New York: Random House, 1994), which gives many examples of such regulation.

21. The point has been made by Hans-Georg Gadamer, *Truth and Method*, trans. Joel Weinsheimer and Donald G. Marshall, rev. ed. (New York: Continuum, 1989), 40, by James Nichols in his Introduction to the *Gorgias*, by Plato, trans.

James H. Nichols, Jr. (Ithaca, N.Y.: Cornell University Press, 1998), 7–9; and by Victoria Kahn, *Rhetoric, Prudence, and Skepticism in the Renaissance* (Ithaca, N.Y.: Cornell University Press, 1985), 189–190.

22. See Jay Heinrichs, "How Harvard Destroyed Rhetoric," *Harvard Magazine* (July/August 1995).

23. For a debate on the aestheticization of rhetoric, though not on politics, see the following: Steve Whitson and John Poulakos, "Nietzsche and the Aesthetics of Rhetoric," *Quarterly Journal of Speech* 79 (1993): 131–145; James W. Hikins, "Nietzsche, Eristic, and the Rhetoric of the Possible: A Commentary on the Whitson and Poulakos 'Aesthetic' View of Rhetoric." *Quarterly Journal of Speech* 81 (1995): 353–377.

24. See Joe Klein, "Where's the Music: Why No One's Listening to What the Candidates Have to Say," *New Yorker*, September 27, 1999, 37–42; Henry Fairlie, "The Decline of Oratory," *New Republic*, May 28, 1984, 15–19; "Notes and Comment," *New Yorker*, January, 1961, 23–24. Cicero, *On the Ideal Orator (De oratore)*, trans. James M. May and Jakob Wisse (New York: Oxford University Press, 2001).

25. David Hume, "Of Eloquence," in *Essays, Moral, Political and Literary*, ed. Eugene F. Miller (Indianapolis, Ind.: Liberty Fund, 1985), 97–110; Edward Gibbon, *An Essay on the Study of Literature* (London: Becket, 1764), XII; Denis Diderot, "Pensées détachées ou Fragments politiques échappés du portefeuille d'un philosophe," in *Oeuvres complètes* (Paris, 1971), vol. 10, 80–81.

26. Tacitus, *Dialogue on Oratory*, in *Agricola; Germania; Dialogus de Oratoribus* (Cambridge, Mass.: Harvard University Press, 1970), 36.4.

27. Ibid., 40.1.

28. Ibid., 40.2–4.

29. Ibid., 41.1–4.

30. For Tacitus on Tiberius, see his *Annals*. For the shouting matches in the senate, see his *Histories* 1.85, cited by Rousseau in the *Social Contract* 4.2. Jean-Jacques Rousseau, *On the Social Contract with Geneva Manuscript and Political Economy*, ed. Roger D. Masters, trans. Judith R. Masters (New York: St. Martin's Press, 1978), 110.

31. I do not deny the persistence of a kind of moral Puritanism, especially in America, but simply suggest that it is not the only important source of political dogmatism today. For a fascinating account of the ways in which the Puritan jeremiad has remained a force throughout American political history, see James A. Morone, *Hellfire Nation: The Politics of Sin in American History* (New Haven, Conn.: Yale University Press, 2003).

32. Recent examples include William Safire, ed., *Lend Me Your Ears: Great Speeches in History* (New York: W. W. Norton, 1997) and Josh Gottheimer, ed., *Ripples of Hope: Great American Civil Rights Speeches* (New York: Basic Civitas Books, 2003).

33. For a good account of some of these changes, see Kathleen Hall Jamieson, *Eloquence in an Electronic Age: The Transformation of Political Speechmaking* (New York: Oxford University Press, 1988).

34. Thomas M. Conley, *Rhetoric in the European Tradition* (Chicago, Ill.: University of Chicago Press, 1990). Other useful works that aim to recount this tradition include George A. Kennedy, *Classical Rhetoric and Its Christian and Secular Tradition from Ancient to Modern Times* (Chapel Hill: University of North Carolina Press, 1999); Thomas Cole, *Origins of Rhetoric in Ancient Greece* (Baltimore, Md.: Johns Hopkins Press, 1991); Marc Fumaroli, *Histoire de la rhétorique dans l'Europe moderne: 1450–1950* (Paris: Presses Universitaires de France, 1999); Brian Vickers, *In Defense of Rhetoric* (New York: Oxford University Press, 1989).

35. A representative example of the recent champions of the sophists is Stanley Fish. See Stanley Fish, *Doing What Comes Naturally* (Durham, N.C.: Duke University Press, 1989) and Stanley Fish, *The Trouble with Principle* (Cambridge, Mass.: Harvard University Press, 1999).

36. See Sheldon S. Wolin, "Fugitive Democracy," *Constellations* 1 (1994): 11–25; Sheldon S. Wolin, "Norm and Form: The Constitutionalizing of Democracy," in *Athenian Political Thought and the Reconstruction of American Democracy,* ed. J. Peter Euben, John R. Wallach, and Josiah Ober (Ithaca, N.Y.: Cornell University Press, 1994).

37. See, for example, Karen Callaghan and Frauke Schnell, eds., *Framing American Politics* (Pittsburgh, Penn.: University of Pittsburgh Press, 2005); Thomas E. Nelson and Donald R. Kinder, "Issue Frames and Group-Centrism in American Public Opinion," *Journal of Politics* 58 (November, 1996): 1055–1078; Thomas E. Nelson, Zoe M. Oxley, and Rosalee. A. Clawson, "Media Framing of a Civil Rights Conflict and Its Effect on Tolerance," *American Political Science Review* 91 (1997): 567–583; and Diane C. Mutz, Paul M. Sniderman, and Richard Brody, eds., *Political Persuasion and Attitude Change* (Ann Arbor: University of Michigan Press, 1996).

1. The Rhetoric against Rhetoric: Hobbes

1. Thomas Hobbes, *Leviathan,* ed. Richard Tuck (Cambridge: Cambridge University Press, 1996), 52.

2. Ibid., 254.

3. For detailed analysis of the frontispieces, see Keith Brown, "The Artist of the *Leviathan* Title-Page," *British Library Journal* 4 (1978): 24–36; and M. M. Goldsmith, "Hobbes's Ambiguous Politics," *History of Political Thought* 12 (1990): 639–673. See also Geoffrey M. Vaughan, "The Audience of Hobbes's *Leviathan* and the Audience of Hobbes's Political Philosophy," *History of Political Thought* 22 (Autumn 2001): 464–471; and Danielle Allen, *Talking to Strangers: Anxieties of Citizenship since Brown v. Board of Education* (Chicago, Ill.: University of Chicago Press, 2004), 80–84.

4. Thomas Hobbes, *On the Citizen,* ed. and trans. Richard Tuck and Michael Silverthorne (Cambridge: Cambridge University Press, 1998), 71, 140–141.

5. Commentators who take up the issue of Hobbes's rhetoric and remark on this puzzle include Victoria Kahn, *Rhetoric, Prudence, and Skepticism in the Renaissance*

(Ithaca, N.Y.: Cornell University Press, 1985), 157; David Johnston, *The Rhetoric of* Leviathan: *Thomas Hobbes and the Politics of Cultural Transformation* (Princeton, N.J.: Princeton University Press, 1986); Sheldon Wolin, *Hobbes and the Epic Tradition of Political Theory,* ed. Richard E. Ashcroft (Los Angeles: University of California Press, 1970), 38; Frederick G. Whelan, "Language and Its Abuses in Hobbes' Political Philosophy," *American Political Science Review* 75 (1981): 59–75; Raia Prokhovnik, *Rhetoric and Philosophy in Hobbes'* Leviathan (New York: Garland Publishing, 1991), 110; Tom Sorrell, "Hobbes's UnAristotelian Political Rhetoric," *Philosophy and Rhetoric* 23 (1990); and Quentin Skinner, *Reason and Rhetoric in the Philosophy of Hobbes* (Cambridge: Cambridge University Press, 1996), 363.

6. J. W. N. Watkins, *Hobbes's System of Ideas: A Study in the Political Significance of Philosophical Ideas,* 2d ed. (London: Hutchinson, 1973); M. M. Goldsmith, *Hobbes's Science of Politics* (New York: Columbia University Press, 1966); Thomas Spragens, *The Politics of Motion: The World of Thomas Hobbes* (Lexington, Ky.: University Press of Kentucky, 1973).

7. Skinner, *Reason and Rhetoric;* Johnston, *The Rhetoric of Leviathan;* Prokhovnik, *Rhetoric and Philosophy.*

8. For the connection between classical-humanist rhetoric and controversy, see especially Thomas M. Conley, *Rhetoric in the European Tradition* (Chicago, Ill.: University of Chicago Press, 1990), 37, 132, 162, 176, 178; and Thomas O. Sloane, *Donne, Milton, and the End of Humanist Rhetoric* (Berkeley, Calif.: University of California Press, 1985), 78–83 passim. On controversy in Hobbes, see Harvey C. Mansfield, "Hobbes and the Science of Indirect Government," *American Political Science Review* 65 (1971): 100: "For Aristotle, men come to government because political controversy is natural; for Hobbes, men are forced to consent to government to escape the consequences of political controversy."

9. Victoria Kahn reaches a similar conclusion about Hobbes's relation to humanist rhetoric, though she puts more emphasis than I do on Hobbes's skepticism and less on the dangers posed by the Puritan rhetoric of conscience. For Hobbes, she argues, Pyrrhonism undermined the idea that debate and dialogue could be practiced with regard to a shared criterion of judgment, and therefore "the invention of a political science *depends* on the exclusion of the humanist notion of rhetoric." Kahn, *Rhetoric, Prudence, and Skepticism,* 190.

10. See Leo Strauss, *The Political Philosophy of Hobbes: Its Basis and Its Genesis,* trans. Elsa M. Sinclair (Oxford: Clarendon Press, 1936), xiv–xv: "Hobbes's intention is not only to expound his view of human life as the expression of his own experience, but above all to justify this view as the only true and universally valid view. It is by starting from this intention that we can grasp the ultimate reason for the contradictions which are to be found in his writings."

11. Hobbes, *Leviathan,* 306.

12. The technique of *paradiastole* to which Quentin Skinner devotes so much attention is closely linked to the controversial character of Renaissance rhetoric. Quentin Skinner, "The Study of Rhetoric as an Approach to Cultural History:

The Case of Hobbes," in *Main Trends in Cultural History: Ten Essays*, ed. Willem Melching and Wyger Velema (Amsterdam: Rodopi, 1994), 17–53.

13. See Walter Ong, *Ramus, Method, and the Decay of Dialogue* (Cambridge, Mass.: Harvard University Press, 1958). See also Richard Tuck, *Philosophy and Government, 1572–1651* (Cambridge: Cambridge University Press, 1993), 24–26.

14. Skinner, *Reason and Rhetoric*, 4–5.

15. Ibid., 3.

16. Aristotle, *Rhetoric*, 1404a13; Thomas Wilson, *The Art of Rhetoric (1560)*, ed. Peter E. Medine (University Park, Penn.: Pennsylvania State University Press, 1994), 45.

17. Skinner, *Reason and Rhetoric*, 3. In an earlier article on the subject Skinner argues that Hobbes's political theory should be understood as offering a new solution to the uncertainty and controversy that was associated with the rhetorical technique of *paradiastole*, or redescription. Skinner's argument in that article is compelling and closely related to my argument here. The crucial point of difference between his account and my interpretation is the question of whether Hobbes's solution should be understood to be within the classical-humanist tradition of rhetoric or whether he began something new. Skinner, "The Study of Rhetoric as an Approach to Cultural History."

18. Hobbes, *On the Citizen*, 79, 120, 122, 124.

19. Geoffrey Vaughan reaches similar conclusions from different but equally compelling arguments about Hobbes's intended audiences. Vaughan, "The Audience of Hobbes's *Leviathan*."

20. Thomas Hobbes, *The Elements of Law, Natural and Politic*, ed. Ferdinand Tönnies (London: Frank Cass, 1969), 24.

21. Hobbes, *Leviathan*, 10, 13.

22. Ibid., 181–182; Thomas Hobbes, *Behemoth, or The Long Parliament*, ed. Ferdinand Tönnies, with an introduction by Stephen Holmes (Chicago, Ill.: University of Chicago Press, 1990), 95.

23. Richard Tuck, "Introduction," in Hobbes, *Leviathan*, xx.

24. Skinner, *Reason and Rhetoric*, 97, 99. See also pp. 27–30, 97–99, 116, 172. For an account that makes the practice of arguing on both sides central to the "climate of thought" of the Italian Renaissance in general, see James Hankins, "Humanism and Modern Political Thought," in Jill Kraye, ed., *The Cambridge Companion to Renaissance Humanism* (Cambridge: Cambridge University Press, 1996), 121.

25. Skinner, *Reason and Rhetoric*, 16.

26. Skinner suggests that if we are seeking sources of John Locke's antipathy for the practice of arguing *in ultramque partem*, we can cite only the Hobbes of the *Elements* and not the Hobbes who conceded the use of rhetoric in *Leviathan*. Skinner, *Reason and Rhetoric*, 374–375.

27. See Vaughan, "The Audience of Hobbes's *Leviathan*" and Johnson, *The Rhetoric of* Leviathan for complementary interpretations.

28. Niccolò Machiavelli, *Discourses on Livy*, trans. Harvey C. Mansfield and Nathan Tarcov (Chicago, Ill.: University of Chicago Press, 1996), 2.52–60; Niccolò

Machiavelli, *The Prince*, trans. Harvey C. Mansfield (Chicago, Ill.: University of Chicago Press, 1998), 61.

29. Machiavelli, *Discourses* 1.52.

30. Ibid., 3.1.

31. Ibid., 3.3.

32. For an account that distinguishes the late Renaissance Tacitists (or "new humanists") from the Ciceronians (or "old humanists"), see Richard Tuck, *Philosophy and Government*, 31–64. For a detailed survey of Tacitism in the Renaissance, see Kenneth C. Schellhase, *Tacitus in Renaissance Political Thought* (Chicago, Ill.: University of Chicago Press, 1976).

33. Schellhase, *Tacitus*, 111: "Bodin's reevaluation of Tacitus constitutes one of the most significant moments in the history of Tacitus in Renaissance political thought. Enlarged and refined by others, it was eventually to lead to 'reason of state.'" Tuck describes Bodin as an anticipation of the new Tacitist humanism rather than the beginning of it, focusing instead on Bodin's Ramism. Tuck, *Philosophy and Government*, 26–30.

34. Jean Bodin, *Methodus ad facilem historiarum cognitionem* (1567), as quoted in Jean Bodin, *Method for the Easy Comprehension of History*, trans. Beatrice Reynolds (New York: Columbia University Press, 1945), 154. See also Schellhase, *Tacitus*, 109.

35. Bodin, *Method*, 54.

36. Ibid., 267.

37. Jean Bodin, *Six Books of the Commonwealth*, trans. M. J. Tooley (Oxford: Basil Blackwell, 1955), 4.7.

38. Ibid.

39. Thomas Hobbes, "A Discourse upon the Beginning of Tacitus," in Noel B. Reynolds and Arlene W. Saxonhouse, eds., *Thomas Hobbes: Three Discourses: A Critical Modern Edition of Newly Identified Work of the Young Hobbes* (Chicago, Ill.: University of Chicago Press, 1995), 36, 35, 38, 42–43. For recent evidence that this work is indeed by Hobbes, see the introduction to Reynolds and Saxonhouse, *Thomas Hobbes*, and Noel B. Reynolds and John L. Hilton, "Thomas Hobbes and Authorship of *Horae Subsecivae*," *History of Political Thought* 14 (1993): 361–380.

40. Thomas Wilson, *The Art of Rhetoric*, 41–42. See also Henry Peacham, epistle dedicatory, *The Garden of Eloquence* (1593), facsimile reproduction (Gainesville, Fla.: Scholars' Facsimiles and Reprints, 1954). The epistle appears only in the second and longer 1593 edition of Peacham's work. Cicero, *De inventione*, in *De inventione; De optimo genere oratorum; Topica*, trans. H. M. Hubbell (Cambridge, Mass.: Harvard University Press, 1949), 1.1–2. I take on Skinner's authority the idea that Wilson and Peacham were representative of the rhetorical tradition in which Hobbes was trained. See Skinner, *Reason and Rhetoric*, 52, 56, 73.

41. Cicero, *De oratore* 1.33–38.

42. See Skinner, *Reason and Rhetoric*, 99.

43. Wilson, *Art of Rhetoric*, 42.

44. Peacham, epistle dedicatory, *Garden of Eloquence*.

45. Hobbes, *Leviathan*, 147.

46. On the link between practical judgment and rhetoric more generally, see Marjorie O'Rourke Boyle, introduction, *Rhetoric and Reform: Erasmus' Civil Dispute with Luther* (Cambridge, Mass.: Harvard University Press, 1983); Hans-Georg Gadamer, *Truth and Method*, trans. Joel Weinsheimer and Donald G. Marshall rev. ed. (New York: Continuum Publishing, 1989), 19–21, 71–72, 189, 376, 485; and Kahn, *Rhetoric, Prudence, and Skepticism in the Renaissance.*

47. For a history of this notion of judgment as it relates to art, see David Summers, *The Judgement of Sense: Renaissance Naturalism and the Rise of Aesthetics* (Cambridge: Cambridge University Press, 1987). On the connection between judgment and rhetoric, see 39–40, 127–132, 333–134.

48. Aristotle, *Rhetoric*, 1355a14–18, 1391b7–20, 1420b2–5; *Politics* 1281b34–1281b6; Cicero, *De oratore* 3.195.

49. Aristotle, *Rhetoric*, 1420b2–5.

50. Giambattista Vico, *On the Study Methods of Our Time*, trans. Elio Gianturco (Ithaca, N.Y.: Cornell University Press, 1990), 13, 34.

51. Hobbes, *On the Citizen*, 123.

52. Hobbes, *Leviathan*, 33.

53. Hobbes, *Elements*, 1.14.8, 10.

54. "For in these things private judgements may differ, and beget controversy. This common measure, some say, is right reason: with whom I should consent, if there were any such thing to be found or known *in rerum natura*. But commonly they that call for right reason to decide any controversy, do mean their own. But this is certain, seeing right reason is not existent, the reason of some man, or men, must supply the place thereof; and that man, or men, is he or they, that have the sovereign power." Hobbes, *Elements*, 2.10.8.

55. Hobbes, *Leviathan*, 120.

56. Hobbes, *Leviathan*, 111.

57. Skinner offers detailed discussions of *paradiastole* in the Renaissance tradition and in Hobbes. See Skinner, *Reason and Rhetoric*, 142–153, 156–172, 174–180, 279–284, 317–326, 338–343, and Skinner, "The Study of Rhetoric as an Approach to Cultural History."

58. See Tuck, *Philosophy and Government*, 313.

59. Vaughan reaches a similar conclusion. See Vaughan, "The Audience of *Leviathan*," 470.

60. Hobbes, *Leviathan*, 479–480. See Richard Tuck, *The Rights of War and Peace: Political Thought and the International Order From Grotius to Kant* (Oxford: Oxford University Press, 1999), 214n.

61. See Tuck's note on the scribal manuscript that accompanies the end of the chapter on religion early in *Leviathan*, which described the priests who "presumed most of Reformation" as reducing religion "to private fancy" and thereby reducing government to "the naturall Condition of Private force." Hobbes, *Leviathan*, 86n2.

62. Hobbes, *Leviathan*, 298–299.

63. In the same way, the sovereign can choose to allow a more direct sort of representation, including elections. See Hobbes, *Leviathan*, chaps. 19, 22.

64. See Tuck, *Rights of War and Peace*, 131: "The prime source of the conflicts of the state of nature, for Hobbes, is thus epistemic in character . . . These judgements need not, strictly speaking, be driven by self-interest *at all*, since they may arise simply from the fact that there is no objective standard of truth." See also Kahn, *Rhetoric, Prudence, and Skepticism*, 20, 190.

65. Erasmus, *Diatriba*, as quoted in Boyle, *Rhetoric and Reform*, 155.

66. See Erasmus, *Hyperaspistis Opera omnia* X.1258a–1262d, as quoted in Boyle, *Rhetoric and Reform*, 23. On Erasmus's skepticism and deliberation more generally, see Thomas O. Sloane, *Donne, Milton, and the End of Humanist Rhetoric* (Berkeley, Calif.: University of California Press, 1985), 73–74.

67. According to Michael Walzer, "Hobbes' private judgment, it may be suggested, was a secularized reduction of the Calvinist conscience." Michael Walzer, *The Revolution of the Saints: A Study in the Origins of Radical Politics* (New York: Atheneum, 1968), 42.

68. William Perkins, *The Arte of Prophecying; A Discourse on Conscience*; and *The Whole Treatise of Cases of Conscience*, in *William Perkins, 1558–1602, English Puritanist: His Pioneer Works in Casuistry*, ed. Thomas F. Merrill (Netherlands: de Graaf, 1966). For Perkins's influence on Puritan preaching, see Perry Miller, *The New England Mind: The Seventeenth Century* (Cambridge, Mass.: Harvard University Press, 1954), 335.

69. William Perkins, *A Discourse of Conscience*, in *William Perkins, 1558–1602, English Puritanist: His Pioneer Works in Casuistry*, ed. Thomas F. Merrill (Netherlands: de Fraaf, 1966), 11.

70. Ibid., 9.

71. Ibid., 7.

72. Hobbes, *Leviathan*, 48. The earlier part of the passage, which seems close to Perkins's etymology, is this: "When two, or more men, know of one and the same fact, they are said to be CONSCIOUS of it one to another; which is as much as to know it together. And because such are fittest witnesses of the facts of one another, or of a third; it was, and ever will be reputed a very Evill act, for any man to speak against his Conscience; or to corrupt, or force another so to do: Insomuch that the plea of *Conscience*, has been always hearkened unto very diligently in all times. Afterwards . . ."

73. Hobbes, *Leviathan*, 236; *Elements* 2.6.12.

74. Hobbes, *Leviathan*, 223.

75. Hobbes, *Elements* 2.6.12.

76. Hobbes, *Leviathan*, 297.

77. Aristotle, *The Politics*, trans. Carnes Lord (Chicago, Ill.: University of Chicago Press, 1984), 1284a1–10.

78. Hobbes, *Leviathan*, 306.

79. Ibid.

80. Ibid., 301. See also *Leviathan*, 246.

81. Miller, *The New England Mind,* 155–156.

82. Frederic Beurhusius's commentary to P. Rami, *Dialecticae Libros Duos* (London, 1581), quoted in Miller, *The New England Mind,* 159.

83. Thomas Hobbes, *A Briefe of the Arte of Rhetorique,* in *The Rhetorics of Thomas Hobbes and Bernard Lamy,* ed. John T. Harwood (Carbondale, Ill.: Southern Illinois University Press, 1986), 45, 47, 56, 63. There was also a tradition of thinking about rhetoric as an art of "coloring" one's argument. Ramists, who saw the argument itself as a work of logic, came to describe rhetoric as the work of applying alluring colors to an already completed argument; rhetoric "put lively colours upon common truths" (Miller, *The New England Mind,* 326). Wilson's *The Arte of Rhetorique* argued that reason had to be embellished and made attractive by rhetoric, which "useth gaie painted sentences, & setteth forth those matters with freshe colours and goodly ornaments." (Miller, *The New England Mind,* 306). Huarte, a Spaniard, similarly thought that rhetoric "might beautifie the speech with polished words, with fine phrases, and with stirring affections and gratious colours" (John Huarte, *Examen de Ingenios* [London, 1596], 128, quoted in Miller, *The New England Mind,* 306). Therefore, the more analytic sermons often worked to understand biblical passages by stripping off the imagery as a secondary quality, to reach the logical argument beneath it (Miller, *The New England Mind,* 342).

84. In this paragraph I follow Richard Tuck, "Hobbes and Descartes," in G. A. J. Rogers and Alan Ryan, eds., *Perspectives on Thomas Hobbes* (Oxford: Oxford University Press, 1988).

85. Hobbes, *Elements* 2.10.

86. Hobbes, *Leviathan,* 15.

87. Ibid., 75, 270, 274, 440.

88. Ibid., 257, 298, 300, 480–482. For similar examples, see *Leviathan,* 18, 275, 428, 445, 446.

89. Ibid., 19.

90. Hobbes, *Elements* 1.2.

91. Ibid., 7.1–3.

92. Hobbes, *Leviathan,* 10.

93. Ibid., 90.

94. Hobbes, *Elements* 1.14.2.

95. Hobbes, *Leviathan,* 39, 110–111.

96. Edward Hyde, Earl of Clarendon, "A Brief View and Survey of the Dangerous and Pernicious Errors to Church and State in Mr Hobbes's Book, Entitled Leviathan (1676)," in G. A. J. Rogers, ed., *Leviathan: Contemporary Responses to the Political Theory of Thomas Hobbes* (Bristol, U.K.: Thoemmes Press, 1995), 180–300.

97. Hobbes, *Elements* 1.4; *Leviathan,* chap. 3.

98. Hobbes, *Leviathan,* 39.

99. Ibid., 110–111.

100. Aristotle, *De anima: Books II and III (with passages from Book I)*, trans. D. W. Hamlyn (Oxford: Clarendon Press, 1993), 430a26.
101. Hobbes, *Leviathan*, chap. 8.
102. Ibid., 120.

2. Persuading without Convincing: Rousseau

1. Jean-Jacques Rousseau, *Émile, or On Education*, trans. Allan Bloom (New York: Basic Books, 1979), 321. Jean-Jacques Rousseau, *On the Social Contract with Geneva Manuscript and Political Economy*, ed. Roger D. Masters, trans. Judith R. Masters (New York: St. Martin's Press, 1978), 2.7. Citations to the *On the Social Contract* will give book and chapter numbers.
2. John Rawls, *A Theory of Justice* (Cambridge, Mass.: Harvard University Press, 1971), 11. John Rawls, *The Law of Peoples* (Cambridge, Mass.: Harvard University Press, 1999), 7, 13.
3. Anne M. Cohler, *Rousseau and Nationalism* (New York: Basic Books, 1970); Marc E. Plattner, "Rousseau and the Origins of Nationalism," in *The Legacy of Rousseau*, ed. Clifford Orwin and Nathan Tarcov (Chicago, Ill.: University of Chicago Press, 1997); Arthur Melzer, "Rousseau, Nationalism, and the Politics of Sympathetic Identification," in *Educating the Prince: Essays in Honor of Harvey Mansfield*, ed. Mark Blitz and William Kristol (Lanham, Md.: Rowman and Littlefield Publishers, 2000), 111–128.
4. Rousseau, *Émile*, 321. On the language of signs, see *Émile*, 237, 321–323, 342.
5. Jean-Jacques Rousseau, *Essay on the Origin of Languages*, in *The First and Second Discourses Together with the Replies to Critics and Essay on the Origin of Languages*, trans. Victor Gourevitch (New York: Harper and Row, 1986). Citations to this work give the chapter and page number. Starobinski briefly calls attention to Rousseau's admiration for "mute eloquence." See Jean Starobinski, "Rousseau et l'éloquence," in *Rousseau After Two Hundred Years: Proceedings of the Cambridge Bicentennial Colloquium*, ed. R. A. Leigh (Cambridge: Cambridge University Press, 1982), 204.
6. Rousseau, *Essay on the Origin of Languages*, 1.241. Niccolò Machiavelli, *The Prince*, 2d ed., trans. Harvey C. Mansfield (Chicago: University of Chicago Press, 1998), 6.29–30. Niccolò Machiavelli, *Discourses on Livy*, trans. Harvey C. Mansfield and Nathan Tarcov (Chicago: University of Chicago Press, 1996), 3.3.
7. Jean-Jacques Rousseau, *Discourse on the Sciences and Arts, or First Discourse*, in *The First and Second Discourses Together with the Replies to Critics and Essay on the Origin of Languages*, trans. Victor Gourevitch (New York: Harper and Row, 1986), 27.
8. Rousseau, *Discourse on the Sciences and Arts*, 12.
9. Rousseau, *On the Social Contract*, 4.6.
10. Rousseau, *Émile*, 322–323.
11. Rousseau, *Essay on the Origin of Languages*, 1.242.
12. Cicero, *De inventione* I.i–ii.

13. Jean-Jacques Rousseau, *Discourse on Inequality, or Second Discourse*, in *The First and Second Discourses*, trans. Victor Gourevitch (New York: Harper and Row, 1986), 182–184.

14. See Rousseau, Geneva Manuscript, in *On the Social Contract*, 182–183.

15. Rousseau, letter to Malesherbes as quoted in Starobinski, "Rousseau et l'éloquence," 190 (my translation): "Avais-je quelque vrai talent pour écrire? Je ne sais. Une vive persuasion m'a toujours tenu lieu d'éloquence et j'ai toujours écrit lâchement et mal quand je n'ai pas été fortement persuadé."

16. Rousseau, *Émile*, 243. See also 251.

17. Rousseau, *Essay on the Origin of Languages*, 11.275, 20.294.

18. Ibid., 20.294.

19. Rousseau, *On the Social Contract*, 2.3, 4.1.

20. Ibid., 4.2.

21. Rousseau, *Émile*, 290. Arash Abizadeh also treats Rousseau's retreat to the inner voice of conscience and its relation to the tradition of rhetoric, but he focuses on the connection between conscience and Descartes's *bon sens*. The interpretation offered here supplements his reading by offering more insight into the way in which conscience is made public—by an internalization of Hobbesian sovereignty. See Arash Abizadeh, "Banishing the Particular: Rousseau on Rhetoric, *Patrie*, and the Passions," *Political Theory* 29 (August 2001): 556–582.

22. Rousseau, *On the Social Contract*, 3.12–15, 17–19; 1.6; 2.4; Jean-Jacques Rousseau, "Political Economy," in *On the Social Contract with Geneva Manuscript and Political Economy*, ed. Roger D. Masters, trans. Judith R. Masters (New York: St. Martin's Press, 1978), 223, 211, 214; Rousseau, *Émile*, 40; Rousseau, *On the Social Contract*, 4.8.

23. Rousseau, "Political Economy," 212–213; Rousseau, "Letter to Grimm," in Rousseau, *First and Second Discourses*, 62.

24. Rousseau, *On the Social Contract*, 2.3, 4.1–2, 4.8.

25. Rousseau, *Discourse on Inequality*, 125.

26. Thomas Hobbes, *Leviathan*, ed. Richard Tuck (Cambridge: Cambridge University Press, 1996), chap. 17, 112. See Cicero, *On the Ideal Orator* [*De oratore*], trans. James M. May and Jakob Wisse (New York: Oxford University Press, 2001), 2.102. I discuss the contrast between Hobbes's view of representation and Cicero's in chapter 5.

27. Jean-Jacques Rousseau, *Politics and the Arts: Letter to M. D'Alembert on the Theatre*, trans. Allan Bloom (Ithaca, N.Y.: Cornell University Press, 1960), 17.

28. Rousseau, *Second Discourse*, 198; Rousseau, *Émile*, 230.

29. Rousseau, *Émile*, 317.

30. Rousseau, *On the Social Contract*, 2.7.

31. Hobbes, *Leviathan*, chap. 21, 152.

32. Hobbes, *Leviathan*, chap. 17, 120.

33. Rousseau, *Émile*, 40.

34. Hobbes, *Leviathan*, chap. 17, 118–119.

35. Rousseau, *On the Social Contract*, 1.8.

36. As Pierre Manent writes, "Rousseau's antiliberal thought is going to provide content to the hypothetical being on which liberalism constructed itself, the individual." Pierre Manent, *An Intellectual History of Liberalism*, trans. Rebecca Balinski (Princeton, N.J.: Princeton University Press, 1994), 77.

37. On the topic of rhetoric and music in Rousseau, see Christopher Kelly, "'To Persuade Without Convincing': The Melodious Language of Rousseau's Legislator," *American Journal of Political Science* 31 (May 1987): 321–335; Starobinski, "Rousseau et l'éloquence," 185–200; Baczko, "La cité et ses langages," in *Rousseau After Two Hundred Years*, 87–108; John T. Scott, "Rousseau and the Melodious Language of Freedom," *Journal of Politics* 59 (August, 1997): 803–829; Neil Saccamano, "Rhetoric, Consensus, and the Law in Rousseau's *Contrat Social*," French issue, *MLN* 107 (September 1992): 730–751; Abizadeh, "Banishing the Particular." On music in Rousseau more generally, see Robert Wokler, *Rousseau on Society, Politics, Music and Language: An Historical Interpretation of His Early Writings* (New York: Garland Pub., 1987); Jean Starobinski, *Le remède du mal: Critique et légitimation de l'artifice à l'âge des Lumières* (Paris: Gallimard, 1989), 208–232; and John T. Scott, "The Harmony Between Roussesau's Musical Theory and His Philosophy," *Journal of the History of Ideas* 59 (1998): 287–308.

38. Compare Baczko, who suggests that Rousseau did not leave behind the model of ancient oratory so much as seek to restrict it to moments of crisis or founding. Baczko, "La cité et ses langages," 93.

39. See, for example, Abizadeh, "Banishing the Particular," 569–576.

40. Rousseau, *Essay on the Origin of Languages*, 4.248.

41. Ibid.

42. See Rousseau, *Dictionary of Music* and "The Principle of Melody," in *The Collected Writings of Rousseau*, vol. 7, ed. Roger D. Masters and Christopher Kelly (Hanover, N.H.: University of New England Press, 1998).

43. Rousseau, *Essay on the Origin of Languages*, 4.248; 16.287–288; 2.245; 13.278; 16.285–88; 17.288.

44. Rousseau, *Essay on the Origin of Languages*, 2.245; *Émile*, 290.

45. Rousseau, *Émile*, 290.

46. Ibid., 289.

47. Hobbes, *Leviathan*, chap. 15, 109.

48. Rousseau, *Émile*, 245.

49. Rousseau, *Discourse on Inequality*, 163; *Émile*, 235n.

50. Ibid., 161–164. On the role of pity and the origin of languages, see especially Jacques Derrida, *Of Grammatology*, corrected ed., trans. Gayatri Chakravorty Spivak (Baltimore, Md.: Johns Hopkins University Press, 1997), 165–192.

51. Rousseau, *Discourse on Inequality*, 162–163. See also Rousseau, Geneva Manuscript, 1.2, 160: "It is false that in the state of independence, reason leads us to cooperate."

52. Rousseau, *Émile*, 219–235.

53. "Men are not naturally kings, or lords, or courtiers, or rich men. All are born naked and poor; all are subject to the miseries of life, to sorrows, ills, needs, and pains of every kind. Finally, all are condemned to death. This is what truly belongs to man . . . what best characterizes humanity." Rousseau, *Émile*, 222.

54. Ibid., 235. Rousseau, *On the Social Contract*, 2.7.

55. Ibid., 40.

56. Rousseau, *On the Social Contract* 2.4. In *Émile*, too, the project of turning the pupil into a moral being is wholly dominated by deepening and directing this natural sentiment. Rousseau, *Émile*, 219–235. A full account of Rousseau's view of the development of man's moral and political nature would also have to take account of the way in which amour propre is transformed and enlarged. For a recent treatment of this development, see Joseph R. Reisert, *Jean-Jacques Rousseau: A Friend of Virtue* (Ithaca, N.Y.: Cornell University Press, 2003), 186.

57. Rousseau, *Essay on the Origin of Languages*, 9.261–262, 9.271–272.

58. Ibid., 1.240.

59. On this point, see Melzer, "Rousseau, Nationalism, and the Politics of Sympathetic Identification," 123.

60. Rousseau, *Discourse on Inequality*, 153, 155, 157–158.

61. Ibid., 156.

62. Rousseau, *On the Social Contract*, 1.8 (emphasis added).

63. Rousseau, *Essay on the Origin of Languages*, 12.278.

64. Ibid., 15.283–284.

65. Hobbes, *Leviathan*, chap. 4.

66. Hobbes, *Leviathan*, chap. 5.

67. Hobbes, *Elements*, 2.10.8; Hobbes, *Leviathan*, chap. 17 and introduction.

68. Rousseau, *On the Social Contract*, 2.7 (emphasis added).

69. Rousseau, *Essay on the Origin of Languages*, 11.275.

70. Rousseau, Geneva Manuscript, 160, 197.

71. Rousseau, *Émile*, 312n. See Rousseau, *Discourse on Inequality*, 192, where he argues that religion "spares more blood than fanaticism causes to flow." See also Rousseau, *On the Social Contract*, 4.8.

72. Rousseau, *Émile*, 85, 66, 102, 120. See J. S. Maloy, "The Very Order of Things: Rousseau's Tutorial Republicanism," *Polity* 37 (April 2005): 235–261.

73. Rousseau, *Émile*, 85.

3. The Sovereignty of Scholars: Kant

1. See Barbara Herman, *The Practice of Moral Judgment* (Cambridge, Mass.: Harvard University Press, 1993); Christine Korsgaard, *Creating a Kingdom of Ends* (Cambridge: Cambridge University Press, 1996); Nancy Sherman, *Making a Necessity of Virtue: Aristotle and Kant on Virtue* (Cambridge: Cambridge University Press, 1997); Onora O'Neill, *Constructions of Reason: Explorations of Kant's Practical Philosophy* (Cambridge: Cambridge University Press, 1989); Ronald Beiner,

Political Judgment (Chicago, Ill.: University of Chicago Press, 1983); Samuel Fleischacker, *A Third Concept of Liberty: Judgment and Freedom in Kant and Adam Smith* (Princeton, N.J.: Princeton University Press, 1999).

2. Hannah Arendt, *Lectures on Kant's Political Philosophy*, ed. Ronald Beiner (Chicago, Ill.: University of Chicago Press, 1982), 19.

3. Hannah Arendt, "The Crisis in Culture: Its Social and Political Significance," in *Between Past and Future: Eight Exercises in Political Thought* (New York: Viking Press, 1968), 221.

4. Arendt, "The Crisis in Culture," 221.

5. On the relation of Arendt's treatment of judgment to other aspects of her thought and to the question of moral judgment in general, see Seyla Benhabib, *Situating the Self: Gender, Community and Postmodernism in Contemporary Ethics* (New York: Routledge, 1992), chap. 4. For an account that emphasizes the political dimension of judgment, see Ronald Beiner, introduction, in Hannah Arendt, *Lectures on Kant's Political Philosophy*, ed. Ronald Beiner (Chicago, Ill.: University of Chicago Press, 1982), and also Beiner, *Political Judgment*, 12–19.

6. Arendt, "The Crisis in Culture," 214, 217–226. See also Hannah Arendt, "Truth and Politics" in *Between Past and Future: Eight Exercises in Political Thought* (New York: Viking Press, 1968), 233, 241, 262.

7. Immanuel Kant, *Critique of Judgment*, trans. J. H. Bernard (New York: Hafner Press, 1951), §53, 171. References are to section number and page.

8. Ibid., §53, 173.

9. Ibid., §53, 173.

10. Immanuel Kant, "An Answer to the Question: What is Enlightenment?" (1784) in Immanuel Kant, *Political Writings*, ed. Hans Reiss, trans. H. B. Nisbet (Cambridge: Cambridge University Press, 1991), 59–60. Kant here alluded to La Mettrie's *L'homme Machine* (1748) and perhaps also to an actual automaton which Vaucanson had been displaying in public settings. See Julien Offray de la Mettrie, *Machine Man and Other Writings*, trans. Ann Thomson (Cambridge: Cambridge University Press, 1996), 3–39; and Otto Mayr, *Authority, Liberty and Automatic Machinery in Early Modern Europe* (Baltimore, Md.: Johns Hopkins University Press, 1986), 132–134, 136. On the danger of treating men as machines, see also Kant's description of "political moralists" in Immanuel Kant, "Perpetual Peace: A Philosophical Sketch," in *Political Writings*, 93–130 at 123.

11. Kant, "What is Enlightenment?," 54.

12. Ibid.

13. Kant, *Critique of Judgment*, §53, 172.

14. John Wallis (1616–1703) was a member of the Royal Society who had engaged in a long dispute with Hobbes, originally about mathematics. He famously claimed to have taught two deaf students to speak by showing them the physical actions of the tongue, teeth, lips, and, mouth. Bernard Lamy wrote of having heard of Wallis's experiment from a Monsieur de Monconys,

who had traveled in England. Bernard Lamy, *The Art of Speaking* (1676) 3.1.1, in *The Rhetorics of Thomas Hobbes and Bernard Lamy*, ed. John T. Harwood (Carbondale, Ill.: Southern Illinois University Press, 1986), 251–252. See 252n for information on Wallis, and see part 3 of Lamy for a mechanistic approach to rhetoric.

15. Jonathan Swift, "A Discourse Concerning the Mechanical Operation of the Spirit," in *A Tale of a Tub* (Oxford: Clarendon Press, 1920), 281. See in this same essay Swift's association of Hobbes with a mechanistic view of rhetorical invention: "For, it is the Opinion of Choice *Virtuosi*, that the Brain is only a Crowd of little Animals, but with Teeth and Claws extremely sharp, and therefore, cling together in the Contexture we behold, like the Picture of Hobbes's *Leviathan* . . . That all invention is formed by the Morsure of two or more of these Animals, upon certain capillary Nerves, which proceed from thence, whereof three Branches spread into the Tongue, and two in the right Hand." For a general discussion of this essay as a satire on oratorical treatises and religious enthusiasm, see Denis Donoghue, *Jonathan Swift: A Critical Introduction* (Cambridge: Cambridge University Press, 1969). That Kant had in fact read Swift's *A Tale of a Tub* is suggested by his quotation of it in "Perpetual Peace." He also referred to Swift (though not to *A Tale of a Tub*) in Immanuel Kant "On the Common Saying: 'This May Be True in Theory, but It Does Not Apply in Practice,'" Immanuel Kant, in *Political Writings*, 102n with 276n8 and 92. Cited hereafter as "Theory and Practice." See also Thomas M. Conley, *Rhetoric in the European Tradition* (Chicago, Ill.: University of Chicago Press, 1990), 189.

16. Kant also criticized rhetoric briefly in another context, when introducing the subject of logic. He distinguished analytic logic from dialectic, which was an "art of semblance": "Amongst the Greeks the dialecticians were advocates and rhetoricians who could lead the populace wherever they chose, because the populace lets itself be deluded with semblance . . . for so long all logic and philosophy was the cultivation by certain chatter-heads of the art of semblance. But nothing can be more unworthy of a philosopher than the cultivation of such an art." Immanuel Kant, *Introduction to Logic*, trans. Thomas Kingsmill Abbott (New York: Philosophical Library, 1963), 2.1, 7.

17. Immanuel Kant, "What is Orientation in Thinking?" in *Political Writings*, 246–247.

18. For the same line of reasoning in moral theory, see Immanuel Kant, *Groundwork of The Metaphysics of Morals*, in *Practical Philosophy*, trans. Mary J. Gregor (Cambridge: Cambridge University Press, 1996), 94–95. See also Christine Korsgaard, "Morality as Freedom" in *Creating the Kingdom of Ends* (Cambridge: Cambridge University Press, 1996), 163.

19. Immanuel Kant, *Critique of Pure Reason*, trans. Norman Kemp Smith (New York: St. Martin's Press, 1965), B vii, xv, xxxi, 17, 21, 30. Kant, "What is Orientation in Thinking?," 246, 248, 249n.

20. Kant, *Critique of Pure Reason*, B xxv, 27.

21. Ibid., A 751–752 / B 779–780, 601. This passage was first brought to my attention by Richard Tuck, who points to it as evidence of the "Hobbesianism" of

Kant in Richard Tuck, *The Rights of War and Peace: Political Thought and the International Order from Grotius to Kant* (New York: Oxford University Press, 1999), 213.

22. Kant, *Critique of Pure Reason*, A 709 / B 737, 574; A 711 / B 739, 576.

23. Ibid., A 752–753 / B 780–781, 601–602.

24. Ibid., A 755–756 / B 784–785, 603–604.

25. Kant, *Critique of Judgment*, §40, 137n.

26. Kant, *Critique of Pure Reason*, B xxxv–xxxvi, 32.

27. Ibid., A 738–39 / B 766–67, 593. Onora O'Neill, *Constructions of Reason*, 37. See chaps. 1–2 for her defense of Kant along the lines summarized here.

28. Kant, *Critique of Pure Reason*, A 752 / B 780, 602 (emphasis added).

29. O'Neill, *Construction of Reason*, 37. See Ibid., A 738–739 / B 766–767, 593.

30. O'Neill, *Constructions of Reason*, 38.

31. Ibid., 42.

32. Kant, *Critique of Judgment*, §41, 139.

33. Arendt, "The Crisis in Culture," 218.

34. Arendt, *Lectures on Kant's Political Philosophy*, 63–64, 65–66.

35. There is another sense in which Kant's thought might be said to be Ciceronian—both philosophers defend moral duties. There are clear echoes of Cicero's Stoicism in Kantian moral theory. This link, however, was not the one that Arendt discussed in the *Lectures on Kant's Political Philosophy*. She drew instead from Cicero's writings on rhetoric to explain Kant's notion of communicability, and this is the connection that ultimately seems implausible.

36. See Kant, *Critique of Pure Reason*, A x–xii, 8–9; Kant, *Introduction to Logic* 4. 23.

37. Helpful accounts of the popular philosophers and their relation to Kant can be found in the following sources: Lewis White Beck, *Early German Philosophy: Kant and His Predecessors* (Cambridge, Mass.: Harvard University Press, 1969), 319–324; Frederick C. Beiser, *The Fate of Reason: German Philosophy from Kant to Fichte* (Cambridge, Mass.: Harvard University Press, 1987), 165–192; Johan van der Zande, "In the Image of Cicero: German Philosophy between Wolff and Kant," *Journal of the History of Ideas* 56 (July 1995): 419–442; Johan van der Zande, "The Microscope of Experience: Christian Garve's Translation of Cicero's *De officiis* (1783)," *Journal of the History of Ideas* 59 (1998): 75–94; John H. Zammito, *Kant, Herder, and the Birth of Anthropology* (Chicago, Ill.: University of Chicago Press, 2002).

38. Georg Friedrich Wilhelm Hegel, *Über das Wesen der philosophischen Kritik überhaupt und ihr Verhältnis zum gegenwärtigen Zustand der Philosophie insbesondere*, *Werke* (20 vols.; Stuttgart, 1970), II.182, as cited in van der Zande, "In the Image of Cicero," 422n.

39. See Beiser, *The Fate of Reason*, 166, for a description of these "Lockeans" as "self-conscious eclectics."

40. For this broad characterization of the popular philosophers I am indebted to van der Zande, "In the Image of Cicero," 434–437.

41. Zammito, *Kant, Herder, and the Birth of Anthropology*, 6, 88.

42. Kant, *Critique of Pure Reason*, A x–xii, 8–9. For similar references to "indifference," see Immanuel Kant, *Prolegomena to Any Future Metaphysics*, trans. Paul Carus, rev. trans. James W. Ellington (Indianapolis, Ind.: Hackett Publishing, 1977), 106–107, 120.

43. Kant, *Critique of Pure Reason*, A x, 8.

44. The review is available in English: Unsigned review, "*Critique of Pure Reason* by Immanuel Kant, 1781, 856 pages in Octavo," *Zugabe zu den Göttingischen Anzeigen von gelehrten Sachen*, January 19, 1782: 40–48, in *Kant's Early Critics: The Empiricist Critique of the Theoretical Philosophy*, trans. and ed. Brigitte Sassen (Cambridge: Cambridge University Press, 2000), 53–58. Referred to here as the Göttingen review.

45. Göttingen review, 53, 58. Both points of criticism—that Kant does not offer anything fundamentally new and that his technical style represents some sort of failure—appeared in Garve's original, unedited review. See Christian Garve, "*Critique of Pure Reason* by Immanuel Kant. Riga, 1781. 856 pages in 8," supplement to vols. 37–52 (1783): 838–862, in *Kant's Early Critics*, 59, 76.

46. See, for instance, Beiser, *The Fate of Reason*, 172–173; Sassen, *Kant's Early Critics*, 7–11; R. C. S. Walker, ed., *The Real in the Ideal: Berkeley's Relation to Kant* (New York: Garland Publishers, 1989).

47. Kant, *Critique of Pure Reason*, B xliii–xliv, 36–37.

48. For an exploration of the philosophical implications of this ugliness see Stephen F. Barker, "The Style of Kant's Critique of Reason," in *The Philosopher as Writer: The Eighteenth Century*, ed. Robert Ginsburg (London: Associated University Presses, 1987), 75–93.

49. Christian Garve to Kant, July 13, 1783, in Immanuel Kant, *Correspondence*, trans. Arnulf Zweig (Cambridge: Cambridge University Press, 1999), 193. The same criticism was on display in Garve's original review. Garve, "*Critique of Pure Reason*," 59.

50. Kant, *Critique of Pure Reason*, A xviii–xx, 12–13; B xliv, 37.

51. Kant, *Critique of Pure Reason*, A xviii, 13; B xxxvi, 32.

52. Garve to Kant, July 13, 1783; Garve, "*The Critique of Pure Reason*," 59–60.

53. Moses Mendelssohn, "On the Question: What Is Enlightenment?" trans. James Schmidt, in *What is Enlightenment?: Eighteenth-Century Answers and Twentieth-Century Questions*, ed. James Schmidt (Berkeley, Calif.: University of California Press, 1996), 53–57.

54. Mendelssohn, "On the Question: What is Enlightenment?" 54.

55. Moses Mendelssohn, "Soll man der einreissenden Schwämerey durch Satyre oder durch äussere Verbindung entgegenarbeiten?" *Berlinische Monatsschrift* 5 (February 1785): 133–137, as quoted in Schmidt, *What is Enlightenment?*, 57.

56. Kant, *Critique of Pure Reason*, B xxxiv, 31–32.

57. Kant, *Metaphysics of Morals*, 366.

58. See Manfred Kuehn, *Scottish Common Sense in Germany, 1768–1800: A Contribution to the History of Critical Philosophy* (Kingston, Can.: McGill-Queen's University Press, 1987), 74–85.

59. Thomas Reid, *An Inquiry into the Human Mind on the Principle of Common Sense,* in *The Works of Thomas Reid,* ed. William Hamilton, vol. 1 (Bristol, U.K.: Thoemmes Press, 1994), 101b.

60. Reid, *Inquiry into the Human Mind,* 102b.

61. The influence of Reid on Garve and Feder shows up even in small details, as when Garve criticized Kant for focusing only on the sense of sight and leaving out consideration of the other senses (Garve, "*Critique of Pure Reason,*" 75). Reid's *Inquiry* began with the sense of smell and proceeded through each of the other four senses in turn.

62. Johann Georg Heinrich Feder, *On Space and Causality: An Examination of Kantian Philosophy,* §16 (title), in Sassen, *Kant's Early Critics,* 140.

63. Garve, "*Critique of Pure Reason,*" 71. See also the beginning of the review, where Garve announced his intention to try to bring the "daylight of common sense" to Kant's ideas.

64. Garve, "*Critique of Pure Reason,*" 77.

65. Kant, *Prolegomena,* 4–5.

66. Kant, *Prolegomena,* 108–109. See also Kant, *Introduction to Logic,* 10. 72 on probability and 2. 7 on *sensus communis.*

67. Kant, *Prolegomena,* 109.

68. Ibid., 5.

69. Thomas Reid, *Essays on the Intellectual Powers of Man* (1785) in *The Works of Thomas Reid,* vol. 1, 424b. For a brief summary of Buffier's rhetoric and its link to common sense see Conley, *Rhetoric in the European Tradition,* 194–197.

70. George Campbell, *The Philosophy of Rhetoric,* ed. Lloyd F. Bitzer (Carbondale, Ill.: Southern Illinois University Press, 1963), 38–42.

71. Kant, *Critique of Judgment,* §40, 136.

72. Kant laid out the same three maxims in section 7 of his *Introduction to Logic* and pointed out in *Critique of Judgment,* §40 that they were somewhat out of place. Thus it seems reasonable to view them as maxims of reasoning in general.

73. Kant, *Critique of Judgment,* §40, 137.

74. Reid, *Inquiry into the Human Mind,* 209b.

75. On the insufficiency of the "naturalistic" method used by those who adopt "common reason" as their standard, see Kant, *Critique of Pure Reason,* A 855 / B 883, 668.

76. Reid, *Inquiry into the Human Mind,* 209b.

77. Arendt, *Lectures on Kant's Political Philosophy,* 72.

78. Reid, *Inquiry into the Human Mind,* 424b.

79. For a comprehensive assessment of the importance of community in Kant's thought, see Susan Meld Shell, *The Embodiment of Reason: Kant on Spirit, Generation, and Community* (Chicago, Ill.: University of Chicago Press, 1996), 133–160.

80. Kant, *Critique of Pure Reason,* A 820 / B848, 645.

81. See also Kant, *Critique of Pure Reason,* A 782 / B 810, 620, for Kant's dismissal of private opinion.

82. Arendt, *Lectures on Kant's Political Philosophy,* 73.

83. Ibid., 74.
84. Kant, *Prolegomena,* 108.
85. Arendt, *Lectures on Kant's Political Philosophy,* 163n155.
86. On "sympathy and detachment," see Beiner, *Political Judgment,* chap. 6.
87. Kant, "Perpetual Peace," 126.
88. O'Neill, *Constructions of Reason,* 34.
89. Kant, "Perpetual Peace," 125.
90. Kant, "Theory and Practice," 83.
91. Kant, "Perpetual Peace," 126–127 and Kant, *The Metaphysics of Morals,* 143–145. See also his discussion of the absence of a provision for rebellion in the English constitution in Kant, "Theory and Practice," 83–84.
92. Kant, "Theory and Practice," 81. See also 75, 84.
93. Ibid., 80.
94. Ibid., 81n. See also Kant, *Metaphysics of Morals,* §52, 480.
95. Richard Tuck makes the point with reference to the parallel passage in §44 of "The Doctrine of Right" in *Metaphysics of Morals.* See Tuck, *The Rights of War and Peace,* 207–208.
96. Kant, "Theory and Practice," 81. See also 79–80, including Kant's note on why the people are not entitled to judge the appropriateness of a war tax so long as it is equitably imposed.
97. Kant, "What is Enlightenment?," 55.
98. Kant, "Theory and Practice," 84–85.
99. See Kant's note on the horror of formal executions of monarchs. Kant, *Metaphysics of Morals,* 145n.
100. Kant, "What is Orientation in Thinking?," 247.
101. Kant, "What is Enlightenment?," 55.
102. For a more sympathetic account of Kant's thought on publicity that emphasizes this point and suggests that it was in fact quite progressive in its context, see John Christian Laursen, "The Subversive Kant: The Vocabulary of 'Public' and 'Publicity,'" in Schmidt, *What Is Enlightenment?,* 253–269.
103. Kant, "Perpetual Peace," 108.
104. Immanuel Kant, "The Contest of the Faculties," in *Political Writings,* 187. See also 184n: "The best way of making a nation content with its constitution is to *rule* autocratically and at the same time to *govern* in a republican manner, i.e. to govern in the spirit of republicanism and by analogy with it."
105. See Michael Clarke, "Kant's Rhetoric of Enlightenment," *Review of Politics* 59 (Winter, 1997): 53–73.
106. Kant, "Contest of the Faculties," as quoted in Laursen, "The Subversive Kant," 261.
107. Kant, "Perpetual Peace," 115.
108. Ibid., 115: "Although it may seem humiliating for the legislative authority of a state, to which we must naturally attribute the highest degree of wisdom, to seek instruction from *subjects* (the philosophers) regarding the principles on which it should act in its relations with other states, it is nevertheless ex-

tremely advisable that it should do so. That state will therefore invite their help silently, making a secret of it. In other words, it will *allow them to speak freely and publicly on the universal maxims of warfare and peacemaking.*" See also Kant, "Theory and Practice," 86.

109. Kant, "Contest of the Faculties," 186.

110. Ibid., 186–187n; Kant, "Perpetual Peace," 114–115.

111. Susan Shell, in a more sympathetic treatment of this point, suggests that Kant is best seen as asking philosophers to be teachers encouraging enlightenment and that unlike some of his followers (Fichte and Marx) he took pains to distinguish that role from one of rulership. The indirectness with which the scholars' enlightened point of view was meant to guide the rulers can thus be interpreted in different ways. But the effectual truth of Kant's position seems to have been that it pointed the way toward a rhetoric of sovereign public reason. See Susan Meld Shell, "Kantian Idealism," in *Educating the Prince: Essays in Honor of Harvey Mansfield,* ed. Mark Blitz and William Kristol (Lanham, Md.: Rowman and Littlefield Publishers, 2000), 135–136.

112. In addition to the popular philosophers Kant seems also to have had in his sights Edmund Burke, whose *Reflections on the Revolution in France* had recently been translated into German. See Hans Reiss's editor's note in Kant, *Political Writings,* 274n3.

113. Kant, "Theory and Practice," 63.

114. Kant, "Perpetual Peace," 129.

115. Ibid., 115.

116. Ibid., 114.

117. Jean-Jacques Rousseau, *On the Social Contract with Geneva Manuscript and Political Economy,* ed. Roger D. Masters, trans. Judith R. Masters (New York: St. Martin's Press, 1978), 3.1.

118. Kant, "Perpetual Peace," 114. See also Kant, *Metaphysics of Morals,* §45, 457. Garve expresses bewilderment about this passage in his review. Garve, "*Critique of Pure Reason,*" 67.

119. Kant, *Critique of Pure Reason* A 322 / B 378–379, 316.

120. Kant, "Perpetual Peace," 100–102.

121. Ibid., 114. Compare Baron Charles Louis de Secondat Montesquieu, *The Spirit of the Laws: A Compendium of the First Edition,* ed. David Wallace Carrithers, trans. Thomas Nugent (Berkeley, Calif.: University of California Press, 1977), 8.2, 171; and Rousseau, *Social Contract,* 3.4.

4. Drawing upon Judgment: Aristotle

1. Among the many authors articulating and praising Aristotle's emphasis on judgment, see especially Ronald Beiner, *Political Judgment* (Chicago, Ill.: University of Chicago Press, 1983), chap. 4; Jill Frank, *A Democracy of Distinction: Aristotle and the Work of Politics* (Chicago, Ill.: University of Chicago Press, 2005);

Jill Frank, "Democracy and Distribution: Aristotle on Just Desert," *Political Theory* 26 (1998): 784–802; Jonathan Lear, *Aristotle: The Desire to Understand* (Cambridge: Cambridge University Press, 1988), 150–151; Martha C. Nussbaum, *The Fragility of Goodness: Luck and Ethics in Greek Tragedy and Philosophy* (Cambridge: Cambridge University Press, 1986), chap. 10; Stephen G. Salkever, *Finding the Mean: Theory and Practice in Aristotelian Political Philosophy* (Princeton, N.J.: Princeton University Press, 1990), chap. 3; Nancy Sherman, *Making a Necessity of Virtue: Aristotle and Kant on Virtue* (Cambridge: Cambridge University Press, 1997), chap. 6; Jeremy Waldron, "The Wisdom of the Multitude: Some Reflections on Book III, Chapter 11 of Aristotle's *Politics*," *Political Theory* 23 (1995): 563–584. Iris Murdoch's writings, though not studies of Aristotle, articulate much of what is attractive in an Aristotelian approach to ethics. See especially Iris Murdoch, *The Sovereignty of Good* (New York: Schocken Books, 1971).

2. Thomas Hobbes, *Leviathan*, ed. Richard Tuck (Cambridge: Cambridge University Press, 1996), 306.

3. Aristotle, *The Politics*, trans. Carnes Lord (Chicago, Ill.: University of Chicago Press, 1984), 1284a1–10. See also 1322b17–29.

4. Eugene Garver also cites the priority of deliberative over judicial rhetoric as a key innovation. Eugene Garver, *Aristotle's Rhetoric: An Art of Character* (Chicago, Ill.: University of Chicago Press, 117). But he is also committed to the "political irrelevance" of this innovation. Eugene Garver, "The Political Irrelevance of Aristotle's *Rhetoric*," *Philosophy and Rhetoric* 29 (1996): 179–199.

5. Aristotle, *Rhetoric*, 1358b, 1377b21, 1420b. I have consulted the following translations: Aristotle, *The Art of Rhetoric*, trans. J. H. Freese (Cambridge, Mass.: Harvard University Press, 1926); Aristotle, *On Rhetoric: A Theory of Civic Discourse*, trans. George A. Kennedy (New York: Oxford University Press, 1991); Aristotle, *Treatise on Rhetoric*, trans. Theodore Buckley (New York: Prometheus Books, 1995). All references will be to Kennedy's translation unless noted. For discussions of judgment in the *Rhetoric*, see the following: Arash Abizadeh, "The Passions of the Wise: *Phronesis*, Rhetoric, and Aristotle's Passionate Practical Deliberation," *Review of Metaphysics* 56 (Dec. 2002): 267–297; Danielle Allen, *Talking to Strangers: Anxieties of Citizenship Since Brown v. Board of Education* (Chicago, Ill.: University of Chicago Press, 2004), chap. 10; Beiner, *Political Judgment*, chap. 4; Eugene Garver, *Aristotle's Rhetoric*; Stephen Halliwell, "The Challenge of Rhetoric to Ethical Theory," in *Essays on Aristotle's Rhetoric*, ed. Amelie Rorty (Berkeley, Calif.: University of California Press, 1996), 175–190; Stephen R. Leighton, "Aristotle and the Emotions," in *Essays on Aristotle's Rhetoric*, 206–237; Mary Nichols, "Aristotle's Defense of Rhetoric," *Journal of Politics* 49 (August 1987): 657–677.

6. Aristotle, *Politics*, 1298a4–1299a1.

7. There is a substantial literature on the question of how the beginning of the *Rhetoric*, which does offer brief direct treatment of the ethical issue, fits with the rest of the work. George Kennedy suggests that apparently conflicting

parts of the text were written at different times. George Kennedy, *The Art of Persuasion in Ancient Greece* (Princeton, N.J.: Princeton University Press, 1963), 82–87. Jürgen Sprute and Eckhart Schütrumpf suggest that book 1 described an ideal rhetoric for an ideal state, whereas book 2 descended to the level of practical advice. Jürgen Sprute, "Aristotle and the Legitimacy of Rhetoric," in *Aristotle's Rhetoric: Philosophical Essays,* ed. David J. Furley and Alexander Nehamas (Princeton, N.J.: Princeton University Press, 1994), 119, 127; Eckart Schütrumpf, "Some Observations on the Introduction to Aristotle's *Rhetoric,*" in *Aristotle's Rhetoric: Philosophical Essays,* 105, 115. Glenn Most cleverly suggests that the opening chapter of the *Rhetoric* served the rhetorical function of persuading the reader to accept that a philosopher could be a good teacher of rhetoric. Glenn Most, "The Uses of *Endoxa:* Philosophy and Rhetoric in the *Rhetoric,*" in *Aristotle's Rhetoric: Philosophical Essays,* 188. Garver offers an account closer to the one given here, though he makes *ethos* more central to the art than I do. Garver, *Aristotle's Rhetoric,* especially chap. 7.

8. Aristotle, *Nicomachean Ethics,* trans. Terence Irwin (Indianapolis, Ind.: Hackett Publishing, 1999), 1094a29–b4, 1181a15.

9. See Thomas M. Conley, *Rhetoric in the European Tradition* (Chicago, Ill.: University of Chicago Press, 1990), 4–5, 7.

10. Plato, *Gorgias,* trans. James H. Nichols, Jr. (Ithaca, N.Y.: Cornell University Press, 1998), 454b, 480a–d, 521c–522e. Gorgias does include "assemblies" when defining the work of rhetoric (452e), but when pressed, he makes clear that he does not regard the assemblies as sites of deliberation; he redescribes his sphere of competence as "persuasion in law courts and in other mobs" (454b).

11. The authorship of the *Constitution of Athens* is not known with certainty, but the work is widely accepted as a product of Aristotle's academy, which collected and interpreted actual constitutions, a practice that Aristotle recommended in the *Ethics* (Aristotle, *Nicomachean Ethics,* 1181b7–12). Without insisting on Aristotle as its author, I use the *Constitution of Athens* as a source for an Aristotelian point of view about the development of the Athenian constitution. Aristotle, *The Constitution of Athens,* in *The Politics and The Constitution of Athens,* ed. Stephen Everson (Cambridge: Cambridge University Press, 1996).

12. *Constitution of Athens,* IX; XXIV.3–XXVII.5; XLV; XLI.2.

13. On confiscations through the courts, see Aristotle, *Politics,* 1320a5. On oligarchs revolting, Aristotle offered the example of Rhodes, where the nobles "on account of the suits brought against them, were compelled to stand together and overthrow [the rule of] the people." He then adduced a number of examples to show that the ordinary cause of revolution in democracies was "the wanton behavior of the popular leaders," by which he meant their treating the nobles unfairly, taking their property and slandering them (1304b21–1305a7); see also 1305b34 on oligarchies. On orators becoming tyrants, see 1310b15: "This is evident from events: most tyrants arose from popular leaders who were trusted because of their slander of the notables." On

encouraging the people to rule by decree, Aristotle stated that popular leaders were "responsible for decrees having authority rather than the laws because they bring everything before the people. For they become great through the people's having authority in all matters, and through having authority themselves over the opinion of the people, since the multitude is persuaded by them" (1292a5–38). On the parallel between rule by decree and tyranny, see 1293a5–32.

14. Aristotle, *Politics*, 1292a15–38, 1313b33–1314a5.

15. Ibid., 1274a5. Aristotle agreed with the correlation between the rise of the courts and the move toward more extreme democracy, but he did not think that Solon had intended for this to happen when he had introduced his reforms.

16. Plato, *Gorgias*, 464c–466a.

17. For an example of the metaphors equating persuasion with force, see Gorgias, *Encomium of Helen*, in Aristotle, *On Rhetoric: A Theory of Civic Discourse*, 283–288. Gorgias argued that if Helen was persuaded to go to Troy, she was as blameless as if she had been forced to go.

18. Aristotle, *Rhetoric*, 1354b (Buckley translation).

19. Aristotle, *Rhetoric*, 1354b10 *(to idion hedu e luperon)* and b30 *(pros charin)*. Though *charis* can mean kindliness or grace, translators have generally agreed about the connotation of this passage: the listeners are listening "merely for their own pleasure" (Freese) or "with partiality" (Kennedy) or "with a view to amusement" (Buckley).

20. Plato, *Gorgias*, 462c–d, 463b.

21. Ibid., 464d–465d.

22. *Constitution of Athens*, XXXV.3.

23. See, for example, Sprute, "Aristotle and the Legitimacy of Rhetoric," 119, 127; Schütrumpf, "Some Observations on the Introduction to Aristotle's *Rhetoric*," 105, 115; Most, "The Uses of *Endoxa*: Philosophy and Rhetoric in the *Rhetoric*," 188; and Kennedy, *The Art of Persuasion in Ancient Greece*, 82–87.

24. For recent work showing how emotions help to constitute Aristotelian deliberation and judgment, see Sherman, *Making a Necessity of Virtue*, chap. 2; Garver, *Aristotle's Rhetoric*, chap. 4; Martha Nussbaum, "Aristotle on Emotions and Rational Persuasion," in *Essays on Aristotle's Rhetoric*, 303–323; and Abizadeh, "The Passions of the Wise."

25. Aristotle, *Rhetoric*, 1377b–1378a.

26. Ibid., 1354a–b.

27. Ibid., 1354a.

28. Garver makes a similar point about the appropriateness of emotions when commenting on a different part of the text. Garver, *Aristotle's Rhetoric*, 137.

29. Aristotle, *Rhetoric*, 1354a15–30, 1354b5–10.

30. Aristotle, *Nicomachean Ethics*, 1137b27–33.

31. Aristotle, *Rhetoric*, 1354b–1355a.

32. Ibid., 1354b.

33. Aristotle *Politics*, 3.14–18. See also Aristotle, *Nicomachean Ethics*, 1137b12–1138a4, 1143a20; Aristotle, *Rhetoric*, 1374a18–22.

34. *Constitution of Athens*, IX.1–2. Compare to Aristotle, *Politics*, 1274a3–22.

35. Aristotle, *Politics*, 1328b12–15.

36. Ibid., 1299a1.

37. Ibid., 1354b–1355a.

38. Aristotle, *Nicomachean Ethics*, 1112b12–15, b32–35; compare to 1111b26–30, 1113b5.

39. Nussbaum, *Fragility of Goodness*, 297: "Aristotle's point is only that for any given piece of deliberation, there must be something that it is *about*, which is itself not up for question in that particular piece of deliberation." A similar reading of the passage can be found in John M. Cooper, *Reason and Human Good in Aristotle* (Indianapolis, Ind.: Hackett Publishing, 1986), 14. A slightly more restrictive view of what deliberation includes can be found in Lear, *Aristotle: The Desire to Understand*, 146–48. The interpretation I give in this paragraph is indebted to these sources and to a conversation with Jill Frank.

40. Aristotle, *Nicomachean Ethics*, 1141a25, 1141b9, 1142b32.

41. Ibid., 1141b23.

42. Ibid., 1181a17–22.

43. Aristotle, *Politics*, 1340b23–25.

44. Ibid., 1291a22–27. Aristotle seems to associate *sunesis* particularly with deliberation. See the brief discussion of this issue in Harvey C. Mansfield Jr., *Taming the Prince: The Ambivalence of Modern Executive Power* (Baltimore, Md: Johns Hopkins University Press, 1993), 56.

45. Judgment often takes this form for Aristotle. Even the judgment of sense impressions draws various inputs toward one common point. See Aristotle, *De anima: Books II and III (with passages from Book I)*, trans. D. W. Hamlyn (Oxford: Clarendon Press, 1993), 426b8–427a14.

46. "It [*sunesis*] is about what we might be puzzled about and might deliberate about. Hence it is about the same things as intelligence [*phronesis*]." Aristotle, *Nicomachean Ethics*, 1143a6.

47. See Aristotle, *Nicomachean Ethics*, 1094b29, 1140b11.

48. Aristotle, *Politics*, 1280a14, 1330a12–24.

49. Mary Nichols pointed out to me the second implication of the passage.

50. Plato, *Gorgias*, 465d.

51. Aristotle mentioned that the arts of perfumery and cooking seemed to aim at pleasure, but his general position seems to have been that "there is no craft of pleasure." See Aristotle, *Nicomachean Ethics*, 1152b18, 1153a25.

52. Plato, *Gorgias*, 453a.

53. Aristotle, *Rhetoric*, 1355a.

54. Ibid., 1354a10.

55. Aristotle, *Rhetoric*, 1355a. A similar, though slightly more ambiguous, formulation can be found in Aristotle's description of dialectic and rhetoric in the *Topics*: "We shall possess the method [of dialectic] completely when we are

in the same situation as in rhetoric and medicine and such faculties [*dynameis*]: that is, [able] to accomplish what we choose from the available means; for neither will the one with rhetorical skill persuade by every means nor will the doctor heal, but if none of the available means is neglected we shall say that he has knowledge adequately." Aristotle, *Topics* 1.3, 101b, in Aristotle, *On Rhetoric*, trans. George A. Kennedy, 292.

56. Garver makes this important point the centerpiece of his book, applying Alasdair MacIntyre's notion of "internal" ends to the activity of rhetoric in order to show how rhetoric can be a "practice" in the theoretically laden sense of that word. Garver contrasts internal or "guiding" ends with external or "given" ends. See Garver, *Aristotle's Rhetoric*, especially chap. 1.

57. Aristotle, *Rhetoric*, 1354b–1355a.

58. Ibid., 1354a.

59. For a persuasive description of Aristotelian deliberation as a "transmitter of desire," see Lear, *Aristotle: The Desire to Understand*, 145–147.

60. Aristotle, *Rhetoric*, 1397a–1400b.

61. Ibid., 1356b.

62. Ibid., 1356b–1357a.

63. Aristotle, *Nicomachean Ethics*, 1112b10.

64. Aristotle, *Rhetoric*, 1367b–1368a.

65. Plato, *Phaedrus*, trans. James H. Nichols Jr. (Ithaca, N.Y.: Cornell University Press, 1998), 271a–272b.

66. Aristotle, *Rhetoric*, 1365b, 1366a. See also Aristotle, *Politics*, 1289a1–10.

67. Though the example in this passage was deliberative rhetoric, a similar point was made when discussing epideictic rhetoric. Aristotle, *Rhetoric*, 1367b: "Consider also the audience before whom the praise [is spoken]; for, as Socrates used to say, it is not difficult to praise Athenians in Athens. And one should speak of whatever is honored among each people as actually existing [in the subject praised], for example, among the Scythians or Laconians or philosophers."

68. Aristotle, *Nicomachean Ethics*, 1112a28–33.

69. Aristotle, *Rhetoric*, 1366a.

70. Garver argues that emotion *(pathos)* is subordinate to character *(ethos)* and that the presentation of the details about the various emotions was designed principally to enable the speaker to adopt the proper tone and thus present himself as a man of good judgment, character, and goodwill (Garver, *Aristotle's Rhetoric*, 110). There is some evidence for this in the way that Aristotle introduced the emotions, and it was clearly one reason for mastering them. But Aristotle also thought that emotions affected an audience's judgment directly, not through the *ethos* of the speaker. At the end of his account of anger, for example, he accepted it as obvious that a speaker should sometimes try to rouse anger in the audience to influence their judgments directly. See Aristotle, *Rhetoric*, 1380a1–5.

71. Plato, *Gorgias*, 494e.
72. In this way my account is different from that of Garver, who adopts from Plato's *Republic* (462b, 464a) the phrase "a community of pleasure and pain" to describe the background conditions required for artful appeals to emotion. This interpretation implies a uniformity of taste and a level of communal agreement regarding ends that Aristotle's *Rhetoric* did not presume in the audience. Aristotle's account seems to require only that the political regime have enough of an influence on pleasure and pain, through emotion, so as to impart a structure that is knowable and usable. Garver, *Aristotle's Rhetoric*, 111.
73. Aristotle, *Rhetoric*, 1368b–1369a.
74. Ibid., 1378a.
75. See Aristotle, *Nicomachean Ethics* 1149b1–2, where emotions are said to follow reason in a way that appetites *(epithumia)* do not. The main complication for the distinction between emotion and appetite is the passage that Gisela Striker points to in the *Rhetoric*, where Aristotle indicated that we could develop appetites for things of which we had only heard descriptions (1370a18–27). This seems to indicate that *epithumia* might respond to speech or reason, but Aristotle did not in general dwell on this possibility. For a different explanation of why Aristotle treats *epithumia* differently in the two books of the *Rhetoric*, see Gisela Striker, "Emotions in Context: Aristotle's Treatment of the Passions in the Rhetoric and His Moral Psychology," in *Essays on Aristotle's Rhetoric*, 289, 301n10. See also Leighton, "Aristotle and the Emotions," 224.
76. Aristotle, *Rhetoric*, 1378a.
77. Ibid., 1379a.
78. On this point, see Garver, *Aristotle's Rhetoric*, 123, 128, and Nichols, "Aristotle's Defense of Rhetoric," 665–667.
79. On "sympathy and detachment" in judgment, see Beiner, *Political Judgment*, chap. 6 and Anthony T. Kronman, *The Lost Lawyer: Failing Ideals of the Legal Profession* (Cambridge, Mass.: Belknap Press, 1993), 66–74. For reflections on honor and partiality, see Sharon R. Krause, *Liberalism with Honor* (Cambridge, Mass.: Harvard University Press, 2002). On the importance of political emotion in Aristotle more generally, see Barbara Koziak, *Retrieving Political Emotion: Thumos, Aristotle, and Gender* (University Park, Penn.: Pennsylvania State University Press, 2000).
80. Aristotle, *Politics*, 1327b23–42. Aristotle in this passage did distinguish his view from Plato's, quarreling with the contention in the *Republic* that guardians should be harsh to outsiders. But this disagreement does not undermine Aristotle's and Plato's agreement about the importance of *thymos*.
81. Plato, *The Republic*, trans. Allan Bloom (New York: BasicBooks, 1968), 412c.
82. Ibid., 412d–413c.
83. For the usual view of Aristotle's notion of community as one of organic wholeness and uniformity, see Alasdair MacIntyre, *After Virtue: A Study in*

Moral Theory (South Bend, Ind.: University of Notre Dame Press, 1982), 153. For correctives, see Frank, *A Democracy of Distinction;* Arlene Saxonhouse, *Fear of Diversity: The Birth of Political Science in Ancient Greek Thought* (Chicago, Ill.: University of Chicago Press, 1992); Bernard Yack, "Community and Conflict in Aristotle's Political Philosophy," in *Action and Contemplation: Studies in the Moral and Political Thought of Aristotle,* ed. Robert C. Bartlett and Susan D. Collins (Albany, N.Y.: State University of New York Press, 1999), 273–292; Bernard Yack, *The Problems of a Political Animal: Community, Justice and Conflict in Aristotelian Political Thought* (Berkeley, Calif.: University of California Press, 1993).

84. T. H. Irwin reviews some of the differences between Aristotle's account of ethical topics in the *Rhetoric* and that found in the *Nicomachean Ethics.* T. H. Irwin, "Ethics in the *Rhetoric* and in the *Ethics,*" in *Essays on Aristotle's Rhetoric,* 142–174.

5. Conviction and Controversy: Cicero

1. Stanley Fish, *Doing What Comes Naturally* (Durham, N.C.: Duke University Press, 1989), 480–481.

2. Stanley Fish, *The Trouble with Principle* (Cambridge, Mass.: Harvard University Press, 1999), 7, 279.

3. Cicero, *De legibus,* in *De re publica; De legibus,* trans. Clinton Walker Keyes (Cambridge, Mass.: Harvard University Press, 1994), 1.36.

4. Cicero's skepticism is on display in *Academica* and *De natura deorum.* In the *Tusculan Disputations* he summed up the philosophical independence he found in skepticism this way: "I live from day to day; I say anything that strikes my mind as probable; and so I alone am free." Cicero, *Tusculan Disputations,* trans. J. E. King (Cambridge, Mass.: Harvard University Press, 1971), 5.33.

5. Cicero, *Lucullus* in *Academica,* in *De natura deorum; Academica,* trans. H. Rackham (Cambridge, Mass.: Harvard University Press, 1967), 31, 53, 58, 99. This question is explored in a large philosophical literature of its own. See especially M. F. Burnyeat, "Can the Sceptic Live his Scepticism?" and Gisela Striker, "Sceptical Strategies," both in *Doubt and Dogmatism: Studies in Hellenistic Epistemology,* ed. Malcolm Schofield, Myles Burnyeat, and Jonathan Barnes (Oxford: Clarendon Press, 1980). Also helpful are the essays in Myles Burnyeat, ed., *The Skeptical Tradition* (Berkeley, Calif.: University of California Press, 1983) and Gisela Striker, *Essays on Hellenistic Epistemology and Ethics* (Cambridge: Cambridge University Press, 1996), especially chaps. 4, 6, 7.

6. Diogenes Laertius 9.62, in A. A. Long and D. N. Sedley, eds., *The Hellenistic Philosophers* (New York: Cambridge University Press, 1987). The example of walking off a cliff is one that Aristotle used in the *Metaphysics* to argue that "all men form unqualified judgments, if not about all things, at least about what is better or worse." Aristotle, *Metaphysics,* trans. Hugh Tredennick (Cambridge, Mass.: Harvard University Press, 1933), 1008b14.

7. See the editor's note in Cicero, *Lucullus* 61, 544n.

8. See Elizabeth Rawson, *Cicero: A Portrait* (Ithaca, N.Y.: Cornell University Press, 1975), 71: "For far too long Cicero was simply a voice crying in the wilderness."

9. As quoted in Rawson, *Cicero*, 75.

10. Cicero, *Lucullus* 62, 63.

11. Ibid., 63.

12. Cicero, *De legibus*, 1.36; Cicero, *De re publica*, in *De re publica; De legibus*, trans. Clinton Walker Keyes (Cambridge, Mass.: Harvard University Press, 1994), 1.39; Cicero *De legibus*, 1.19–20, 1.20, 1.28, 1.42. Malcolm Schofield points out that Cicero's description of natural law (*De Legibus*, 1.21) was a version of the opening words in the Stoic Chrysippus's *On Law*. See Malcolm Schofield, "Two Stoic Approaches to Justice," in *Justice and Generosity: Studies in Hellenistic Social and Political Philosophy: Proceedings of the Sixth Symposium Hellenisticum*, ed. Andre Laks and Malcolm Schofield (Cambridge: Cambridge University Press, 1995), 192–193.

13. Cicero, *De legibus*, 1.39.

14. John Glucker, "Cicero's Philosophical Affiliations," in *The Question of "Eclecticism,"* ed. J. Dillon and A. A. Long (Berkeley, Calif.: University of California Press, 1988), 34–69.

15. C. Wirszubski, "Cicero's CVM DIGNITATE OTIVM: A Reconsideration," *Journal of Roman Studies* 44 (1954): 1–13.

16. Malcolm Schofield, *Saving the City: Philosopher-Kings and other Classical Paradigms* (London: Routledge, 1999), 178–194.

17. See Thomas N. Mitchell, "Cicero on the Moral Crisis of the Late Republic," *Hermathena* 136 (Summer 1984): 21–41; Christian Habict, *Cicero the Politician* (Baltimore, Md.: Johns Hopkins University Press, 1990); P. F. Izzo, "Cicero and Political Expediency," *Classical Weekly* 42 (1948–1949): 168–172.

18. M. I. Finley, *Politics in the Ancient World* (Cambridge: Cambridge University Press, 1983), 128, with internal quotation from G. Watson, "The Natural Law and Stoicism," in *Problems in Stoicism*, ed. A. A. Long (London: Athlone Press, 1971), 235. Finley follows and cites the negative assessment of Cicero in T. Mommsen, *The History of Rome*, trans. W. P. Dickson (London, 1908), 5: 508. Malcolm Schofield offers a defense of Cicero against Finley's charge in Schofield, *Saving the City*, 178–194.

19. Rawson, *Cicero*, 106–107. More recent biographies do not offer reasons to doubt this view. See Anthony Everitt, *Cicero: A Turbulent Life* (London: John Murray, 2001) and Thomas N. Mitchell, *Cicero: The Senior Statesman* (New Haven, Conn.: Yale University Press, 1991).

20. Compare to Leo Strauss, *Natural Right and History* (Chicago, Ill.: University of Chicago Press, 1971), 143.

21. That Cicero evaluated the various philosophical positions by considering their relation to oratory is confirmed by his discussion of Epicureanism in *De oratore*. He explicitly drew his reader's attention to the practical result of the philos-

ophy for orators: "But the question I am asking now is not which philosophy is the truest, but which has the most affinity with the orator. So let us dismiss these people, but without insulting them, for they are good folk and, since they think so themselves, they are blissful as well. Let us merely remind them to keep their opinion to themselves, and guard it as a holy secret, even if it should be quite true—I mean their claim that it is not the part of a wise man to be involved in politics. If they convince us as well as all the best people of the truth of this, then they themselves will not be able to do what they desire most—that is, to live in undisturbed peace." Cicero, *On the Ideal Orator (De oratore),* trans. James M. May and Jakob Wisse (New York: Oxford University Press, 2001), 3.64. Henceforth referred to as *De oratore.*

22. Cicero, *Tusculan Disputations* 2.9; Cicero, *De oratore* 2.8.

23. Cicero, *On Duties* 2.7–8; 3.20. Cicero, *Tusculan Disputations,* 1.17, 2.9, 4.47.

24. Cicero, *Lucullus,* 99–100.

25. Michael Frede takes up this problem in Michael Frede, "The Skeptic's Two Kinds of Assent and the Question of the Possibility of Knowledge," in *Philosophy in History: Essays in the Historiography of Philosophy,* ed. Richard Rorty, J. B. Schneewind, and Quentin Skinner (Cambridge: Cambridge University Press, 1984), 255–278. See especially 270–271.

26. Cicero, *Orator,* trans. H. M. Hubbell (Cambridge, Mass.: Harvard University Press, 1939), 69. See Glucker, "Cicero's Philosophical Affiliations," 116–117.

27. Cicero, *De oratore,* 1.12, 1.108, 1.219–224.

28. Plato, *Phaedrus,* trans. James H. Nichols, Jr. (Ithaca, N.Y.: Cornell University Press, 1998), 272d–273b.

29. Cicero, *De oratore,* 1.213, 1.223–224.

30. Ibid., 3.65–66; compare to 2.159. See also Cicero, *De finibus bonorum et malorum,* trans. H. Rackham (Cambridge, Mass.: Harvard University Press, 1994), 4.21, 4.7; Cicero, *Pro Murena,* in *In Catilinam I–IV; Pro Murena; Pro Sulla; Pro Flacco,* trans. C. Macdonald (Cambridge, Mass.: Harvard University Press, 1989), 61. Cicero did once experiment with the project of making Stoic tenets more palatable. See Walter Englert, "Bring Philosophy to the Light: Cicero's *Paradoxica Stoicorum,*" *Apeiron* 23 (December 1990): 117–142.

31. Cicero, *De finibus,* 4.52.

32. Cicero, *Lucullus,* 99–100. John Glucker presents evidence that the Latin phrase *veri simile* was often the translation for the Greek for "idea" and thus carried conspicuous traces of Plato's thought, perhaps indicating an effort by Philo of Larissa to bring a concern with transcendent truths back into the Academy. Glucker, "Cicero's Philosophical Affiliations," 34–69.

33. Cicero, *Lucullus,* 8. In the next sentence he identified the approximations as *probabilia.* See also Cicero, *Tusculan Disputations* 1.8, where Cicero claimed his practice of arguing both sides was an imitation of Socrates, who "thought that in this way the probable truth [*veri simillimum*] was most readily discovered," and, 2.9; Cicero, *On Duties,* 2.7–8; Cicero, *De oratore,* 2.8. Recently, Harald

Thorsrud has argued that this "fallibilism" was characteristic not only of the version of Academic skepticism that Cicero and Philo upheld but also of the skepticism of Arcesilaus and Carneades. Harald Thorsrud, "Cicero on His Academic Predecessors: The Fallibilism of Arcesilaus and Carneades," *Journal of the History of Philosophy* 40 (January 2002): 1–18.

34. Cicero, *De oratore,* 2.30.

35. Ibid., 3.145.

36. Thomas Conley seems to incline toward this view, while the introduction to the new translation of *De oratore* by James May and Jakob Wisse offers a correction in the direction I suggest here. Thomas M. Conley, *Rhetoric in the European Tradition* (Chicago, Ill.: University of Chicago Press, 1990), 37; James M. May and Jakob Wisse, introduction to *On the Ideal Orator (De oratore),* by Cicero, trans. James M. May and Jakob Wisse. (New York: Oxford University Press, 2001), 11–12.

37. Cicero, *De oratore,* 1.48, 1.51; 3.55.

38. Ibid., 3.108. For a helpful account of the technical rhetorical issue at stake here, see May and Wisse, introduction, 25, 27–28.

39. Cicero, *De oratore,* 1.263–264, 2.40.

40. Ibid., 1.47, 1.51; 3.24.

41. Ibid., 1.166, 1.51, 1.53, 1.60, 1.75–76.

42. Ibid., 1.28. Compare to Plato, *Phaedrus,* 229a.

43. Plato, *Phaedrus,* 262a. See 261d–262c and 273d–274a.

44. Ibid., 273d.

45. Cicero, *De oratore,* 2.133–134. A position about the importance of the ability to see true likenesses may be also be implicit in Cicero's argument against inappropriate metaphors at 3.162.

46. Ibid., 3.56–81.

47. Aristotle, *Rhetoric,* 1355a.

48. Cicero, *De re publica,* 1.45–64.

49. Aristotle, *Politics,* 1280a1–1281a10, 1282b15–1284a3, 1294a35–1294b40.

50. Cicero, *De oratore,* 2.102.

51. Ibid., 2.189–192.

52. Ibid., 2.193. See Nadia Urbinati, "Representation as Advocacy," *Political Theory* 28 (December 2000): 758–786, a wonderful article I discovered only after writing this chapter.

53. See Gary Remer, "Political Oratory and Conversation: Cicero versus Deliberative Democracy," *Political Theory* 27 (February 1999): 39–65.

54. Cicero, *De oratore,* 1.12, 2.159.

55. See the editor's introduction to Cicero, *On Duties,* xi–xii.

56. Cicero, *De finibus,* 3.7.

57. Cicero, *De oratore,* 1.102–104.

58. Plato, *Gorgias,* 462b.

59. Cicero, *De oratore,* 1.56–57.

60. Ibid., 1.112.

61. Ibid., 2.75–76.
62. Ibid., 1.263–264, 2.66–68, 2.133, 2.362, 2.40–43. The last statement echoes one made by Scaevola when Crassus reveals his learning on the first day (1.165) and anticipates one Catulus makes about Crassus in the third book (3.82).
63. Cicero, *De oratore,* 1.99, 111–112, 224–226, 2.156, 2.4. 2.40–41, Although Crassus claims that he might avoid philosophy simply because he lacks knowledge about the subject (1.99), that claim must be taken ironically, both because Cicero presents him as the greatest orator and because Crassus eventually discourses at great length on just the topics he claims not to understand.
64. Cicero, *Brutus,* trans. G. L. Hendrickson (Cambridge, Mass.: Harvard University Press, 1939), 92; Cicero, *Orator,* trans. H. M. Hubbell. (Cambridge, Mass.: Harvard University Press, 1939), 130. Hanna Gray notices that such deference became central to the rhetorical culture of the Renaissance, where terms of rhetoric such as *imitatio* and *decorum* gained moral connotations, indicating an ethic of conformity. Hanna H. Gray, "Renaissance Humanism: The Pursuit of Eloquence," *Journal of the History of Ideas* 24 (1963): 506.
65. Cicero, *De legibus,* 1.8–14.
66. Cicero, *Brutus,* 256.
67. Cicero, *Tusculan Disputations,* 5.33.
68. Plato, *Gorgias,* 456e, 457c. Cicero, *De oratore,* 3.5.
69. In this section I follow Malcolm Schofield's article "Cicero's Definition of *Res Publica*" in presenting the *res publica* as a criterion of legitimacy and focusing on *De re publica* 1.39 and 3.43 as crucial passages. I add to Schofield's argument in emphasizing the way in which Cicero's use of Stoic ideas aimed to preserve the conditions of deliberative rhetoric. See Schofield, *Saving the City,* 178–194.
70. Cicero, *De re publica,* 1.39, 3.43. See Schofield, "Cicero's Definition of *Res Publica,*" 178–194.
71. Cicero, *De re publica,* 3.45.
72. Ibid., 1.41, 1.44, 1.51, 1.53, 3.48.
73. Cicero, *De oratore,* 1.141. Cicero sometimes used *conciliare* as one of the three functions of oratory. See 2.128, 2.310; 3.104. The quoted passage is at 1.199.
74. Cicero, *De legibus* 3.40. See also 3.28.
75. Cicero, *On Duties* 1.26, 38, 64–65, 68, 73–74, 83. Cicero cited Caesar as the example.
76. A. A. Long outlines the distinction in Long, "Cicero's Politics in *De officiis,*" in Laks and Schofield, *Justice and Generosity,* 213–240.
77. Cicero, *On Duties,* 1.14.
78. Ibid., 1.62, 1.62–68.
79. Ibid., 1.65.
80. Ibid., 1.66–67.
81. Cicero, *On Duties,* 3.26; Cicero, *De legibus,* 1.40; Cicero, *De re publica,* 3.33, 6.13, 6.29; Cicero, *On Duties,* 3.36, 3.84–85.
82. Cicero, *On Duties,* 3.84; Cicero, *De re publica,* 3.23, 3.24, 3.27; Cicero, *De finibus,* 5.84–85; Cicero, *On Duties,* 3.36.

83. Cicero, *De re publica,* 1.60.

84. Cicero, *De legibus,* 3.23–26 on the tribunate, 1.40–52 on morals.

85. Michel de Montaigne, "Of Custome," in *Essays,* trans. John Florio (New York: Dutton, 1965), 165.

86. René Descartes, *Discourse on Method,* trans. Donald A. Cress (Cambridge: Hackett Publishing, 1998), 23.

87. Richard Tuck, *Philosophy and Government, 1572–1651* (Cambridge: Cambridge University Press, 1993). See also Richard Tuck, introduction to *Leviathan,* by Thomas Hobbes, ed. Richard Tuck (Cambridge: Cambridge University Press, 1996), xxxi–xxxiv.

88. Cicero, *De legibus,* 1.39.

6. Persuasion and Deliberation

1. Jürgen Habermas, *The Structural Transformation of the Public Sphere: An Inquiry into a Category of Bourgeois Society,* trans. Thomas Burger (Cambridge, Mass.: MIT Press, 1999), especially chap. 4.

2. Thomas Hobbes, *Leviathan,* ed. Richard Tuck (Cambridge: Cambridge University Press, 1996), 306.

3. Jean-Jacques Rousseau, "Political Economy," in *On the Social Contract with Geneva Manuscript and Political Economy,* ed. Roger D. Masters, trans. Judith R. Masters (New York: St. Martin's Press, 1978), 213.

4. Melzer draws from Rousseau to find "the seeds of nationalism" in "the politics of sympathetic identification" that the structure of the modern state seems to require. Melzer does not link sympathetic identification to Rousseau's "persuading without convincing" nor to anything like a "rhetoric of prophetic nationalism," however. See Arthur Melzer, "Rousseau, Nationalism, and the Politics of Sympathetic Identification," in *Educating the Prince: Essays in Honor of Harvey Mansfield,* ed. Mark Blitz and William Kristol (Lanham, Md.: Rowman and Littlefield, 2000).

5. Sheldon Wolin does remark upon this starting point of Rawls's *Political Liberalism.* See Sheldon Wolin, *Politics and Vision: Continuity and Innovation in Western Political Thought,* expanded ed. (Princeton, N.J.: Princeton University Press, 2004), 540–542.

6. John Rawls, *Political Liberalism* (N.Y.: Columbia University Press, 1996), xxx.

7. John Rawls, "The Idea of Public Reason Revisited," in *The Law of Peoples with "The Idea of Public Reason Revisited"* (Cambridge, Mass.: Harvard University Press, 1999), §1.1, 132–133.

8. Rawls, *Political Liberalism,* xxviii. See also Rawls, "The Idea of Public Reason Revisited," throughout and especially 7.1, and Rawls, *Political Liberalism,* xxx and xxxix in the introduction to the paperback edition, where he sharpens his question to focus on the problem of religion: "How is it possible for those affirming a religious doctrine that is based on religious authority, for example the Church or the Bible, also to hold a reasonable political conception that supports a just democratic regime?"

9. John Rawls, *The Law of Peoples*, §1.4, 19–21: "Not to be overlooked is the fact that Hitler's demonic conception of the world was, in some perverse sense, religious," followed by quotations from Hitler's speeches.

10. Stephen L. Carter, *The Culture of Disbelief: How American Law and Politics Trivialize Religious Devotion* (New York: Basic Books, 1993), 264.

11. Michael J. Sandel, *Democracy's Discontent: American in Search of a Public Philosophy* (Cambridge, Mass.: Belknap Press, 1996), 322.

12. Jeffrey Stout, *Democracy and Tradition* (Princeton, N.J.: Princeton University Press, 2004), 299. See chaps. 3–4 for a more general argument against Rawlsian public reason that is broadly similar to the one advanced here.

13. Bonnie Honig, *Political Theory and the Displacement of Politics* (Ithaca, N.Y.: Cornell University Press, 1993), 15.

14. Robert A. Burt, *The Constitution in Conflict* (Cambridge, Mass.: Belknap Press, 1992).

15. Ian Shapiro briefly outlines an argument to this effect in Ian Shapiro, *The State of Democratic Theory* (Princeton, N.J.: Princeton University Press, 2003), 25–26.

16. John Rawls, "The Idea of Public Reason Revisited," §4.1, 152.

17. Ibid., §4.2, 154.

18. Ibid., §4.3, 156.

19. Ibid., §3.2, 151–152.

20. Jon Elster, "The Market and the Forum," in *The Foundations of Social Choice Theory*, ed. Jon Elster and A. Aanund (Cambridge: Cambridge University Press, 1986), 103–132; Jürgen Habermas, *The Theory of Communicative Action*, trans. Thomas McCarthy (Cambridge: Polity Press, 1986–1989).

21. See Albert O. Hirschman, *The Passions and the Interests: Political Arguments for Capitalism Before its Triumph* (Princeton, N.J.: Princeton University Press, 1981) and Harvey C. Mansfield, "Self-Interest Rightly Understood," *Political Theory* 23 (February 1995): 48–66, particularly 57.

22. Bernard Manin, "On Legitimacy and Political Deliberation," trans. Elly Stein and Jane Mansbridge, *Political Theory* 15 (August 1987): 338–368.

23. Ibid., 351–352.

24. Ibid., 352–353. In a footnote to this description of deliberative argument, Manin cites Chaim Perelman and Lucie Olbrechts-Tyteca, *The New Rhetoric: A Treatise on Argumentation*, trans. John Wilkinson and Purcell Weaver (Notre Dame, Ind.: University of Notre Dame Press, 1969).

25. Manin, "On Legitimacy and Political Deliberation," 359.

26. Joshua Cohen, "Deliberation and Democratic Legitimacy," in *The Good Polity*, ed. A. Hamlin and P. Pettit (Oxford: Blackwell Publishers, 1989), 17–34; Joshua Cohen, "Procedure and Substance in Deliberative Democracy," in *Democracy and Difference*, ed. Seyla Benhabib (Princeton, N.J.: Princeton University Press, 1996), 95–119.

27. John Rawls, *A Theory of Justice* (Cambridge, Mass.: Harvard University Press, 1971), 139; Rousseau, *On the Social Contract*, 4.2.

28. Jeffrey Stout, whose recent book lays out a position sympathetic to the one taken here, nevertheless makes the case in a different way. He argues for al-

lowing religious arguments into justificatory discourse rather than for making a distinction between that discourse and a discourse of persuasion. See Stout, *Democracy and Tradition*, chap. 3.

29. Joseph M. Bessette, *The Mild Voice of Reason: Deliberative Democracy and American National Government* (Chicago, Ill.: University of Chicago Press, 1994), 46–56.

30. Bruce Ackerman and James Fishkin, *Deliberation Day* (New Haven, Conn.: Yale University Press, 2004).

31. James S. Fishkin, *Democracy and Deliberation: New Directions for Democratic Reform* (New Haven, Conn.: Yale University Press, 1991), chap. 4.

32. Jürgen Habermas, *Between Facts and Norms: Contributions to a Discourse Theory of Law and Democracy*, trans. William Rehg (Cambridge, Mass.: MIT Press, 1996), 1–9.

33. Ibid., 484.

34. Ibid., 448.

35. Alexander Hamilton, *Federalist* #71, in Alexander Hamilton, James Madison, and James Jay, *The Federalist Papers*, ed. Clinton Rossiter, with a new introduction by Charles R. Kesler (New York: Mentor, 1999), 400.

36. Henry Fairlie, "The Decline of Oratory," *New Republic*, May 28, 1984, 17.

37. See, for example: George E. Marcus, *The Sentimental Citizen: Emotion in Democratic Politics* (University Park, Penn.: Pennsylvania State University Press, 2002); George E. Marcus, W. Russell Neuman, and Michael MacKuen, *Affective Intelligence and Political Judgment* (Chicago, Ill.: University of Chicago Press, 2000); Robert Frank, *Passions within Reason* (New York: W. W. Norton, 1988); Ronald de Sousa, *The Rationality of Emotion* (Cambridge, Mass.: MIT Press, 1987); Allen Gibbard, *Wise Choices, Apt Feelings* (Cambridge, Mass.: Harvard University Press, 1990); A. R. Damasio, *Descartes' Error: Emotion, Reason, and the Human Brain* (New York: Putnam, 1994); V. S. Ramachandran, *Phantoms in the Brain: Probing the Mysteries of the Human Mind* (New York: William Morrow, 1998); and Joseph LeDoux, *The Emotional Brain* (New York: Simon and Schuster, 1996). Among political theorists interested in the issue, see Barbara Koziak, *Retrieving Political Emotion: Thumos, Aristotle and Gender* (University Park, Penn.: Pennsylvania State University Press, 2000); Patchen Markell, "Making Affect Safe for Democracy?: On Constitutional Patriotism," *Political Theory* 28 (February 2000): 38–63; Martha Nussbaum, *Upheavals of Thought: The Intelligence of Emotions* (New York: Cambridge University Press, 2001); Simon Blackburn, *Ruling Passions: A Theory of Practical Reasoning* (Oxford: Oxford University Press, 1998); Michael Walzer, "Passion and Politics," *Philosophy and Social Criticism* 28 (2003): 617–633; Cheryl Hall, "'Passions and Constraint': The Marginalization of Passion in Liberal Political Theory," *Philosophy and Social Criticism* 28 (2002): 727–748; and Sharon Krause, "Humean Judgment and Democratic Deliberation" (unpublished manuscript presented at the 2004 annual meeting of the New England Political Science Association).

38. Hobbes, *Leviathan*, chap. 3, 21.

39. Sharon Krause, *Liberalism with Honor* (Cambridge, Mass.: Harvard University Press, 2002), 4.

40. Marcus, *Sentimental Citizen*, chap. 6, especially 101–108.

250   **Notes to Pages 196–203**

41. Jean-Jacques Rousseau, "Geneva Manuscript," in *On the Social Contract with Geneva Manuscript and Political Economy*, ed. Roger D. Masters, trans. Judith R. Masters (New York: St. Martin's Press, 1978), 1.2.

42. Bessette, *Mild Voice of Reason*, 226–227. In this paragraph I have followed Bessette's discussion, 221–228. See also Michael Walzer, *Spheres of Justice: A Defense of Pluralism and Equality* (New York: Basic Books, 1983), 306–309; Fareed Zakaria, *The Future of Freedom: Illiberal Democracy at Home and Abroad* (New York: W. W. Norton, 2004), 171–172; Dale Bumpers, "How the Sunshine Harmed Congress," *New York Times,* January 3, 1999, sec. 4, p. 9.

43. See Alan Binder, "Is Government Too Political?" *Foreign Affairs* (November/December 1997) and Zakaria, who discusses Binder in *Future of Freedom,* 248–250.

44. For related arguments distinguishing Kantian respect from respect for actual persons, see Bonnie Honig, *Political Theory and the Displacement of Politics,* chap. 2; Andreas Teuber, "Kant's Respect for Persons," *Political Theory* 11 (1983): 369–392; and Michael Sandel, "Political Liberalism," *Harvard Law Review* 107 (May 1994): 1794.

45. Seyla Benhabib, *Situating the Self: Gender, Community and Postmodernism in Contemporary Ethics* (New York: Routledge, 1992), chap. 5. See also Stout, *Democracy and Tradition,* 73.

46. Cass Sunstein, *Why Societies Need Dissent* (Cambridge, Mass.: Cambridge University Press, 2003), 160–161. See chaps. 1–6 in general for a good recent account of the dangers of group polarization and conformity in democratic discourse. On the tendency to produce conflict as a difficulty for deliberative democrats, see Shapiro, *State of Democratic Theory,* 25–26.

47. Wolin, *Politics and Vision,* 549.

48. Sheldon S. Wolin, "Fugitive Democracy," *Constellations* 1 (1994): 11–25, particularly 18.

49. See Hannah Arendt, *On Revolution* (New York: Viking Press, 1963).

50. James Madison, *Federalist* #10, 46.

51. Ibid., 49.

52. Ibid., 47; Madison, *Federalist* #51, 292.

53. Madison, "Vices of the Political System"; Madison, *Federalist* #10, 52, and *Federalist* #63, 352. On the paper-money convulsions and the framers' fear of demagogy, see Bessette, *Mild Voice of Reason,* 7–18, which I follow in this paragraph.

54. Madison, *Federalist* #10, 47.

55. Ibid., 48.

56. Kant took precisely the opposite view in arguing for the need for sovereign judgment, insisting that parties could not be left as judges in their own causes. See Immanuel Kant, "On the Common Saying: 'This May Be True in Theory, but It Does Not Apply in Practice,'" in *Political Writings,* ed. Hans Reiss, trans. H. B. Nisbet (Cambridge: Cambridge University Press, 1991), 81.

57. I thus depart from Wolin, who argues that Hobbes is the exemplar of the sort of "boundary" that stands for the "containment of democracy" and further

that "the crucial boundary is a constitution" and that "constitutionalism, especially in its Madisonian version, is designed to strew as many barriers as possible to demotic power." Wolin, "Fugitive Democracy," 11–13, 22.

58. Alexander Hamilton, "The Farmer Refuted," 1 *Hamilton Papers,* 98, as quoted in Burt, *Constitution in Conflict,* 50.

59. Alexander Hamilton, speech to the Constitutional Convention, June 18, 1787, in James Madison, *Notes on the Debates in the Federal Convention of 1787* (New York: W. W. Norton, 1987), 129–139, particularly 131–135. The speech and its relevance were brought to my attention by Burt, *Constitution in Conflict,* 48.

60. Madison, *Federalist* #10, 52. See also *Federalist* #63, where Madison again took up several points specifically in response to Hamilton's speech, including how best to interpret Maryland's actions on the paper-money issue and the question of whether the House of Lords had been successful in resisting impulses from the lower chamber in England.

61. Madison, *Federalist* #49, 282.

62. Ibid., 283–285, and *Federalist* #50, 285–288.

63. Madison, *Federalist* #49, 283–285.

64. Madison, *Federalist* #78, 435–436.

65. Burt, *Constitution in Conflict,* 62–63.

66. Madison, *Federalist* #10, 48.

67. Madison, *Federalist* #51, 293.

68. Madison, *Federalist* #51, 290.

69. My attention has been drawn to these sorts of practices by Andrew Sabl's argument for "governing pluralism," which gives pride of place to the Ciceronian notion of roles or "offices." Sabl notes, "The claim that every political rhetoric and every political relationship should be available to everyone assumes not only an unusual view of human character but an unnecessarily narrow view of political argument." Andrew Sabl, *Ruling Passions: Political Offices and Democratic Ethics* (Princeton, N.J.: Princeton University Press, 2002), 305, 324–325.

70. For characterizations of the Constitution that also emphasize its purpose of sustaining controversy, see Sunstein, *Why Societies Need Dissent,* chap. 7, and Burt, *Constitution in Conflict,* chaps. 2, 10.

71. The view of constitutional government offered here differs from the one presumed by Habermas, who suggests that the constitution exists to transmit the sovereign popular will into administrative action; it is "the medium for transforming communicative power into administrative power." Habermas, *Between Facts and Norms,* 169. Ronald Dworkin's influential view of the constitution also presumes an independent and sovereign popular will. See Ronald M. Dworkin, *Law's Empire* (Cambridge, Mass.: Belknap Press, 1986).

72. This habit of attention may produce a certain relationship over time, one which might approach the sort of political "friendship" described recently in different ways by Danielle Allen and Jill Frank. Both draw in one way or another from Aristotle's broad use of the term "friendship" and make the important point that it arises not as an emotional attachment prior to politics but from practices of citizenship. See Danielle S. Allen, *Talking to Strangers: Anxieties*

of Citizenship since Brown v. Board of Education (Chicago, Ill.: University of Chicago Press, 2004), chap. 9; Jill Frank, *A Democracy of Distinction: Aristotle and the Work of Politics* (Chicago, Ill.: University of Chicago Press, 2005), chap. 5. See also Bernard Yack, *The Problems of a Political Animal: Community, Justice and Conflict in Aristotelian Political Thought* (Berkeley, Calif.: University of California Press, 1993), chap. 4.

73. Thomas Hobbes, *On the Citizen*, ed. and trans. Richard Tuck and Michael Silverthorne (Cambridge: Cambridge University Press, 1998), 10.9.

Bibliography

Abizadeh, Arash. "Banishing the Particular: Rousseau on Rhetoric, *Patrie*, and the Passions." *Political Theory* 29 (August 2001): 556–582.

———. "The Passions of the Wise: *Phronesis*, Rhetoric, and Aristotle's Passionate Practical Deliberation." *Review of Metaphysics* 56 (December 2002): 267–297.

Ackerman, Bruce, and James Fishkin. *Deliberation Day.* New Haven, Conn.: Yale University Press, 2004.

Allen, Danielle S. *Talking to Strangers: Anxieties of Citizenship since Brown v. Board of Education.* Chicago, Ill.: University of Chicago Press, 2004.

Arendt, Hannah. "The Crisis in Culture: Its Social and Political Significance." In *Between Past and Future: Eight Exercises in Political Thought.* New York: Viking Press, 1968.

———. *Lectures on Kant's Political Philosophy,* ed. Ronald Beiner. Chicago, Ill.: University of Chicago Press, 1982.

———. *On Revolution.* New York: Viking Press, 1963.

Aristotle, *The Art of Rhetoric,* trans. J. H. Freese. Cambridge, Mass.: Harvard University Press, 1926.

———. *De anima: Books II and III (with passages from Book I),* trans. D. W. Hamlyn. Oxford: Clarendon Press, 1993.

———. *Metaphysics,* trans. Hugh Tredennick. Cambridge, Mass.: Harvard University Press, 1933.

———. *Nicomachean Ethics,* trans. Terence Irwin. Indianapolis, Ind.: Hackett Publishing, 1999.

———. *On Rhetoric: A Theory of Civic Discourse,* trans. George A. Kennedy. New York: Oxford University Press, 1991.

———. *The Politics,* trans. Carnes Lord. Chicago, Ill.: University of Chicago Press, 1984.

———. *The Politics and The Constitution of Athens,* ed. Stephen Everson, trans. B. Jowett. Cambridge: Cambridge University Press, 1996.

———. *Treatise on Rhetoric,* trans. Theodore Buckley. New York: Prometheus Books, 1995.

Baczko, Bronislaw. "La cité et ses langages." In *Rousseau After Two Hundred Years: Proceedings of the Cambridge Bicentennial Colloquium,* ed. R. A. Leigh. Cambridge: Cambridge University Press, 1982.

————. "Moïse, législateur . . ." In *Reappraisals of Rousseau: Studies in Honor of R. A. Leigh,* ed. Simon Harvey, Marian Hobson, David Kelley, and Samuel S. B. Taylor. Manchester, U.K.: Manchester University Press, 1980.

Barker, Stephen F. "The Style of Kant's Critique of Reason." In *The Philosopher as Writer: The Eighteenth Century,* ed. Robert Ginsburg. London: Associated University Presses, 1987.

Beck, Lewis White. *Early German Philosophy: Kant and His Predecessors.* Cambridge, Mass.: Harvard University Press, 1969.

Beiner, Ronald. *Political Judgment.* Chicago, Ill.: University of Chicago Press, 1983.

Beiser, Frederick C. *The Fate of Reason: German Philosophy from Kant to Fichte.* Cambridge, Mass.: Harvard University Press, 1987.

Benhabib, Seyla. "Deliberative Rationality and Models of Democratic Legitimacy." *Constellations* 1 (April 1994): 25–53.

————. *Situating the Self: Gender, Community and Postmodernism in Contemporary Ethics.* New York: Routledge, 1992.

Bessette, Joseph M. *The Mild Voice of Reason: Deliberative Democracy and American National Government.* Chicago, Ill.: University of Chicago Press, 1994.

Binder, Alan. "Is Government Too Political?" *Foreign Affairs* (November/December 1997): 115–137.

Blackburn, Simon. *Ruling Passions: A Theory of Practical Reasoning.* Oxford: Oxford University Press, 1998.

Bloch, Maurice, ed. *Political Language and Oratory in Traditional Society.* New York: Academic Press, 1975.

Bodin, Jean. *Method for the Easy Comprehension of History,* trans. Beatrice Reynolds. New York: Columbia University Press, 1945.

————. *Six Books of the Commonwealth,* trans. M. J. Tooley. Oxford: Basil Blackwell, 1955.

Bohman, James and William Rehg, eds. *Deliberative Democracy: Essays on Reason and Politics.* Cambridge, Mass.: MIT Press, 1997.

Boyle, Marjorie O'Rourke. *Rhetoric and Reform: Erasmus' Civil Dispute with Luther.* Cambridge, Mass.: Harvard University Press, 1983.

Brown, Keith. "The Artist of the *Leviathan* Title-Page," *British Library Journal* 4 (1978): 24–36.

Bruni, Leonardo. *Laudatio Florentinae urbis.* English translation in *The Earthly Republic: Italian Humanists on Government and Society,* ed. Benjamin G. Kohl and Ronald G. Witt. Philadelphia: University of Pennsylvania Press, 1978.

Bumpers, Dale. "How the Sunshine Harmed Congress," *New York Times,* January 3, 1999.

Burnyeat, M. F. "Can the Sceptic Live his Scepticism?" In *Doubt and Dogmatism: Studies in Hellenistic Epistemology,* ed. Malcolm Schofield, Myles Burnyeat, and Jonathan Barnes. Oxford: Clarendon Press, 1980.

————. ed. *The Skeptical Tradition.* Berkeley: University of California Press, 1983.

Burt, Robert A. *The Constitution in Conflict.* Cambridge, Mass.: Belknap Press, 1992.

Campbell, George. *The Philosophy of Rhetoric,* ed. Lloyd F. Bitzer. Carbondale: Southern Illinois University Press, 1963.

Callaghan, Karen and Franke Schnelle, eds. *Framing American Politics.* Pittsburgh, Penn.: University of Pittsburgh Press, 2005.

Carter, Stephen L. *The Culture of Disbelief: How American Law and Politics Trivialize Religious Devotion.* New York: Basic Books, 1993.

Cicero, Marcus Tullius. *Brutus,* trans. G. L. Hendrickson. Cambridge, Mass.: Harvard University Press, 1939.

———. *De finibus bonorum et malorum,* trans. H. Rackham. Cambridge, Mass.: Harvard University Press, 1994.

———. *De inventione; De optimo genere oratorum; Topica,* trans. H. M. Hubbell. Cambridge, Mass.: Harvard University Press, 1949.

———. *De natura deorum; Academica,* trans. H. Rackham. Cambridge, Mass.: Harvard University Press, 1967.

———. *De officiis,* trans. Walter Miller. Cambridge, Mass.: Harvard University Press, 1997.

———. *De re publica; De legibus,* trans. Clinton Walker Keyes. Cambridge, Mass.: Harvard University Press, 1977.

———. *In Catilinam 1–4. Pro Murena. Pro Sulla. Pro Flacco,* trans. C. Macdonald. Cambridge, Mass.: Harvard University Press, 1989.

———. *On the Ideal Orator (De oratore),* trans. James M. May and Jakob Wisse. New York: Oxford University Press, 2001.

———. *Orator,* trans. H. M. Hubbell. Cambridge, Mass.: Harvard University Press, 1939.

———. *Tusculan Disputations,* trans. J. E. King. Cambridge, Mass.: Harvard University Press, 1971.

Clarke, Michael. "Kant's Rhetoric of Enlightenment." *Review of Politics* 59 (Winter 1997): 53–73.

Cohen, Joshua. "Deliberation and Democratic Legitimacy." In *The Good Polity,* ed. A. Hamlin and P. Pettit. Oxford: Blackwell Publishers, 1989.

———. "Procedure and Substance in Deliberative Democracy." In *Democracy and Difference,* ed. Seyla Benhabib. Princeton, N.J.: Princeton University Press, 1996.

Cohler, Anne M. *Rousseau and Nationalism.* New York: Basic Books, 1970.

Cole, Thomas. *Origins of Rhetoric in Ancient Greece.* Baltimore, Md.: Johns Hopkins Press, 1991.

Conley, Thomas M. *Rhetoric in the European Tradition.* Chicago, Ill.: University of Chicago Press, 1990.

Cooper, John M. *Reason and Human Good in Aristotle.* Indianapolis, Ind.: Hackett Publishing, 1986.

Damasio, A. R. *Descartes' Error: Emotion, Reason, and the Human Brain.* New York: Putnam, 1994.

Derrida, Jacques. *Of Grammatology,* corrected ed., trans. Gayatri Chakravorty Spivak. Baltimore, Md.: Johns Hopkins University Press, 1997.

Descartes, René. *Discourse on Method,* trans. Donald A. Cress. Cambridge: Hackett Publishing, 1998.

de Sousa, Ronald. *The Rationality of Emotion.* Cambridge, Mass.: MIT Press, 1987.

Diderot, Denis. "Pensées détachees ou Fragments politique échappés du portefeuille d'un philosophe." In *Oeuvres complètes.* Paris: le Club Français du Livre, 1969.

Donoghue, Denis. *Jonathan Swift: A Critical Introduction*. Cambridge: Cambridge University Press, 1969.

Dryzek, John S. *Discursive Democracy: Politics, Policy, and Political Science*. Cambridge: Cambridge University Press, 1990.

Dworkin, Ronald M. *Law's Empire*. Cambridge, Mass.: Belknap Press, 1986.

Elster, Jon. "The Market and the Forum." In *The Foundations of Social Choice Theory*, ed. Jon Elster and A. Aanund. Cambridge: Cambridge University Press, 1986.

Ely, John Hart. *Democracy and Distrust: A Theory of Judicial Review*. Cambridge, Mass.: Harvard University Press, 1980.

Englert, Walter. "Bring Philosophy to the Light: Cicero's *Paradoxica Stoicorum*." *Apeiron* 23 (December 1990): 117–142.

Everitt, Anthony. *Cicero: A Turbulent Life*. London: John Murray, 2001.

Fairlie, Henry. "The Decline of Oratory," *New Republic*, May 28, 1984, 15–19.

Farrell, Thomas B. *Norms of Rhetorical Culture*. New Haven, Conn.: Yale University Press, 1993.

Feder, Johann Georg Heinrich. *On Space and Causality: An Examination of the Kantian Philosophy*. Göttingen: Dietrich, 1787. In *Kant's Early Critics: The Empiricist Critique of the Theoretical Philosophy*, trans. and ed. Brigitte Sassen. Cambridge: Cambridge University Press, 2000.

Finley, M. I. *Politics in the Ancient World*. Cambridge: Cambridge University Press, 1983.

Fish, Stanley. *Doing What Comes Naturally*. Durham, N.C.: Duke University Press, 1989.

———. *The Trouble with Principle*. Cambridge, Mass.: Harvard University Press, 1999.

Fishkin, James S. *Democracy and Deliberation: New Directions for Democratic Reform*. New Haven, Conn.: Yale University Press, 1991.

Fleischacker, Samuel. *A Third Concept of Liberty: Judgment and Freedom in Kant and Adam Smith*. Princeton, N.J.: Princeton University Press, 1999.

Fontana, Benedetto, Cary J. Nederman, and Gary Remer, eds. *Talking Democracy: Historical Perspectives on Rhetoric and Democracy*. University Park, Penn.: Pennsylvania State University Press, 2004.

Frank, Jill. "Democracy and Distribution: Aristotle on Just Desert," *Political Theory* 26 (1998): 784–802.

———. *A Democracy of Distinction: Aristotle and the Work of Politics*. Chicago, Ill.: University of Chicago Press, 2005.

Frank, Robert. *Passions within Reason*. New York: W. W. Norton, 1988.

Frede, Michael. "The Skeptic's Two Kinds of Assent and the Question of the Possibility of Knowledge." In *Philosophy in History: Essays in the Historiography of Philosophy*, ed. Richard Rorty, J. B. Schneewind, and Quentin Skinner. Cambridge: Cambridge University Press, 1984.

Fumaroli, Marc. *Histoire de la rhétorique dans l'Europe moderne: 1450–1950*. Paris: Presses Universitaires de France, 1999.

Gadamer, Hans-Georg. *Truth and Method*, rev. ed., trans. Joel Weinsheimer and Donald G. Marshall. New York: Continuum Publishing, 1989.

Garve, Christian. "*Critique of Pure Reason* by Immanuel Kant." In *Kant's Early Critics: The Empiricist Critique of the Theoretical Philosophy,* trans. and ed. Brigitte Sassen. Cambridge: Cambridge University Press, 2000.

[Garve, Christian]. "*Critique of Pure Reason* by Immanuel Kant, 1781." In *Kant's Early Critics: The Empiricist Critique of the Theoretical Philosophy,* trans. and ed. Brigitte Sassen. Cambridge: Cambridge University Press, 2000.

Garver, Eugene. *Aristotle's Rhetoric: An Art of Character.* Chicago, Ill.: University of Chicago Press, 1994.

———. "The Political Irrelevance of Aristotle's *Rhetoric*." *Philosophy and Rhetoric* 29 (1996): 179–199.

Gaus, Gerald F. *Justificatory Liberalism: An Essay on Epistemology and Political Theory.* New York: Oxford University Press, 1996.

Gibbard, Allen. *Wise Choices, Apt Feelings.* Cambridge, Mass.: Harvard University Press, 1990.

Gibbon, Edward. *An Essay on the Study of Literature.* London: Becket, 1764.

Glucker, John. "Cicero's Philosophical Affiliations." In *The Question of "Eclecticism,"* ed. J. Dillon and A. A. Long. Berkeley, Calif.: University of California Press, 1988.

Goldsmith, M. M. "Hobbes's Ambiguous Politics." *History of Political Thought* 11 (1990): 639–673.

———. *Hobbes's Science of Politics.* New York: Columbia University Press, 1966.

Goodin, Robert E. *Manipulatory Politics.* New Haven, Conn.: Yale University Press, 1980.

Gorgias. *Encomium of Helen.* In *On Rhetoric: A Theory of Civic Discourse,* ed. and trans. George Kennedy. New York: Oxford University Press, 1991.

Gottheimer, Josh, ed. *Ripples of Hope: Great American Civil Rights Speeches.* New York: Basic Civitas Books, 2003.

Gray, Hanna H. "Renaissance Humanism: The Pursuit of Eloquence." *Journal of the History of Ideas* 24 (Oct.–Dec. 1963): 497–514.

Gutmann, Amy and Dennis Thompson. *Democracy and Disagreement: Why Moral Conflict Cannot Be Avoided in Politics, and What Should Be Done about It.* Cambridge, Mass.: Belknap Press, 1996.

———. "Why Deliberative Democracy is Different." *Social Philosophy and Policy* 17 (Winter 2000): 161–180.

Habermas, Jürgen. *Between Facts and Norms: Contributions to a Discourse Theory of Law and Democracy,* trans. William Rehg. Cambridge, Mass.: MIT Press, 1996.

———. "Deliberative Politics." In *Democracy,* ed. David Estlund. Oxford: Blackwell Publishers, 2002.

———. "The European Nation-State: On the Past and Future of Sovereignty and Citizenship." In *The Inclusion of the Other: Studies in Political Theory.* Cambridge, Mass.: MIT Press, 1998.

———. *The Structural Transformation of the Public Sphere: An Inquiry into a Category of Bourgeois Society,* trans. Thomas Burger. Cambridge, Mass.: MIT Press, 1999.

———. *The Theory of Communicative Action,* trans. Thomas McCarthy. Cambridge, Mass: Polity Press, 1986–1989.

Habict, Christian. *Cicero the Politician.* Baltimore, Md.: Johns Hopkins University Press, 1990.

Hall, Cheryl. "'Passions and Constraint': The Marginalization of Passion in Liberal Political Theory," *Philosophy and Social Criticism* 28 (2002): 727–748.

Halliwell, Stephen. "The Challenge of Rhetoric to Ethical Theory." In *Essays on Aristotle's Rhetoric,* ed. Amelie Rorty. Berkeley, Calif.: University of California Press, 1996.

Hamilton, Alexander, James Madison, and John Jay. *The Federalist Papers,* ed. Clinton Rossiter, with a new introduction by Charles Kesler. New York: Mentor, 1999.

Hankins, James. "Humanism and Modern Political Thought." In *The Cambridge Companion to Renaissance Humanism,* ed. Jill Kraye, Cambridge: Cambridge University Press, 1996.

Heinrichs, Jay. "How Harvard Destroyed Rhetoric." *Harvard Magazine,* July/August 1995.

Herman, Barbara. *The Practice of Moral Judgment.* Cambridge, Mass.: Harvard University Press, 1993.

Hikins, James W. "Nietzsche, Eristic, and the Rhetoric of the Possible: A Commentary on the Whitson and Poulakos 'Aesthetic' View of Rhetoric." *Quarterly Journal of Speech* 81 (1995): 353–377.

Hirschman, Albert O. *The Passions and the Interests: Political Arguments for Capitalism Before Its Triumph.* Princeton, N.J.: Princeton University Press, 1981.

Hobbes, Thomas. *Behemoth, or The Long Parliament,* ed. Ferdinand Tönnies, with an introduction by Stephen Holmes. Chicago, Ill.: University of Chicago Press, 1990.

———. *A Briefe of the Arte of Rhetorique.* In *The Rhetorics of Thomas Hobbes and Bernard Lamy,* ed. John T. Harwood. Carbondale, Ill.: Southern Illinois University Press, 1986.

———. "A Discourse upon the Beginning of Tacitus." In *Thomas Hobbes: Three Discourses: A Critical Modern Edition of Newly Identified Work of the Young Hobbes,* ed. Noel B. Reynolds and Arlene W. Saxonhouse. Chicago, Ill.: University of Chicago Press, 1995.

———. *The Elements of Law, Natural and Politic,* ed. Ferdinand Tönnies. London: Frank Cass, 1969.

———. *Leviathan,* ed. Richard Tuck. Cambridge: Cambridge University Press, 1996.

———. *On the Citizen,* ed. and trans. Richard Tuck and Michael Silverthorne. Cambridge: Cambridge University Press, 1998.

Holmes, Stephen. *Passions and Constraint: On the Theory of Liberal Democracy.* Chicago, Ill.: University of Chicago Press, 1995.

Honig, Bonnie. *Political Theory and the Displacement of Politics.* Ithaca, N.Y.: Cornell University Press, 1993.

Howard, Philip K. *The Death of Common Sense: How Law Is Suffocating America.* New York: Random House, 1994.

Hume, David. *An Enquiry Concerning Human Understanding,* ed. Eric Steinberg. Indianapolis, Ind.: Hackett Publishing, 1977.

———. "Of Eloquence." In *Essays, Moral, Political and Literary,* ed. Eugene F. Miller. Indianapolis, Ind.: Liberty Fund, 1985.

Hyde, Edward, Earl of Clarendon. "A Brief View and Survey of the Dangerous and Pernicious Errors to Church and State in Mr Hobbes's Book, Entitled Leviathan" (1676). In *Leviathan: Contemporary Responses to the Political Theory of Thomas Hobbes*, ed. G. A. J. Rogers. Bristol, U.K.: Thoemmes Press, 1995.

Irwin, T. H. "Ethics in the *Rhetoric* and in the *Ethics*." In *Essays on Aristotle's Rhetoric*, ed. Amelie Rorty. Berkeley, Calif.: University of California Press, 1996.

Izzo, P. F. "Cicero and Political Expediency." *Classical Weekly* 42 (1948–1949): 168–172.

Jamieson, Kathleen Hall. *Eloquence in an Electronic Age: The Transformation of Political Speechmaking*. New York: Oxford University Press, 1988.

Johnston, David. *The Rhetoric of Leviathan: Thomas Hobbes and the Politics of Cultural Transformation*. Princeton, N.J.: Princeton University Press, 1986.

Kahn, Victoria. *Rhetoric, Prudence, and Skepticism in the Renaissance*. Ithaca, N.Y.: Cornell University Press, 1985.

Kant, Immanuel. "An Answer to the Question: What is Enlightenment?" In *Political Writings*, ed. Hans Reiss, trans. H. B. Nisbet. Cambridge: Cambridge University Press, 1991.

———. "The Contest of the Faculties." In *Political Writings*, ed. Hans Reiss, trans. H. B. Nisbet. Cambridge: Cambridge University Press, 1991.

———. *Correspondence*, trans. Arnulf Zweig. Cambridge: Cambridge University Press, 1999.

———. *Critique of Judgment*, trans. J. H. Bernard. New York: Hafner Press, 1951.

———. *Critique of Pure Reason*, trans. Norman Kemp Smith. New York: St. Martin's Press, 1965.

———. *Groundwork of The Metaphysics of Morals*. In *Practical Philosophy*, trans. Mary J. Gregor. Cambridge: Cambridge University Press, 1996.

———. *Introduction to Logic*, trans. Thomas Kingsmill Abbott. New York: Philosophical Library, 1963.

———. *Metaphysics of Morals*. In *Practical Philosophy*, trans. Mary J. Gregor. Cambridge: Cambridge University Press, 1996.

———. "On the Common Saying: 'This May be True in Theory, but It Does Not Apply in Practice." In *Political Writings*, ed. Hans Reiss, trans. H. B. Nisbet. Cambridge: Cambridge University Press, 1991.

———. "Perpetual Peace: A Philosophical Sketch." In *Political Writings*, ed. Hans Reiss, trans. H. B. Nisbet. Cambridge: Cambridge University Press, 1991.

———. *Prolegomena to Any Future Metaphysics*, trans. Paul Carus, rev. trans. James W. Ellington. Indianapolis, Ind.: Hackett Publishing, 1977.

———. "What Is Orientation in Thinking?" In *Political Writings*, ed. Hans Reiss, trans. H. B. Nisbet. Cambridge: Cambridge University Press, 1991.

Kelly, Christopher. "'To Persuade without Convincing': The Language of Rousseau's Legislator." *American Journal of Political Science* 31 (May, 1987): 321–335.

Kennedy, George A. *The Art of Persuasion in Ancient Greece*. Princeton, N.J.: Princeton University Press, 1963.

———. *Classical Rhetoric and Its Christian and Secular Tradition from Ancient to Modern Times*. Chapel Hill: University of North Carolina Press, 1999.

Klein, Joe. "Where's the Music: Why No One's Listening to What the Candidates Have to Say." *New Yorker,* September 27, 1999, 37–42.

Kochin, Michael. *Gender and Rhetoric in Plato's Political Thought.* Cambridge: Cambridge University Press, 2002.

Korsgaard, Christine. *Creating the Kingdom of Ends.* Cambridge: Cambridge University Press, 1996.

Koziak, Barbara. *Retrieving Political Emotion: Thumos, Aristotle, and Gender.* University Park, Penn.: Pennsylvania State University Press, 2000.

Krause, Sharon R. "Humean Judgment and Democratic Deliberation." Unpublished manuscript presented at the 2004 annual meeting of the New England Political Science Association.

———. *Liberalism with Honor.* Cambridge, Mass.: Harvard University Press, 2002.

———. "Partial Justice." *Political Theory* 29 (2001): 315–336.

Kronman, Anthony T. *The Lost Lawyer: Failing Ideals of the Legal Profession.* Cambridge, Mass.: Belknap Press, 1993.

Kuehn, Manfred. *Scottish Common Sense in Germany, 1768–1800: A Contribution to the History of Critical Philosophy.* Kingston: McGill-Queen's University Press, 1987.

Laks, Andre and Malcolm Schofield, eds. *Justice and Generosity: Studies in Hellenistic Social and Political Philosophy: Proceedings of the Sixth Symposium Hellenisticum.* Cambridge: Cambridge University Press, 1995.

La Mettrie, Julien Offray de. *Machine Man and Other Writings,* trans. Ann Thomson. Cambridge: Cambridge University Press, 1996.

Lamy, Bernard. *The Art of Speaking.* In *The Rhetorics of Thomas Hobbes and Bernard Lamy,* ed. John T. Harwood. Carbondale, Ill.: Southern Illinois University Press, 1986.

Larmore, Charles. *The Morals of Modernity.* Cambridge: Cambridge University Press, 1996.

Lear, Jonathan. *Aristotle: The Desire to Understand.* Cambridge: Cambridge University Press, 1988.

LeDoux, Joseph. *The Emotional Brain.* New York: Simon and Schuster, 1996.

Leigh, R. A., ed. *Rousseau After Two Hundred Years: Proceedings of the Cambridge Bicentennial Colloquium.* Cambridge: Cambridge University Press, 1982.

Leighton, Stephen R. "Aristotle and the Emotions." In *Essays on Aristotle's Rhetoric,* ed. Amelie Rorty. Berkeley, Calif.: University of California Press, 1996.

Long, A. A. "Cicero's Politics in *De officiis.*" In *Justice and Generosity: Studies in Hellenistic Social and Political Philosophy: Proceedings of the Sixth Symposium Hellenisticum,* ed. Andre Laks and Malcolm Schofield. Cambridge: Cambridge University Press, 1995.

Long, A. A., ed. *Problems in Stoicism.* London: Athlone Press, 1971.

Long, A. A. and D. N. Sedley, eds. *The Hellenistic Philosophers.* New York: Cambridge University Press, 1987.

Macedo, Stephen. *Liberal Virtues: Citizenship, Virtue, and Community in Liberal Constitutionalism.* Oxford: Clarendon Press, 1990.

Machiavelli, Niccolò. *Discourses on Livy,* trans. Harvey C. Mansfield and Nathan Tarcov. Chicago, Ill.: University of Chicago Press, 1996.

————. *The Prince*, trans. Harvey C. Mansfield. Chicago, Ill.: University of Chicago Press, 1998.

MacIntyre, Alasdair. *After Virtue: A Study in Moral Theory.* Notre Dame, Ind.: University of Notre Dame Press, 1982.

Madison, James. *Notes on the Debates in the Federal Convention of 1787.* New York: W. W. Norton, 1987.

————. "Vices of the Political System." In *Papers,* ed. William T. Hutchinson and William M. E. Rachal. Chicago, Ill.: University of Chicago Press, 1962–1991.

Maloy, J. S. "The very order of things: Rousseau's tutorial republicanism." *Polity* 37 (April 2005): 235–261.

Manent, Pierre. *An Intellectual History of Liberalism,* trans. Rebecca Balinksi. Princeton, N.J.: Princeton University Press, 1994.

Manin, Bernard. "On Legitimacy and Political Deliberation," trans. Elly Stein and Jane Mansbridge. *Political Theory* 15 (August 1987): 338–368.

Mansbridge, Jane J. *Beyond Adversary Democracy.* Chicago, Ill.: University of Chicago Press, 1983.

Mansfield, Harvey C., Jr. *America's Constitutional Soul.* Baltimore, Md.: Johns Hopkins University Press, 1991.

————. "Bruni and Machiavelli on Civic Humanism." In *Renaissance Civic Humanism: Reappraisals and Reflections,* ed. James Hankins. Cambridge: Cambridge University Press, 2000.

————. "Hobbes and the Science of Indirect Government." *American Political Science Review* 65 (1971): 97–110.

————. "Self-Interest Rightly Understood." *Political Theory* 23 (February 1995): 48–66.

————. *Taming the Prince: The Ambivalence of Modern Executive Power.* Baltimore, Md.: Johns Hopkins University Press, 1993.

Marcus, George E. *The Sentimental Citizen: Emotion in Democratic Politics.* University Park, Penn.: Pennsylvania State University Press, 2002.

Marcus, George E., W. Russell Neuman, and Michael MacKuen. *Affective Intelligence and Political Judgment.* Chicago, Ill.: University of Chicago Press, 2000.

Markell, Patchen. "Making Affect Safe for Democracy?: On Constitutional Patriotism." *Political Theory* 28 (February 2000): 38–63.

Mayhew, David. *Congress: The Electoral Connection.* New Haven, Conn.: Yale University Press, 1974.

Mayr, Otto. *Authority, Liberty and Automatic Machinery in Early Modern Europe.* Baltimore, Md.: Johns Hopkins University Press, 1986.

McCloskey, Donald. *The Rhetoric of Economics.* Madison, Wisc.: University of Wisconsin Press, 1985.

Mendelssohn, Moses. "On the Question: What Is Enlightenment?" trans. James Schmidt. In *What is Enlightenment?: Eighteenth-Century Answers and Twentieth-Century Questions,* ed. James Schmidt. Berkeley, Calif.: University of California Press, 1996.

Melzer, Arthur. *The Natural Goodness of Man.* Chicago, Ill.: University of Chicago Press, 1990.

————. "Rousseau, Nationalism, and the Politics of Sympathetic Identification." In *Educating the Prince: Essays in Honor of Harvey Mansfield,* ed. Mark Blitz and William Kristol. Lanham, Md.: Rowman and Littlefield Publishers, 2000.

Miller, Perry. *The New England Mind: The Seventeenth Century.* Cambridge, Mass.: Harvard University Press, 1954.

Mitchell, Thomas N. "Cicero on the Moral Crisis of the Late Republic." *Hermathena* 136 (Summer 1984): 21–41.

————. *Cicero: The Senior Statesman.* New Haven, Conn.: Yale University Press, 1991.

Montaigne, Michel de. "Of Custome." In *Essays,* trans. John Florio. New York: Dutton, 1965.

Montesquieu, Baron Charles Louis de Secondat. *The Spirit of the Laws: A Compendium of the First Edition,* ed. David Wallace Carrithers, trans. Thomas Nugent. Berkeley, Calif.: University of California Press, 1977.

Morone, James A. *Hellfire Nation: The Politics of Sin in American History.* New Haven, Conn.: Yale University Press, 2003.

Most, Glenn. "The Uses of *Endoxa:* Philosophy and Rhetoric in the *Rhetoric.*" In *Aristotle's Rhetoric: Philosophical Essays,* ed. David J. Furley and Alexander Nehamas. Princeton, N.J.: Princeton University Press, 1994.

Murdoch, Iris. *The Sovereignty of Good.* New York: Schocken Books, 1971.

Mutz, Diane C., Paul M. Sniderman, and Richard Brody, eds. *Political Persuasion and Attitude Change.* Ann Arbor, Mich.: University of Michigan Press, 1996.

Nelson, John S., Allan Megill, and Donald N. McCloskey, eds. *Rhetoric of the Human Sciences: Language and Argument in Scholarship and Public affairs.* Madison, Wisc.: University of Wisconsin Press, 1987.

Nelson, Thomas E. and Donald R. Kinder, "Issue Frames and Group-Centrism in American Public Opinion." *Journal of Politics* 58 (November, 1996): 1055–1078.

Nelson, Thomas E., Zoe M. Oxley, and Rosalee A. Clawson. "Media Framing of a Civil Rights Conflict and Its Effect on Tolerance." *American Political Science Review* 91 (1997): 567–583.

Nichols, Mary. "Aristotle's Defense of Rhetoric." *Journal of Politics* 49 (August 1987): 657–677.

————. *Citizens and Statesmen: A Study of Aristotle's Politics.* Lanham, Md.: Rowman and Littlefield Publishers, 1992.

Nussbaum, Martha. "Aristotle on Emotions and Rational Persuasion." In *Essays on Aristotle's Rhetoric,* ed. Amelie Rorty. Berkeley, Calif.: University of California Press, 1996.

————. *The Fragility of Goodness: Luck and Ethics in Greek Tragedy and Philosophy.* Cambridge: Cambridge University Press, 1986.

————. *Love's Knowledge: Essays on Philosophy and Literature.* New York: Oxford University Press, 1990.

————. *Upheavals of Thought: The Intelligence of Emotions.* New York: Cambridge University Press, 2001.

O'Neill, Onora. *Constructions of Reason: Explorations of Kant's Practical Philosophy.* Cambridge: Cambridge University Press, 1989.

Ong, Walter. *Ramus, Method, and the Decay of Dialogue.* Cambridge, Mass.: Harvard University Press, 1958.

Peacham, Henry. Epistle dedicatory. In *The Garden of Eloquence* (1593). Facs. reprod., Gainesville, Fla.: Scholars' Facsimiles and Reprints, 1954.

Perelman, Chaim and Lucie Olbrechts-Tyteca. *The New Rhetoric: A Treatise on Argumentation,* trans. John Wilkinson and Purcell Weaver. Notre Dame, Ind.: University of Notre Dame Press, 1969.

Perkins, William. *The Arte of Prophecying.* In *William Perkins, 1558–1602, English Puritanist: His Pioneer Works on Casuistry,* ed. Thomas F. Merrill. Netherlands: de Graaf, 1966.

———. *A Discourse of Conscience.* In *William Perkins, 1558–1602, English Puritanist: His Pioneer Works on Casuistry,* ed. Thomas F. Merrill. Netherlands: de Graaf, 1966.

———. *The Whole Treatise of Cases of Conscience.* In *William Perkins, 1558–1602, English Puritanist: His Pioneer Works on Casuistry,* ed. Thomas F. Merrill. Netherlands: de Graaf, 1966.

Plato. *Gorgias,* trans. James H. Nichols, Jr. Ithaca, N.Y.: Cornell University Press, 1998.

———. *Phaedrus,* trans. James H. Nichols, Jr. Ithaca, N.Y.: Cornell University Press, 1998.

———. *The Republic,* trans. Allan Bloom. New York: Basic Books, 1968.

Plattner, Marc E. "Rousseau and the Origins of Nationalism." In *The Legacy of Rousseau,* ed. Clifford Orwin and Nathan Tarcov. Chicago, Ill.: University of Chicago Press, 1997.

Prokhovnik, Raia. *Rhetoric and Philosophy in Hobbes'* Leviathan. New York: Garland Publishing, 1991.

Ramachandran, V. S. *Phantoms in the Brain: Probing the Mysteries of the Human Mind.* New York: William Morrow, 1998.

Rawls, John. "The Idea of an Overlapping Consensus (1987)." In *Collected Papers,* ed. Samuel Freeman. Cambridge, Mass.: Harvard University Press, 1999.

———. *The Law of Peoples with "The Idea of Public Reason Revisited."* Cambridge, Mass.: Harvard University Press, 1999.

———. *Political Liberalism.* New York: Columbia University Press, 1996.

———. *A Theory of Justice.* Cambridge, Mass.: Harvard University Press, 1971.

Rawson, Elizabeth. *Cicero: A Portrait.* Ithaca, N.Y.: Cornell University Press, 1975.

Reid, Thomas. *Essays on the Intellectual Powers of Man.* In *The Works of Thomas Reid,* ed. William Hamilton, vol. 1. Bristol, U.K.: Thoemmes Press, 1994.

———. *An Inquiry into the Human Mind on the Principle of Common Sense.* In *The Works of Thomas Reid,* ed. William Hamilton, vol. 1. Bristol, U.K.: Thoemmes Press, 1994.

Reisert, Joseph. *Jean-Jacques Rousseau: A Friend of Virtue.* Ithaca, N.Y.: Cornell University Press, 2003.

Remer, Gary. "Political Oratory and Conversation: Cicero versus Deliberative Democracy." *Political Theory* 27 (February 1999): 39–65.

Reynolds, Noel B. and John L. Hilton. "Thomas Hobbes and Authorship of *Horae Subsecivae.*" *History of Political Thought* 14 (1993): 361–380.

Richards, I. A. *The Philosophy of Rhetoric.* London: Oxford University Press, 1936.

Riley, Patrick. "Hannah Arendt on Kant, Truth and Politics." In *Essays on Kant's Political Philosophy,* ed. Howard Williams. Cardiff, U.K.: University of Wales Press, 1992.

Rogers, G. A. J., ed. *Leviathan: Contemporary Responses to the Political Theory of Thomas Hobbes.* Bristol, U.K.: Thoemmes Press, 1995.

Rorty, Amelie, ed. *Essays on Aristotle's Rhetoric.* Berkeley, Calif.: University of California Press, 1996.

Rousseau, Jean-Jacques. *Dictionary of Music.* In *The Collected Writings of Rousseau,* vol. 7, ed. Roger D. Masters and Christopher Kelly. Hanover, N.H.: University of New England Press, 1998.

———. *Discourse on Inequality, or Second Discourse,* in *The First and Second Discourses,* trans. Victor Gourevitch. New York: Harper and Row, 1986.

———. *Discourse on the Sciences and Arts, or First Discourse.* In *The First and Second Discourses Together with the Replies to Critics and Essay on the Origin of Languages,* trans. Victor Gourevitch. New York: Harper and Row, 1986.

———. *Essay on the Origin of Languages.* In *The First and Second Discourses Together with the Replies to Critics and Essay on the Origin of Languages,* trans. Victor Gourevitch. New York: Harper and Row, 1986.

———. *Émile, or On Education,* trans. Allan Bloom. Basic Books, 1979.

———. *Essai sur l'origine des langues, où il est parlé de la mélodie et de l'imitation musicale,* ed. Jean Starobinski. Paris: Gallimard, 1990.

———. *On the Social Contract with Geneva Manuscript and Political Economy,* ed. Roger D. Masters, trans. Judith R. Masters. New York: St. Martin's Press, 1978.

———. *Politics and the Arts: Letter to M. D'Alembert on the Theatre,* trans. Allan Bloom. Ithaca, N.Y.: Cornell University Press, 1960.

Sabl, Andrew. *Ruling Passions: Political Offices and Democratic Ethics.* Princeton, N.J.: Princeton University Press, 2002.

Saccamano, Neil. "Rhetoric, Consensus, and the Law in Rousseau's *Contrat Social.*" French issue, *MLN* 107 (September 1992): 730–751.

Safire, William, ed. *Lend Me Your Ears: Great Speeches in History.* New York: W. W. Norton, 1997.

Salkever, Stephen G. *Finding the Mean: Theory and Practice in Aristotelian Political Philosophy.* Princeton, N.J.: Princeton University Press, 1990.

Sandel, Michael. *Democracy's Discontent: America in Search of a Public Philosophy.* Cambridge, Mass.: Belknap Press, 1996.

———. *Liberalism and the Limits of Justice,* 2d ed. Cambridge: Cambridge University Press, 1998.

———. "Political Liberalism." *Harvard Law Review* 107 (May 1994): 1765–1794.

Sassen, Brigette, trans. and ed. *Kant's Early Critics: The Empiricist Critique of the Theoretical Philosophy.* Cambridge: Cambridge University Press, 2000.

Saxonhouse, Arlene. *Fear of Diversity: The Birth of Political Science in Ancient Greek Thought.* Chicago, Ill.: University of Chicago Press, 1992.

Schellhase, Kenneth C. *Tacitus in Renaissance Political Thought.* Chicago, Ill.: University of Chicago Press, 1976.

Schofield, Malcolm. *Saving the City: Philosopher-Kings and Other Classical Paradigms.* London: Routledge, 1999.

———. "Two Stoic Approaches to Justice." In *Justice and Generosity: Studies in Hellenistic Social and Political Philosophy: Proceedings of the Sixth Symposium Hellenisticum,* ed. Andre Laks and Malcolm Schofield. Cambridge: Cambridge University Press, 1995.

Schütrumpf, Eckart. "Some Observations on the Introduction to Aristotle's *Rhetoric.*" In *Aristotle's Rhetoric: Philosophical Essays,* ed. David J. Furley and Alexander Nehamas. Princeton, N.J.: Princeton University Press, 1994.

Scott, John T. "The Harmony Between Rousseau's Musical Theory and His Philosophy." *Journal of the History of Ideas* 59 (1998): 287–308.

———. "Rousseau and the Melodious Language of Freedom." *Journal of Politics* 59 (August, 1997): 803–829.

Shapiro, Ian. *The State of Democratic Theory.* Princeton, N.J.: Princeton University Press, 2003.

Shell, Susan Meld. *The Embodiment of Reason: Kant on Spirit, Generation, and Community.* Chicago, Ill.: University of Chicago Press, 1996.

———. "Kantian Idealism." In *Educating the Prince: Essays in Honor of Harvey Mansfield,* ed. Mark Blitz and William Kristol. Lanham, Md.: Rowman and Littlefield Publishers, 2000.

Sherman, Nancy. *Making a Necessity of Virtue: Aristotle and Kant on Virtue.* Cambridge: Cambridge University Press, 1997.

Shklar, Judith. "The Liberalism of Fear." In *Liberalism and the Moral Life,* ed. Nancy Rosenblum. Cambridge, Mass.: Harvard University Press, 1989.

———. *Men and Citizens: A Study of Rousseau's Social Theory.* Cambridge: Cambridge University Press, 1969.

Skinner, Quentin. *Reason and Rhetoric in the Philosophy of Hobbes.* Cambridge: Cambridge University Press, 1996.

———. "The Study of Rhetoric as an Approach to Cultural History: The Case of Hobbes." In *Main Trends in Cultural History: Ten Essays,* ed. Willem Melching and Wyger Velema. Amsterdam: Rodopi, 1994.

Sleeper, Jim. *Liberal Racism.* New York: Viking Press, 1997.

Sloane, Thomas O. *Donne, Milton, and the End of Humanist Rhetoric.* Berkeley, Calif.: University of California Press, 1985.

Sorrell, Tom. "Hobbes's UnAristotelian Political Rhetoric." *Philosophy and Rhetoric* 23 (1990).

Spragens, Thomas. *The Politics of Motion: the World of Thomas Hobbes.* Lexington, Ky.: University Press of Kentucky, 1973.

Sprute, Jürgen. "Aristotle and the Legitimacy of Rhetoric." In *Aristotle's Rhetoric: Philosophical Essays,* ed. David J. Furley and Alexander Nehamas. Princeton, N.J.: Princeton University Press, 1994.

Starobinski, Jean. "Eloquence and Liberty." *Journal of the History of Ideas* 38 (1977): 195–210.

———. *Le remède du mal: Critique et légitimation de l'artifice à l'âge des Lumières.* Paris: Gallimard, 1989.

———. "Rousseau et l'éloquence." In *Rousseau After Two Hundred Years: Proceedings of the Cambridge Bicentennial Colloquium*, ed. R. A. Leigh. Cambridge: Cambridge University Press, 1982.

Stout, Jeffrey. *Democracy and Tradition*. Princeton, N.J.: Princeton University Press, 2004.

Strauss, Leo. *Natural Right and History*. Chicago, Ill.: University of Chicago Press, 1971.

———. *The Political Philosophy of Hobbes: Its Basis and Its Genesis*, trans. Elsa M. Sinclair. Oxford: Clarendon Press, 1936.

Striker, Gisela. "Emotions in Context: Aristotle's Treatment of the Passions in the *Rhetoric* and His Moral Psychology." In *Essays on Aristotle's* Rhetoric, ed. Amelie Rorty. Berkeley, Calif.: University of California Press, 1996.

———. *Essays on Hellenistic Epistemology and Ethics*. Cambridge: Cambridge University Press, 1996.

———. "Sceptical Strategies." In *Doubt and Dogmatism: Studies in Hellenistic Epistemology*, ed. Malcolm Schofield, Myles Burnyeat, and Jonathan Barnes. Oxford: Clarendon Press, 1980.

Summers, David. *The Judgement of Sense: Renaissance Naturalism and the Rise of Aesthetics*. Cambridge: Cambridge University Press, 1987.

Sunstein, Cass R. *Why Societies Need Dissent*. Cambridge, Mass.: Harvard University Press, 2003.

Swift, Jonathan. "A Discourse Concerning the Mechanical Operation of the Spirit." In *A Tale of a Tub*. Oxford: Clarendon Press, 1920.

Tacitus. *Dialogue on Oratory*. In *Agricola; Germania; Dialogus de Oratoribus*. Cambridge, Mass.: Harvard University Press, 1970.

Tanner, J. R. *English Constitutional Conflicts of the Seventeenth Century, 1603–1689*. Cambridge: Cambridge University Press, 1962.

Teuber, Andreas. "Kant's Respect for Persons." *Political Theory* 11 (1983): 369–392.

Thorsrud, Harald. "Cicero on His Academic Predecessors: The Fallibilism of Arcesilaus and Carneades." *Journal of the History of Philosophy* 40 (January 2002): 1–18.

Tocqueville, Alexis de. *Democracy in America*, trans. Harvey C. Mansfield and Delba Winthrop. Chicago, Ill.: University of Chicago Press, 2000.

Tuck, Richard. "Hobbes and Descartes." In *Perspectives on Thomas Hobbes*, ed. G. A. J. Rogers and Alan Ryan. Oxford: Oxford University Press, 1988.

———. *Philosophy and Government, 1572–1651*. Cambridge: Cambridge University Press, 1993.

———. *The Rights of War and Peace: Political Thought and the International Order from Grotius to Kant*. New York: Oxford University Press, 1999.

Tulis, Jeffrey. *The Rhetorical Presidency*. Princeton, N.J.: Princeton University Press, 1987.

Urbinati, Nadia. "Representation as Advocacy." *Political Theory* 28 (December 2000): 758–786.

van der Zande, Johan. "In the Image of Cicero: German Philosophy between Wolff and Kant." *Journal of the History of Ideas* 56 (July 1995): 419–442.

———. "The Microscope of Experience: Christian Garve's Translation of Cicero's *De officiis* (1783)." *Journal of the History of Ideas* 59 (1998): 75–94.

Vaughan, Geoffrey M. "The Audience of Hobbes's *Leviathan* and the Audience of Hobbes's Political Philosophy." *History of Political Thought* 22 (Autumn 2001): 448–471.

Vickers, Brian. *In Defense of Rhetoric.* New York: Oxford University Press, 1989.

Vico, Giambattista. *On the Study Methods of Our Time*, trans. Elio Gianturco. Ithaca, N.Y.: Cornell University Press, 1990.

Villa, Dana. *Socratic Citizenship.* Princeton, N.J.: Princeton University Press, 2001.

Waldron, Jeremy. *Liberal Rights: Collected Papers, 1981–1991.* Cambridge: Cambridge University Press, 1993.

———. "The Wisdom of the Multitude: Some Reflections on Book III, Chapter 11 of Aristotle's *Politics.*" *Political Theory* 23 (1995): 563–584.

Walker, R. C. S., ed. *The Real in the Ideal: Berkeley's Relation to Kant.* New York: Garland Publishers, 1989.

Walzer, Michael. "Passion and Politics." *Philosophy and Social Criticism* 28 (2003): 617–633.

———. *The Revolution of the Saints: A Study in the Origins of Radical Politics.* New York: Atheneum, 1968.

———. *Spheres of Justice: A Defense of Pluralism and Equality.* New York: Basic Books, 1983.

Watkins, J. W. N. *Hobbes's System of Ideas: A Study in the Political Significance of Philosophical Ideas*, 2d ed. London: Hutchinson, 1973.

Watson, G. "The Natural Law and Stoicism." In *Problems in Stoicism*, ed. A. A. Long. London: Athlone Press, 1971.

Whelan, Frederick G. "Language and Its Abuses in Hobbes' Political Philosophy." *American Political Science Review* 75 (1981): 59–75.

Whitson, Steve and John Poulakos. "Nietzsche and the Aesthetics of Rhetoric." *Quarterly Journal of Speech* 79 (1993): 131–145.

Wilson, Thomas. *The Art of Rhetoric (1560)*, ed. Peter E. Medine. University Park, Penn.: Pennsylvania State University Press, 1994.

Winthrop, Delba. "Aristotle and Political Responsibility." *Political Theory* 3 (1975): 406–422.

———. "Aristotle and Theories of Justice." *American Political Science Review* 72 (1978): 1201–1216.

Wirszubski, C. "Cicero's CVM DIGNITATE OTIVM: A Reconsideration." *The Journal of Roman Studies* 44 (1954): 1–13.

Wokler, Robert. *Rousseau: A Very Short Introduction.* Oxford: Oxford University Press, 2001.

———. *Rousseau on Society, Politics, Music and Language: An Historical Interpretation of His Early Writings.* New York: Garland Publishing, 1987.

Wolin, Sheldon S. "Fugitive Democracy." *Constellations* 1 (1994): 11–25.

———. *Hobbes and the Epic Tradition of Political Theory*, ed. Richard E. Ashcroft. Los Angeles: University of California Press, 1970.

———. "Norm and Form: The Constitutionalizing of Democracy." In *Athenian Political Thought and the Reconstruction of American Democracy*, ed. J. Peter Euben, John R. Wallach, and Josiah Ober. Ithaca, N.Y.: Cornell University Press, 1994.

———. *Politics and Vision: Continuity and Innovation in Western Political Thought*, expanded ed. Princeton, N.J.: Princeton University Press, 2004.

Yack, Bernard. "Community and Conflict in Aristotle's Political Philosophy." In *Action and Contemplation: Studies in the Moral and Political Thought of Aristotle*, ed. Robert C. Bartlett and Susan D. Collins. Albany, N.Y.: State University of New York Press, 1999.

———. *The Problems of a Political Animal: Community, Justice and Conflict in Aristotelian Political Thought*. Berkeley, Calif.: University of California Press, 1993.

Yunis, Harvey. *Taming Democracy: Models of Political Rhetoric in Classical Athens*. Ithaca, N.Y.: Cornell University Press, 1996.

Zakaria, Fareed. *The Future of Freedom: Illiberal Democracy at Home and Abroad*. New York: W. W. Norton, 2004.

Zammito, John H. *Kant, Herder, and the Birth of Anthropology*. Chicago, Ill.: University of Chicago Press, 2002.

Index